PROFESSIONALIZING MULTIMODAL COMPOSITION

PROFESSIONAL
COMPOSITES

PROFESSIONALIZING MULTIMODAL COMPOSITION

EDITED BY
**SANTOSH KHADKA
AND SHYAM B. PANDEY**

UTAH STATE UNIVERSITY PRESS
Logan

© 2023 by University Press of Colorado

Published by Utah State University Press
An imprint of University Press of Colorado
1624 Market Street, Suite 226
PMB 39883
Denver, Colorado 80202-1559

All rights reserved
Printed in the United States of America

 The University Press of Colorado is a proud member of the Association of University Presses.

The University Press of Colorado is a cooperative publishing enterprise supported, in part, by Adams State University, Colorado State University, Fort Lewis College, Metropolitan State University of Denver, University of Alaska Fairbanks, University of Colorado, University of Denver, University of Northern Colorado, University of Wyoming, Utah State University, and Western Colorado University.

∞ This paper meets the requirements of the ANSI/NISO Z39.48-1992 (Permanence of Paper).

ISBN: 978-1-64642-416-0 (hardcover)
ISBN: 978-1-64642-417-7 (paperback)
ISBN: 978-1-64642-418-4 (ebook)
https://doi.org/10.7330/9781646424184

Library of Congress Cataloging-in-Publication Data

Names: Khadka, Santosh, 1977– editor. | Pandey, Shyam B., editor.
Title: Professionalizing multimodal composition / edited by Santosh Khadka and Shyam B. Pandey.
Description: Logan : Utah State University Press, [2023] | Includes bibliographical references and index.
Identifiers: LCCN 2023010607 (print) | LCCN 2023010608 (ebook) | ISBN 9781646424160 (hardcover) | ISBN 9781646424177 (paperback) | ISBN 9781646424184 (ebook)
Subjects: LCSH: English language—Composition and exercises—Study and teaching (Higher)—United States. | English language—Rhetoric—Study and teaching (Higher)—United States. | Multimedia communications—Study and teaching (Higher)—United States. | English teachers—Training of—United States. | College teachers—Training of—United States. | Curriculum change—United States. | LCGFT: Essays.
Classification: LCC PE1405.U6 P756 2023 (print) | LCC PE1405.U6 (ebook) | DDC 808/.0420711—dc23/eng/20230413
LC record available at https://lccn.loc.gov/2023010607
LC ebook record available at https://lccn.loc.gov/2023010608

Cover art: ©Aliaksandr Famin/Shutterstock

CONTENTS

Professionalizing Multimodal Composition: An Introduction
Santosh Khadka and Shyam B. Pandey   3

PART I: FACULTY PREPAREDNESS   23

1. Graduate Student and Faculty Development in Multimodal Composing
    Wilfredo Flores, Teresa Williams, Christina Boyles, Kristin Arola, and Dànielle Nicole DeVoss   25

2. (E)merging Expertise: Multivocal, Multimodal Preparation and Development of Graduate Teaching Assistants in Writing Programs
    Kelly Moreland, Sarah Henderson Lee, and Kirsti Cole   43

3. Practicing (Antiracist and Anti-ableist) Multimodality: TA Training and Student Responses to Implementing a Multimodal Curriculum in First-Year Writing
    Megan McIntyre and Jennifer Lanatti Shen   61

4. Professional Development for Multimodal Composition: Preparing Graduate Teaching Assistants for the Twenty-First Century
    Tiffany Bourelle   78

5. Incorporating Multimodal Literacies across an FYW Program: Graduate Instructors' Preparation and Experiences
    Lauren Brawley, Morgan Connor, Meghalee Das, Aliethia Dean, Claudia Diaz, Michael J. Faris, Michelle Flahive, Maeve Kirk, Max Kirschenbaum, Joshua Kulseth, Alfonsina Lago, Kristina Lewis, Lance Lomax, Brook McClurg, Zachary Ostraff, Anthony Ranieri, Sierra Sinor, Rebekah Smith, and Yifan Zhang   95

PART II: INSTITUTIONAL INITIATIVES AND SUPPORT   113

6. DMAC at Fifteen: Professionalizing Digital Media and Composition
    Scott Lloyd DeWitt and John Jones   115

7. Looking beyond the Writing Program: Institutional Allies to Support Professional Development in the Teaching of Digital Writing

Alison Witte, Stacy Kastner, and Kerri Hauman   139

8. A Fresh Catalyst: Invigorating the University with Integrated Modalities

Daniel Schafer and Josh Ambrose   158

9. Embedding Multimodal Writing across a University at the Institutional, Administrative, and Curricular Level: The Undergraduate Professional Writing and Rhetoric Major as Agent of Change

Li Li, Michael Strickland, and Paula Rosinski   175

PART III: ACADEMIC LEADERSHIP   195

10. The Art of Responsiveness: The Ongoing Development of a Master of Arts in Composition, Rhetoric, and Digital Media (CRDM)

Claire Lutkewitte   197

11. "Go *Make* Things Happen": Professionalizing Graduate Students through Multimodal Composing

Shauna Chung, Stephen Quigley, and Tia Dumas   213

12. Centering Translingualism in Multimodal Practice: A Reflective Case Study of a Linguistically Diverse Graduate Program

Megan E. Heise and Matthew A. Vetter   233

13. Multimodality as a Key Consideration in Developing a New Communications Degree at UMass, Dartmouth

Anthony F. Arrigo   250

Epilogue: Multimodal Professionalization during and after the COVID-19 Pandemic

Santosh Khadka and Shyam B. Pandey   271

Index   275
About the Authors   281

PROFESSIONALIZING MULTIMODAL COMPOSITION

PROFESSIONALIZING MULTIMODAL COMPOSITION
An Introduction

Santosh Khadka and Shyam B. Pandey

It took us three decades to get to where we stand today in terms of programmatic implementation of multimodality. Over the years, there have been multiple calls to incorporate multimodal and digital literacies into writing curricula (Kress 1999; Kress and Van Leeuwen 2001; New London Group 1996; Selber 2005; Selfe 1999; Takayoshi and Selfe 2007; Wysocki et al. 2004; Yancey 2004). Even though some scholars argue that multimodal predates digital and that writing has always been multimodal (Palmeri 2012; Shipka 2009), the urgent call for embracing multimodal composition in the field of English/writing studies came with New London Group's "A Pedagogy of Multiliteracy" in 1996. NCTE later responded to this call with a position statement on multimodality in 2005. This institutional call was echoed again in 2009 by the past CCCC's chair, Kathleen Blake Yancey, who noted, "We can and should respond to these new composings and new sites of composing with new energy and a new composing agenda" (7). She further maintained that given the technological moment we are in, we have an opportunity to foster "new models of writing; designing a new curriculum supporting those models; and creating models for teaching that curriculum" (1). No question, that was an opportune moment for multimodal intervention in curricula and programs; however, the instances of actual design and implementation of multimodal writing curricula and programs are rare even today in 2022. Most of the published scholarship on curriculum design and implementation is at the course level—either as an addition of a multimodal component to an existing first-year composition curriculum or development of a new course on multimodal and/or digital composition. There are hardly any accounts of programs built completely around multimodal or digital composition and emerging media. For instance, Dànielle Nicole DeVoss, Cheryl Ball, Cynthia L. Selfe, and Scott Lloyd DeWitt (2015), Chanon Adsanatham, Phill

https://doi.org/10.7330/9781646424184.c000

Alexander, Kerrie Carsey, Abby Dubisar, Wioleta Fedeczko, Denise Landrum, Cynthia Lewiecki-Wilson, Heidi McKee, Kristen Moore, Gina Patterson, and Michele Polak (2013), and Ericsson et al. (2016) describe processes and challenges of introducing a multimodal component or course curriculum at their respective institutions. But these attempts, as Carrie Leverenz (2008) notes, have yielded results only thanks to individual teachers' drive and motivation, not because of a program-wide endeavor (41). Adsanatham et al. (2013) actually discuss some programmatic, curricular, and classroom changes initiated in the composition program at Miami University to "promote the teaching and learning of multimodal composition" (282). They actually created the Digital Writing Collaborative (DWC) at the same time "to develop and sustain a culture and community of digital writing, learning, and teaching in all areas of English studies, especially in composition" (282). In order to materialize this multimodal initiative, they had to go through a process of institutional change—"from building alliances across campus to integrating the teaching and learning of multimodal digital composition into our first-year composition curriculum, classroom practices, and teacher training" (282). While this is a notable initiative, it is still an attempt to add a multimodal component to a first-year curriculum, not an initiative to develop and launch a full-fledged multimodal program.

While multimodal instruction itself is a relatively recent phenomenon in US higher education, the last two decades have witnessed exponential growth in multimodal composition research. That research has then seeped into disciplinary publications, conference presentations, and some upper-division and graduate seminar courses in the larger field of rhetoric and composition. In fact, multimodal composition, a progenitor of other cognate study areas, such as digital rhetoric, computer and composition, and digital writing, has emerged as an exciting subfield within writing studies, with its own unique identity and an impressive set of professional activities. Not just that, even mainstream rhetoric and composition as a field regularly features multimodal composition and/or digital rhetoric as an integral part of larger disciplinary conversations, even though there is a slight difference between the former and the latter. While multimodal composition relates to the production of digital or nondigital texts in more than one modality, digital rhetoric is primarily an analytic method and a heuristic for production and dissemination of digital texts in different platforms, including today's pervasive social media. Gloria E. Jacobs (2013), in fact, clarifies fine distinctions between the terms *multimodal* and *digital*. According to her, "Multimodal communication refers to the simultaneous use of more than one textual form to make meaning (Kress and

Van Leeuwen, 2001)" (102), but multimodal composing does not necessarily require the use of digital tools or technology, "although digital tools have democratized the production and distribution of multimodal texts (NCTE 2008)" (102). In that sense, there is a distinction between but also a significant overlap in these modes of composing.

Since multimodal composition is a predecessor of digital composition and encompasses both digital and nondigital texts, this collection clearly chooses to engage multimodal composition in its broader sense. One salient fact about multimodal composition as an academic subject and as a composing praxis is that it coevolves with advancements in information and communication technologies. From visual and spatial arrangement of typefaces, white spaces, and images on a print page, to 3D animations, AR and VR simulations, and a rapid development of artificial intelligence, multimodal composition has expanded substantially in both its scope and its varied forms of composing. Some popular forms of multimodal composing college students are routinely assigned these days include video/audio remixes, visual analysis, PSA, video/audio documentaries, podcasts, posters, infographics, memes, web and database design, 3D animations, and app development, among others. This range and variety of multimodal assignments reflect the field's effort to keep up with innovations in composing technologies taking place outside the academy. The good news is that the effort has been worthwhile. Multiple research studies into student responses to multimodal and traditional assignments have shown students, in fact, prefer multimodal projects over traditional essay assignments for their real-life applications. For instance, Santosh Khadka, in his monograph, *Multiliteracies, Emerging Media, and College Writing Instruction* (2019), reports findings from a research study on the writing practices of diverse college students. While analyzing interview data around a documentary production project in his multiliteracies-based sophomore-level course, he found students in his class "preferred new literacy practices over the traditional ones. The traditional essayist or critical literacies are not in their list of favorites, but digital, multimodal, visual, and social media literacies are, even though, to many of them, these new literacies meant hard work, and [a] steep learning curve" (102–3). In their reflections and interviews with him, "most students said that they preferred documentary or web design assignment over an academic essay even though many of them also agreed that documentary filmmaking in particular was much more complex and labor intensive than writing an essay because it involved technology, and multiple semiotic modes of composition" (98). Based on this and similar findings, he claims,

> Students these days are more into technology than into alphabetic literacy practices. They are immersed into digital and emerging media technology since early childhood, but their alphabetic literacy practices, in the traditional sense of the term, have become mostly limited to academy. This has raised some serious questions about disconnect between our students' literate practices outside and inside the academy. (98)

Given these exciting new developments and research findings, faculty members, academic leaders, and students have come to recognize that traditional and new technologies have enabled and even demanded they use more than one mode of composing to communicate, solve problems, and engage in public discourse. However, as different faculty members and programs are situated in their own specific institutional contexts, their recognition and implementation of multimodality in their research and teaching vary drastically.

In fact, as Khadka and Jennifer Lee, in their recently edited book *Bridging the Multimodal Gap: From Theory to Practice* (2019), succinctly note, "Attempts at implementing multimodal approaches are sporadic at best" (4). They further maintain that despite increased productivity in scholarship, attempts at integrating multimodal/digital components into the curriculum have been limited to a handful of individual faculty members and programs across the country. This glaring gap between theory and practice can be attributed to a number of factors, including complex and differing understandings of what writing is and what goals the writing curriculum should have, varied professional-development opportunities for faculty across institutions, and wide-ranging programmatic and institutional support for faculty to pursue multimodality in their scholarship and in their classrooms. Rory Lee (2020), in his recent work, argues along similar lines, noting implementation of multimodality is largely influenced by institutional and departmental contexts and distribution of labor in a given institution. Therefore, being mindful of the given institution's contextual constraints and possibilities should be the first priority while reimagining any writing curricula to incorporate multimodality (267).

So, a critical question many faculty members and higher education leaders are asking at this moment is how to expand the implementation of multimodality across programs and institutions. They are in unanimity that we must create or allocate more curricular space for multimodality in both its traditional and contemporary forms. However, the departmental or programmatic adoption of this new study area and these new forms of composing has not gained momentum at the level or velocity expected by multimodal scholars and instructors because of some obvious challenges. The first among them is our or our institution's inability or unwillingness to expand our faculty pool with new members capable of developing, redesigning, or reimagining writing curricula and programs with multimodal focus or components, and then implementing them effectively across different course or degree levels. The other related challenge is bringing the existing faculty pool on board to take up multimodality and/or digitality in their courses or programs. As Cynthia Selfe (1999) said some twenty years ago, instructors identify themselves as either protechnology or antitechnology when it comes to reimagining writing curricula, and it is always easier to preach to a convert than to someone who disagrees or is outright hostile to the whole notion of multimodal and/or digital composition. A similar challenge is bridging the existing disconnect between what position statements of our major professional organizations, such as CCCC, NCTE and CWPA, encourage writing programs and faculty members to do and what faculty members across institutions are actually capable of or equipped to do. In her empirical qualitative study titled "Technology Professional Development of Writing Faculty: The Expectations and the Needs," Lilian W. Mina (2020) analyzes forty CCCC, NCTE and CWPA position statements to study technology-related teaching expectations for college writing faculty and characteristics of technology professional-development programs. The findings of her study revealed there was a critical gap between the desired and the actual qualifications of many faculty members. She learned that the conceptual, pedagogical and technological knowledge necessary to comfortably and effectively teach writing curricula with technological components in them was expected of writing faculty. However, when the faculty members were asked to teach with technology and achieve technology-related outcomes, they were found to be lacking one or more of those qualifications. In fact, Mina found problems with the workings and the thought processes behind the position statements themselves. All these statements brilliantly articulate the expectations or outcomes for different writing courses; however, Mina asserts, they are silent about what institutions or programs need to do in order to bring their faculty on par with the expectations.

> The leading organizations in the field have invested large resources to clearly articulate the conceptual, pedagogical, and technological expectations of teaching writing with technology (92 clauses coded), with less emphasis on describing the need for and characteristics of robust TPD programs for in-service writing faculty (39 clauses coded) to be able to meet those expectations.

This lack of desired qualifications among a large number of writing faculty is further complicated by the fact that many of our faculty members are contingent (part timers, adjuncts, and graduate teaching assistants), and there exists a significant opportunity gap between full-time and contingent faculty members. Full-time and tenure-line faculty members in R1 institutions and four-year colleges usually have access to some form of funding and benefits package, which allows them to enroll into new courses or attend workshops and professional conferences to learn new or advanced theoretical insights and functional digital skills necessary to teach writing courses with multimodal focus. However, the same opportunity is not available to contingent faculty members and even full-time faculty members in two-year colleges. These faculty members are, in fact, overworked and underpaid, and they lack access to funds and opportunities to learn and experiment with digital media and technologies in their classrooms. This opportunity gap is the single most impactful factor in the slow adoption of multimodality and/or digitality in our writing classrooms and is partly an outcome of the neoliberalization of higher education, which has pushed faculty positions into precarity and dramatically cut funding and resources for teaching and research activities. As such, higher education in the United States is reeling under severe budget cuts, reduction of permanent positions, and increased reliance on contingent staff for both teaching and research. This is concerning because federal or state budget cuts trickle down to department and program levels, compelling them to prioritize teaching over professional-development programs or even faculty research. On the other hand, contingent positions come without security, decent pay, or benefits, which keeps faculty at the edge all the time and forces them to overwork or take jobs at multiple institutions just to support themselves. No doubt, this less-than-ideal state of educational institutions and faculty status is undermining the overall quality of teaching and research, but it is also severely impacting the implementation or expansion of multimodality in college curricula because this initiative requires not just funding and resources but also time and eagerness on the part of faculty members to learn new forms and technologies of composing.

Thus, we will need to square multiple dimensions of academia to get to the bottom of the causes behind the slow and differential professionalization of multimodal composition across programs and institutions. However, scholars differ in their views when it comes to placing value on different factors causing the sluggish adoption of multimodality. For instance, Michael J. Faris (2019) finds WPAs to be key players in the professionalization of multimodal composition. Faris argues, "WPAs can and should be at the forefront of this work, regarding technology as central to their advocacy work in ways that adjust to and change the local rhetorical ecologies of their programs and institutions" (110). Mina (2020) also notes that involving WPAs in advocacy for multimodality matters because professionalizing multimodal composition is contingent on their awareness of this new field and the goals they set for their respective writing programs.

In fact, academic leaders, including WPAs, department chairs, deans, and so on, can be instrumental in realizing the expectations or outcomes as outlined in the position statements of our professional organizations. To invoke academic leaders here is basically to invoke institutional, programmatic, and faculty-level initiatives to bridge the existing theory-praxis gap in our field by professionalizing faculty of all standings to engage multimodality effectively in their classrooms. Given this context, the authors in this book discuss three major areas these initiatives must focus on at the moment: (1) faculty preparedness to take up multimodality in their curricula; (2) institutional support to professionalize faculty to incorporate multimodal composition in their curricula or programs; and (3) academic leadership and those leaders' willingness to introduce and support multimodal composition in different levels of writing courses and/or degree programs. All these areas definitely intersect and work in tandem. For instance, faculty preparedness to engage multimodality/digitality in their research and pedagogies is contingent on the kind of institutional support and academic leadership faculty get in their home institutions. As a result, institutional support for faculty can come in different forms. Direct funding for research and professional development is one form of institutional support; the other form could be tuition remission or financial assistance for faculty to enroll in courses, institutes, or boot camps to learn or upgrade their multimodal composing knowledge and skills. Yet another form of support could be faculty-development programs and opportunities made available to them right there in their own academic units or institutions. Workshops and boot camps run in-house are examples of such opportunities. Faculty-development opportunities could also come in the form of year- or semester-long teaching practica or extensive orientations for incoming faculty or teaching associates at the beginning of an academic year. All these different programs and events can serve as gateways for the majority of our faculty to enter into the world of multimodality. Professional-development programs, particularly the workshops and boot camps, could also be instrumental in introducing this exciting subfield to many non-writing specialists. However, academic coursework or research would be the most important of all these initiatives. Be it mentoring our graduate teaching assistants or training our doctoral students with adequate coursework and research assignments on emerging media and composing, our graduate programs are and should be at the heart of producing some top-notch next-gen multimodal instructors and scholars for the field (more on this below in the "Defining Professionalization" section).

Two major points become evident in our discussion here. First, our current understanding of professional development through GTA mentoring and graduate course offerings is a necessary but not sufficient step to expand the implementation of multimodality in our field because a large body of contingent faculty do not have access to professional-development opportunities, nor do they hold a terminal degree with multimodal focus that makes it possible for them to initiate or enact changes in their curricular and pedagogical practices. Second, while there is an increasing interest among individual faculty and programs to incorporate multimodality, there still is a dearth of research studies that present clear evidence that writing instructors have the knowledge and skills to implement multimodality at the programmatic, departmental, or institutional level. Even more critically, there are not many published accounts of successful academic interventions or faculty-development initiatives launched to prepare or mentor faculty of all standings at a programmatic, departmental, or institutional level to teach multimodal or digital composition. This chilling absence has two major implications. First, there is no exchange of experiences and lessons learned within the communities of practice, and second, such a lack of exchange has considerably delayed the process of integrating multimodality into the larger college writing curriculum. Therefore, we must expand both the definition and implementation of multimodal professionalization and publish and circulate the results or findings of such initiatives throughout a wider community of practice.

DEFINING PROFESSIONALIZATION

Numerous studies speak to the condition of the majority of our institutions and faculty, one that calls for immediate actions. Our programs and field must focus on pedagogically based rather than tool-based training, make professional development ongoing, discipline-specific, and rhetorically situated to the institutional and teaching contexts. This training basically is what professionalizing with/through/for multimodality requires.

To begin with, Felice J. Levine and Nathan E. Bell (2015), in their article "Social Sciences Professions and Professionalization," define professionalization as "the development of skills, identities, norms, and values associated with becoming part of a professional group" (679). They note that through professionalization, "individuals pursuing careers in specific social sciences acquire both substantive and methodological knowledge and develop understandings of their roles that permit them to function as professionals in their fields" (679). In general, the definition of professionalization includes some concrete criteria, such as a body of knowledge, exclusiveness, lengthy training, practitioner autonomy, and a code of ethics. As per Saul Carliner (2012), professionalization is primarily connected with infrastructures, which typically include five common components: professional organizations, bodies of knowledge, education, professional activities, and certification. Armin Krishnan (2009), however, takes a sociological perspective on professionalization and describes it as "a social process through which an activity becomes a means for people to make a living. A professional is someone who can carry out a certain activity with a higher level of skill and knowledge than an amateur and someone who is paid for it sufficiently to base their own livelihood on that activity" (26–27). However, as Richard Ohmann (1990) discusses in his *College English* article, the process and practices of professionalization are contentious in nature.

> Professions are . . . socially made categories, and processes. A group that is doing a particular kind of work organizes itself in a professional association; appropriates, shares, and develops a body of knowledge as its own; discredits other practitioners performing similar work; establishes definite routes of admission, including but not limited to academic study; controls access; and gets recognition as the only group allowed to perform that kind of work, ideally with state power backing its monopoly. The process doesn't end there. Every constituted profession must continue to defend its rights and its borders. (250)

If we were to extend such a definition of professionalization to multimodal composition, we would have to generate a list of criteria for members to enter the profession of teaching multimodal composition, which, sure enough, would be contentious as well. Ideally, the members should earn a degree in writing studies with a focus on multimodal composition, produce and read bodies of knowledge in the field, engage in professional activities, and be affiliated with professional organizations. These would sound like minimal professionalizing expectations in other fields because fields like medicine and law have even more stringent requirements, such as certifications or credentialing and their maintenance over the life of the profession, but the field of multimodal composition doesn't have any agreed-upon set of expectations for multimodal faculty, even though they would need academic and professional preparation to be able to teach courses on multimodal composing. The same is roughly the case with first-year composition. Faculty teaching first-year writing courses are not required to have any particular academic or professional preparation other than a degree in English studies or a cognate field. Wouldn't it be contentious if we started talking about a need for a degree in a particular subject area, let alone certification or credentialing to qualify as a faculty member to teach multimodal composition, or first-year composition for that matter? We are not arguing here that we devise gatekeeping measures, as Ohmann (1990) describes above, but we must ensure our faculty have academic and professional preparation to teach multimodal composition competently and effectively.

As per Lisa Meloncon, Peter England, and Alex Ilyasova (2016), our contingent faculty, in particular, lack professional-development opportunities "defined as those opportunities to stay current in the field or improve as a teacher and scholar" (221). They report data and case studies showing "significant gaps in professional development and training opportunities for contingent faculty" (264). Apparently, these faculty require "training, mentoring, and practice" (Cook et al., 2013, p. 311) in order to be able to integrate multimodality into their curriculum. In other words, faculty members would need learning opportunities or professionalization before they could design and implement a multimodal curriculum in their classrooms or in their programs. An upshot of involving faculty in learning opportunities or professionalization would be their participation in educational changes (Voogt et al. 2015). According to Joke Voogt, Therese Laferrière, Alain Breuleux, Rebecca C. Itow, Daniel T. Hickey, and Susan McKenney (2015), faculty can be involved in educational change "through a national/state reform or a local reform, or through collaborative design of instruction or curricular materials, which they adapt to their context" (260). Such an involvement could change the faculty's instructional practice and also help develop a sense of ownership for the reform. This shared process of adaptation through collaborative design of curricular materials offers ample opportunities for faculty professional development (260). Thus, Voogt et al. make it clear that collaborative design of curricular/ instructional materials could be a professionalizing experience for both new and veteran faculty. This experience creates a mutually rewarding situation because when it comes to multimodal composing or learning about new technologies or tools, veteran faculty need as much training, workshopping, or mentorship as the new faculty. In that sense, multimodal composing and new media can serve as equalizers or democratizing forces in our departments and institutions.

When it comes to multimodal professionalization, how to professionalize faculty for multimodal composition is even more important than why to professionalize them. No wonder there are and could be multiple models of professionalization. For instance, Punya Mishra and Matthew J. Koehler (2006) propose a conceptual framework that integrates technology, content, and pedagogical knowledge (popularly known as TPACK). According to Seyum Tekeher Getenet (2017), "TPACK stems from the notion that technology integration benefits from a cautious alignment of content, pedagogy, and technological knowledge" (2630) and, obviously, to integrate multimodality in their teaching practice, faculty must be competent in all three domains. According to Laura McGrath and Letizia Guglielmo (2015), DMAC (Digital Media and Composition Institute) could also serve as a model for faculty professionalization of multimodality. For them, "DMAC offered a model of goal-oriented activity and playful experimentation complemented by ongoing reflection and the support of co-learners and mentors, a model similar to what Barb Blakely Duffelmeyer (2003) described as a community of practice" (45). As the authors argue, this "community of practice" model can be "adapted for use in professional development contexts as well as in the classroom" (46). They actually present some case studies of how they adapted the DMAC model first to facilitate professional technological development of faculty at their institution and then to teach an upper-division Writing in Digital Environments course in their department (46). They found DMAC's "careful framing and community building," which allowed "messing around" and "reflective practice," to be a particularly effective approach both for the professional-development (PD) programs and classroom teaching. Another important insight gained from the DMAC model was that faculty professional development in teaching digital writing and digital writing scholarship is and should be the domain of rhetoric and composition faculty (52). This insight ties back to the TPACK framework discussed above. Any technology PD events divorced from content knowledge and pedagogical practice is simply useless. The DMAC Institute is effective because it's run by faculty members in rhetoric and composition. A chain impact such as that of the DMAC Institute is testimony to the fact that individual professionalization can eventually accumulate into a program-wide and discipline-wide kind of professionalization.

14   KHADKA AND PANDEY

Sharla Berry (2018) concurs with McGrath and Guglielmo and claims departmental colleagues are the best resource for professional-development programs. Berry, in fact, presents the results of a qualitative case study in which she drew on interviews with thirteen faculty members in an online doctoral program to find out how professional-development offerings strengthened distance instructors' technical, pedagogical, and content knowledge. She found both newer and veteran faculty agreed that the most impactful form of professional development was the one "designed for instructors, by instructors" (132). Under this PD model, "Faculty would meet in groups by course to discuss curriculum and instruction for the week's course sessions" (130). Their weekly meetings were productive for a number of reasons: (1) they were designed with instructors in mind, (2) they met instructors' needs by focusing on curriculum and content of the week, and (3) the instructors got the opportunity to learn from the content experts they trusted.

Kristine L. Blair (2014), on the other hand, has a slightly different take on how to professionalize multimodal composition among graduate students and faculty members. She calls for the entire department to be involved in the professional development of its faculty and graduate students. She laments that "all too often the task of technological training is delegated to the single course, the single expert in the program, a technical role those earlier theorists have referred to as the 'white coat syndrome' (Zeni)" (104). Graduate students, in particular, must be afforded learning opportunities across a spectrum of courses, from multimodal composing to the course in research methods. But she also sees value in making graduate students coteachers and researchers and immersing them in multimodal publication processes and editorial work on journals. She notes that this level of student engagement with digital and multimodal literacies is not possible with an individual effort, so the "graduate programs in the field should view the digital-literacy acquisition of graduate students as a shared responsibility among colleagues that includes the students themselves in a reciprocal, recursive mentoring model that will shape their future faculty identities, online and off" (105).

INTERVENTIONS OF THIS COLLECTION

This collection strives to respond to an unusual gap that exists between multimodal theory and practice in the field (Khadka and Lee 2019) and brings together academic leaders, scholars, and instructors who have successfully designed and launched academic programs or faculty-development initiatives, either institutionally or individually, and want to discuss the theoretical and logistical questions considered while designing those initiatives, the outcomes they achieved by successfully running those programs or initiatives, and how others can emulate those initiatives. This exchange of knowledge, insights, experiences, and lessons learned among community members is critical for enabling or inspiring many other programs, departments, and institutions to conceive, design, and launch academic programs or faculty-development initiatives for their own faculty. To be more precise, this collection explores the individual faculty, programmatic, and institutional initiatives for integrating multimodal composition into various writing or writing-intensive courses and programs across institutions. Since the larger goal with professionalizing is to work with teaching faculty to increase their interactional expertise with multimodal composition, this collection offers a set of models (divided into three sections) for how faculty can do that at their own institutions and in their own programs. In that sense, this collection advocates for an approach to professionalizing that works for multimodality, which is detailed in three sections and thirteen individual chapters.

With similar goals in mind, the editors of this collection, Shyam B. Pandey and Shantosh Khadka, recently edited another collection, *Multimodal Composition: Faculty Development Programs and Institutional Change* (2022), focused on faculty development, which has launched conversations on multimodal professionalization of writing faculty. Whereas each of the chapters in these two collections is based on research studies conducted in different institutional settings and with different research questions and participants, and their findings are unique and distinctive, these collections perfectly complement one another, and, taken together, they could provide an array of ideas, approaches, models, and best practices for multimodal professionalization. This particular collection, for instance, focuses more on institutional initiatives, faculty preparedness (primarily grad students/TAs), and institutional academic leadership on those initiatives, whereas *Multimodal Composition* centers more on individual faculty initiatives, curriculum design, faculty-development programs, and writing across the disciplines.

In summary, this collection brings together thirteen ground-breaking essays, which, individually and collectively, address the following set of critical questions about multimodal professionalization:

- What progress have we made in the last twenty years to embrace and implement multimodality in our writing programs? How do university, department, or writing program administrators go about

16   KHADKA AND PANDEY

professionalizing multimodal composition in their respective units? What struggles and successes have they realized?

- How has multimodal composition been part of faculty-development programs? Has it received any priority in faculty hiring processes?
- How are, can, and should graduate teaching assistants be trained to engage multimodality in their coursework, teaching, and scholarship? To what extent do they feel prepared to incorporate multimodality in their course syllabi upon completion of their degree?
- What challenges, struggles, and successes have been identified to integrate multimodality in first-year composition and upper-division writing or writing-intensive courses across the curriculum or disciplines? How can writing faculty better integrate multimodality in their curricula?
- How are writing faculty trained to utilize multimodality to teach the diverse student population more effectively? How do the different variables, such as the age, sex, class, access, abilities, literacy level, and socioeconomic status of students play into the successes and failures of adopting multimodal composition pedagogies in writing classrooms?
- To what extent are writing instructors prepared to implement multimodal pedagogies in multilingual and online spaces? What challenges and opportunities are identified in those spaces?
- What departmental and institutional challenges to and opportunities for studying and teaching multimodal composition exist in today's higher education settings? How can those challenges be turned into opportunities?

CHAPTER SUMMARIES

This book includes thirteen distinct chapters, which are divided into three thematic sections: "Faculty Preparedness," "Institutional Initiatives and Support," and "Academic Leadership." The first section has five chapters, the second has four chapters, and the final section has four chapters.

In chapter 1, "Graduate Student and Faculty Development in Multimodal Composing," Wilfredo Flores, Teresa Williams, Christina Boyles, Kristin Arola, and Dànielle Nicole DeVoss discuss the scholarly landscape to examine how multimodal composing and teacher professional training have run perpendicular to one another and describe the teacher-development and writing center-anchored components of supporting their first-year writing curriculum, specifically one of its shared assignments: a remix composition. In chapter 2, "(E)merging Expertise: Multivocal, Multimodal Preparation and Development of Graduate Teaching Assistants in Writing Programs," Kelly Moreland,

Sarah Henderson Lee, and Kirsti Cole discuss one institution's curricular revision to merge and update three different writing programs in the same English department, while taking into consideration their institutional context and the revision work they were doing to their curriculum for their first-year writing program. They also describe how, in their specific contexts, the faculty worked to mentor their graduate teaching assistants to teach and evaluate multimodal composition for diverse student populations. In chapter 3, "Practicing (Antiracist and Anti-ableist) Multimodality: TA Training and Student Responses to Implementing a Multimodal Curriculum in First-Year Writing," Megan McIntyre (a WPA) and Jennifer Lanatti Shen (a graduate teaching associate) discuss implementing a multimodal pedagogy and offer insight into how multimodal composition supports the professional development of GTAs, how these new instructors apply multimodal theory and praxis when designing their own courses, and how students respond to a multimodal curriculum. In chapter 4, "Professional Development for Multimodal Composition: Preparing Graduate Teaching Assistants for the Twenty-First Century," Tiffany Bourelle argues for administrators to extend opportunities for GTAs to learn and experiment with the theory behind multimodal composition to advance their knowledge and experience as writing instructors in these times of great technological innovations. She also discusses different professional-development opportunities, including developing seminars or practicum courses, facilitating one-on-one mentoring, and conducting ongoing workshops and focus groups, among others. And, finally, in chapter 5, "Incorporating Multimodal Literacies across an FYW Program: Graduate Instructors' Preparation and Experiences," a WPA, Michael J. Faris, and eighteen graduate instructors, Lauren Brawley, Morgan Connor, Meghalee Das, Aliethia Dean, Claudia Diaz, Michelle Flahive, Maeve Kirk, Max Kirschenbaum, Joshua Kulseth, Alfonsina Lago, Kristina Lewis, Lance Lomax, Brook McClurg, Zachary Ostraff, Anthony Ranieri, Sierra Sinor, Rebekah Smith, and Yifan Zhang, share their program's experiences preparing new graduate instructors to teach multimodal composition. Together, they reflect on and discuss four different themes: (1) preparation for teaching multimodality through the practicum course and peer mentoring programs; (2) teaching functional aspects of digital and multimodal literacy; (3) teaching critical and rhetorical aspects of digital and multimodal literacy; and (4) exploration, play, inquiry, and risk taking. They conclude the chapter with discussion of implications for faculty development in any writing programs that incorporate multimodal composition.

The second section of this book, "Institutional Initiatives and Support," starts with chapter 6, "DMAC at Fifteen: Professionalizing Digital Media and Composition," in which authors Scott Lloyd DeWitt and John Jones report the findings of an impact study that examines the influence of the Digital Media and Composition Institute's instructional experience on all past attendees and analyze the significance of associated pedagogical, scholarly, and community outcomes. In chapter 7, "Looking beyond the Writing Program: Institutional Allies to Support Professional Development in the Teaching of Digital Writing," Alison Witte, Kerri Hauman, and Stacy Kastner profile six award-winning writing programs that assign digital writing projects to illustrate how writing programs interact with their broader campus technoecologies to access technology pedagogy professional development and support. As the authors put it, the goals of their chapter are to (1) highlight innovative and effective high-impact strategies for tech-ped PD developed beyond writing programs and (2) discuss how and why writing programs, and individuals within them, access these PD opportunities, in order to (3) ultimately encourage WPAs and faculty to consider leveraging connections/networks across campus in their local contexts. In chapter 8, "A Fresh Catalyst: Invigorating the University with Integrated Modalities," Daniel Schafer and Josh Ambrose discuss the model being developed at McDaniel College—a framework built around internship-based courses in which multimodal composition is integral—and argue that the model can be adapted for implementation at any college or university. Finally, in chapter 9, "Embedding Multimodal Writing across a University at the Institutional, Administrative, and Curricular Level: The Undergraduate Professional Writing and Rhetoric Major as Agent of Change," Li Li, Paula Rosinski, and Michael Strickland present a case study on how multimodal writing has been advocated and implemented at three different levels—institutional and administrative, curricular, and class—at their university (Elon University).

Finally, the third section, "Academic Leadership," begins with chapter 10, "The Art of Responsiveness: The Ongoing Development of a Masters of Arts Degree in Composition, Rhetoric, and Digital Media (CRDM)," in which Claire Lutkewitte uses Nova Southeastern University's masters of arts degree in composition, rhetoric, and digital media (CRDM) as an example to explore the strategies for successfully responding to the multifaceted needs of developing a program focusing on multimodal writing and preparing the faculty to write about and teach multimodal composition effectively. Similarly, in chapter 11, "En(Act)ion: Bridging the Graduate School Digital Divide," Stephen Quigley and Shauna

Chung describe a cutting-edge cross-curricular digital-literacy program designed to address transferable skills, beginning with matriculating graduate students before they arrive on campus and after they have established themselves in their courses of study. In chapter 12, "Centering Translingualism in Multimodal Practice: A Reflective Case Study of a Linguistically Diverse Graduate Program," Megan E. Heise and Matthew A. Vetter explore how a linguistically diverse doctoral program in composition and applied linguistics uses multimodal practices in a course on digital rhetoric in an effort to identify challenges and successes, which sheds light on the intersections between translingual and multimodal theories and practices. Along similar lines, in chapter 13, "Multimodality as a Key Consideration in Developing a New Communications Degree at UMass, Dartmouth," Anthony F. Arrigo presents a case study of how and why faculty at the University of Massachusetts, Dartmouth, focused on multimodality as a key feature in designing a brand-new communications BA degree. This chapter primarily discusses how multimodal writing and communication has been a structural focus throughout the curriculum and what the resulting expectations and opportunities for educators in their program and beyond have been.

REFERENCES

Adsanatham, Chanon, Phill Alexander, Kerrie Carsey, Abby Dubisar, Wioleta Fedeczko, Denise Landrum, Cynthia Lewiecki-Wilson, Heidi McKee, Kristen Moore, Gina Patterson, and Michele Polak. 2013. "Going Multimodal: Programmatic, Curricular, and Classroom Change." In *Multimodal Literacies and Emerging Genres*, edited by T. Bowen, and C. Whithaus, 282–312. Pittsburgh: University of Pittsburgh Press.

Berry, Sharla. 2018. "Professional Development for Online Faculty: Instructors' Perspectives on Cultivating Technical, Pedagogical and Content Knowledge in a Distance Program." *Journal of Computing in Higher Education* 31: 121–36.

Blair, Kristine L. 2014. "Composing Change: The Role of Graduate Education in Sustaining a Digital Scholarly Future." *Composition Studies* 42 (1): 103–6.

Carliner, Saul. 2012. "The Three Approaches to Professionalization in Technical Communication." *Technical Communication* 59 (1): 49–65.

Cook, K. C., & Grant-Davie, K., eds. (2013). *Online Education 2.0: Evolving, Adapting, and Reinventing Online Technical Communication*. Amityville, NY: Baywood.

Ericsson, Patricia, Leeann Downing Hunter, Tialitha Michelle Macklin, and Elizabeth Sue Edwards. 2016. "Composition at Washington State University: Building a Multimodal Bricolage." *Composition Forum* 33. compositionforum.com/issue/33/wsu.php.

Faris, Michael J. 2019. "Writing and Technology in WPA: Toward the WPA as an Advocate for Technological Writing." *WPA: Writing Program Administration* 42 (3): 106–12.

Getenet, Seyum Tekeher. 2017. "Adapting Technological Pedagogical Content Knowledge Framework to Teach Mathematics." *Education and Information Technologies* 22 (5): 2629–44.

Jacobs, Gloria E. 2013. "Multi, Digital, or Technology? Seeking Clarity of Teaching Through a Clarity of Terms." *Journal of Adolescent and Adult Literacy* 57 (2): 99–103.

Khadka, Santosh. 2019. *Multiliteracies, Emerging Media, and College Writing Instruction*. New York: Routledge.

Khadka, Santosh, and J. C Lee. 2019. *Bridging the Multimodal Gap: From Theory to Practice*. Logan: Utah State University Press.

Kress, Gunther. 1999. " 'English' at the Crossroads: Rethinking the Curricula of Communication in the Context of the Turn to the Visual." In *Passions, Pedagogies, and Twenty-First-Century Technologies*, edited by G. F. Hawisher and C. L. Selfe, 66–88. Logan: Utah State University Press.

Kress, Gunther, and Theo Van Leeuwen. 2001. *Multimodal Discourse: The Modes and Media of Contemporary Communication*. London: Arnold.

Krishnan, Armin. 2009. "What Are Academic Disciplines? Some Observations on the Disciplinarity vs. Interdisciplinarity Debate." ESRC National Centre for Research Methods Working Paper. https://eprints.ncrm.ac.uk/id/eprint/783/1/what_are_academic_disciplines.pdf.

Lee, Rory. 2020. "Making the Case: Implementing Multimodality in Undergraduate Major Programs in Writing and Rhetoric." In *Writing Changes: Alphabetic Text and Multimodal Composition*, edited by P. P. Powell, 253–70. New York: MLA.

Levine, Felice J., and Bell, Nathan. E. 2015. "Social Science Professions and Professionalization." *International Encyclopedia of the Social and Behavioral Sciences* 22 (2): 679–86.

Leverenz, Carrie. 2008. "Remediating Writing Program Administration." *WPA: Writing Program Administration: Journal of the Council of Writing Program Administrators* 32 (1): 37–56.

McGrath, Laura, and Letizia Guglielmo. 2015. "Communities of Practice and Makerspaces: DMAC's Influence on Technological Professional Development and Teaching Multimodal Composing." *Computers and Composition* 36: 44–53.

Meloncon, Lisa, England, Peter, & Ilyasova, Alex. (2016). "A Portrait of Non-Tenure-Track Faculty in Technical and Professional Communication." *Journal of Technical Writing and Communication*, 46(2), 206–235. doi:10.1177/0047281616633601.

Mina, Lilian. W. 2020. "Technology Professional Development of Writing Faculty: The Expectations and the Needs." *Composition Forum* 43. https://compositionforum.com/issue/43/professional-development.php.

Mishra, Punya, and Koehler, Matthew J. 2006. "Technological Pedagogical Content Knowledge: A Framework for Teacher Knowledge." *Teachers College Record* 108 (6): 1017–54.

NCTE. (2009). Writing in the 21st Century: A Report from the National Council of Teachers of English. https://archive.nwp.org/cs/public/download/nwp_file/12440/Kathleen_Blake_Yancey_Writing_21st_Century.pdf?x-r=pcfile_d.

The New London Group. 1996. "A Pedagogy of Multiliteracies: Designing Social Futures." *Harvard Educational Review* 66 (1): 60–92.

Ohmann, Richard. 1990. "Graduate Students, Professionals, Intellectuals." *College English* 52 (3): 247–57.

Palmeri, Jason. 2012. *Remixing Composition: A History of Multimodal Writing Pedagogy*. Carbondale: Southern Illinois University Press.

Pandey, Shyam B., and Santosh Khadka. 2022. *Multimodal Composition: Faculty Development Programs and Institutional Change*. New York: Routledge.

Selber, Stuart A. 2005. *Multiliteracies for a Digital Age*. Carbondale: Southern Illinois University Press.

Selfe, Cynthia. 1999. "Technology and Literacy: A Story about the Perils of Not Paying Attention." *College Composition and Communication* 50 (3): 411–36.

Shipka, Jodie. 2009. "Negotiating Rhetorical, Material, Methodological, and Technological Difference: Evaluating Multimodal Designs." *College Composition and Communication* 61: 343–66.

Takayoshi, Pamela, and Cynthia Selfe. 2007. "Thinking about Multimodality." In *Multimodal Composition: Resources for Teachers*, edited by C. Selfe, 1–12. Cresskill, NJ: Hampton Press.

Voogt, Joke, Therese Laferriere, Alaine Breuleux, Rebecca C. Itow, Daniel T. Hickey, and Susan McKenney. 2015. "Collaborative Design as a Form of Professional Development." *Instructional Science* 43: 259–82.

Wysocki, Anne Frances, Johndan Johnson-Eilola, Cynthia L. Selfe, and Geoggrey Sirc. 2004. *Writing New Media: Theory and Applications for Expanding the Teaching of Composition.* Logan: Utah State University Press.

Yancey, Kathleen Blake. 2004. "Made Not Only in Words: Composition in a New Key." *CCC* 56 (2): 297–328. doi:10.2307/4140651.

PART I

Faculty Preparedness

One of the most frequently asked questions in academia when it comes to adopting or integrating multimodal composition is about faculty preparedness. The answer to that question is hard to come by because faculty preparedness is tied to institutional contexts: How has multimodal composition fared in faculty-development events or programs? Has it received any consideration in faculty hiring processes? To what extent are writing instructors prepared to implement multimodal pedagogies in diverse teaching contexts like multilingual classes, online spaces, or post-COVID-19 contexts? What challenges and opportunities are identified in those spaces? How are, can, and should graduate teaching assistants be trained to engage multimodality in their coursework, teaching, and scholarship? To what extent do they feel prepared to incorporate multimodality in their curricula upon completion of their degree? Not all institutions may have the same level and scale of faculty preparedness, as they may be reeling under a myriad of constraints, such as low infrastructure and professional-development funds, budget cuts, overworked faculty, unavailability of mentors, and so on.

The five chapters in this section engage questions and issues such as the ones discussed above. Drawing on their own institutional experiences, authors shed light on their faculty-development initiatives on multimodal composing. Taken together, these chapters discuss how to mentor faculty and graduate students to teach multimodal composing, how to involve graduate teaching assistants in the development of multivocal and multimodal writing curricula, how to center TA training to practice an antiracist and anti-ableist multimodal approach in first-year writing curricula, how to make suggestions for WPAs and other teacher-trainers when implementing multimodal composition so their faculty members are better prepared for the twenty-first-century teaching contexts, how to mentor and model Tas to teach multimodal composition, and how to create an environment where faculty and Tas can share their multimodal teaching experiences.

https://doi.org/10.7330/9781646424184.p001

PART I

Facility Requirements

1

GRADUATE STUDENT AND FACULTY DEVELOPMENT IN MULTIMODAL COMPOSING

Wilfredo Flores, Teresa Williams, Christina Boyles, Kristin Arola, and Dànielle Nicole DeVoss

We imagined and proposed this chapter in the fall of 2019 without, of course, any sense of how much our teaching context would change in the spring of 2020 with the spread of COVID-19. Currently, scholarship is being developed and proposed in our field to document how we navigated our institutions, our teaching, and our professional lives as they moved entirely online in spring 2020. At our institution, the announcement to move entirely online was shared university wide at 10:30 a.m. on Wednesday, March 13. Our university closed its doors to face-to-face teaching at noon that day.

Although some of us anticipated the move, this shift was jarring for most faculty, especially those teaching multimodal composing and leaning heavily on our campus labs, robust internet connections, and access to expensive software (not surprisingly, we have found multimodal composing is tethered in a variety of ways to physical tools and equipment and deeply embedded in institutional infrastructural issues). Although we are sorely tempted to write about the anxieties and the successes of the past months and the COVID transition in this chapter, instead we are using this space to address our original proposal and initial query, which is how to foster and sustain multimodal composing from a teacher-development perspective. As we argue below, it takes a sustained, integrated, deliberate orientation and commitment to do so.

INTRODUCTION

In preparing for a class session, Chris reviews her lesson plans and gathers the materials she wants to combine for a set of slides for class. She

https://doi.org/10.7330/9781646424184.c001

merges existing slides, creates new slides, identifies video content (some of which she downloads and embeds in her slides and some of which she embeds as links to YouTube from her slides). She identifies concepts that lend themselves well to—or even perhaps require—visuals for comprehension. Some visuals she creates within the slideshow-creation software; for other visuals, she does a Google Image search and identifies, downloads, and embeds an existing image that conveys the concept well.

As part of their communications internship with a department that houses the university's first-year writing program, Antonio produces the monthly podcast series for the department. To produce the podcast, they ask students and faculty in the department about possible interviewees. Once they identify the interviewee they want to focus on, they do some background research on them and their work and ask some initial questions over email to get to know them a bit. They share the questions in advance and then arrange to conduct the interview (usually over Zoom, with a test session first to make sure the interviewee has a good enough microphone to capture quality audio). After the interview, they listen a few times to identify places to cut, transitions to create, and edits to perform. Once that editing is done, they add the intro music they found on a copyright-free music-sharing site and record their intro to the podcast.

Melody is a first-year PhD student in biochemistry and molecular biology preparing a poster presentation for a conference. Melody is generally familiar with creating field- and research-specific visuals, having done much reading and researching with the principal investigator (PI) of the study she is working on. Melody has also started drafting manuscripts with her PI and the lab's research team. However, she has never had to create a poster, and she has never presented at a conference this large on her own. She has decided to use Microsoft PowerPoint as her poster-making tool and to prep graphs in Google Sheets. Melody's advisor has suggested the writing center's new multimodal center as a space for support in pulling all the pieces of the poster together. A consultant trained in digital rhetoric and using a variety of digital-visual tools helps Melody create the poster in PowerPoint, transition the graphs from Google Sheets to PowerPoint-ready graphics, and think about visual design (e.g., asking questions like, "How large will heading font sizes need to be for viewers to easily scan the poster from, say, ten feet or so away?"). Melody leaves the session with a plan for how to finish and where to print the poster ahead of the conference.

We share these scenarios because they're fairly commonplace and typical of composing that happens in and around our department and in our writing center. We also share these scenarios to ask, How can our teaching of writing support these practices? Prepare students for this type of robust, cross-software, cross-platform, multimodal composing? How can we support, develop, and sustain the teaching of multimodal composing? What sort of graduate student and faculty development might prepare teachers to support students for this type of robust, cross-software, cross-platform multimodal composing? To support teachers themselves in delivering their teaching with this type of robust, cross-software, cross-platform multimodal compositions? To support grad students to not only engage multimodal composing in their course work and scholarly projects but also to graduate and be technology innovators and multimodal composing advocates in their future work?

In this chapter, we first discuss the scholarly landscape to examine how multimodal composing and teacher professional training have run perpendicular to one another. We then turn to our first-year writing program as a case, focusing specifically on one of its shared assignments: a remix composition. We discuss the teacher-development and writing center-anchored components of supporting the curriculum and specifically this assignment. Our program values multimodal composing as a norm and centers teacher practices and expertise. As such, our commitment to professional development both in our department and across the institution views multimodal production work as requiring, as Jennifer Sheppard (2009)—and others, as we discuss below—argue, "careful attention to both traditional and technological rhetorical considerations" (121). Although we describe a particular institutional context and approach, we share this case and our teacher-engaged, development-focused multimodal composing advocacy work in a way we hope makes these institutional practices malleable, adaptable, and adoptable at a range of institution types and in a variety of programmatic contexts.

THEORIZING MULTIMODAL COMPOSING FROM A TEACHER-SUPPORT APPROACH

Teacher Support in Rhetoric and Composition Studies

In many ways, rhetoric and composition studies—with writing instruction at its pedagogical heart and scholarly core—has maintained a significant, long-term, and ongoing discussion about aspects of faculty support. Multiple books have focused on or included chapters on, for instance, teaching-assistant development and training (e.g., Bullock 1999; Dobrin 2005; Restaino 2012; Ritter and Matsuda 2010), and journal articles have honed in on writing program administration philosophies of and around faculty support (e.g., Artze-Vega et al. 2013; Brunk-Chavez 2010; Fedukovich and Morse 2017; Marshall 2008; Reid 2018; Willard-Traub 2008). However—and this claim certainly resonates with the very *reason* this book exists—there has been no ongoing, focused scholarly conversation about preparing faculty to teach, engage, evaluate, and assess multimodal composing.

Certainly this lack is understandable, given the relative newness of multimodal composition as this collection conceptualizes it. People have been composing with multiple media for millennia, but the newness of multimodal composing relates to the widespread ability of tools for and networked capacity to share writing that includes photos, animations, music, and more broadly and rapidly. Indeed, as Claire Lauer (2009) articulates, we—the global we—are still bouncing around terms like *new media, multimedia,* and *multimodal* (see also Werner 2015). Twitter launched in 2005, the same year the first YouTube video hit the million-view mark, and Facebook didn't claim its status as the most popular social platform until 2009 (a status that is tenuous now as fewer young people head to the space, preferring instead Snapchat and TikTok). True, many of the students in our classes grew up with these tools and these writerly spaces, but many of us witnessed their emergence—they were an add-on and extensions to our rhetorical and scholarly toolkits and foci, not necessarily a default composing space or place.

If we turn to the pages of two landmark, key journals in our field, there are some murmurs of multimodal composing and teacher training, but, again, no sustained focus. Past discussions have oriented toward a particular technological or historical moment or exigency; for instance, Catherine Gouge's (2009) piece focuses on hybrid courses and the future of writing programs, and June Griffin and Deborah Mintner (2013) attend to online writing classrooms vis-a-vis material conditions. Other pieces, for instance the work of Lisa Meloncon and Peter England (2011), focus on particular communities—in their case, training of contingent faculty teaching technical and professional communication.[1]

Cynthia Selfe is clearly the key scholar in rhetoric and composition studies whose scholarly career was oriented toward new-media composing and, moreover, teacher training, development, and support. And perhaps the most significant title related to supporting teacher development is her 2007 book *Multimodal Composition: Resources for Teachers,* which is a theoretically engaged, scholarly informed, and directly pedagogical in nature collection addressing how to effectively engage multimodality in the classroom. Chapters of the book focus on how and why to include multimodality across writing courses and include chapters on crafting assignments, the multimodal composing process itself, assessing multimodal work, and partnering with writing centers to support teacher and student needs.

Other important authors include Lilian Mina, whose work has studied the ways teachers take up new-media technologies in first-year writing. Echoing Stuart Selber (2005) and also Selfe (1999), Mina (2019) attends to the difficult balance between analytical and instrumental approaches. Her mixed-methods study framed by Andrew Feenberg's theory of critical technology included teacher self-reports about new-media technology in teaching first-year writing and revealed that the "majority of writing teachers seem to use new-media technologies instrumentally rather than critically" (12). One suggested response to this uncritical approach is for "designing and implementing locally situated and tailored technology professional development programs" (13) engaged by analysis of social and historical orientations toward the technologies and delivered by ongoing support and mentoring.

In a 2020 piece in *Composition Forum*, Mina continues this work, here focusing on eleven published statements by the Council of Writing Program Administrators (CWPA), the Conference on College Composition and Communication (CCCC), and the National Council of Teachers of English (NCTE) about technology experiences and expectations in writing classrooms. Mina specifically interrogates the how of the statements—that is, how do we best prepare teachers to engage these experiences and expectations? After discussing the conceptual, pedagogical, and technological expectations as expressed in the statements, she offers an integrative model of teaching with technology, one that unites these three expectations through a rhetorical, critical awareness.

Along with Mina, Kerri Hauman, Stacy Kastner, and Alison Witte (2015) conducted a broad, national study of preparation in teaching with technology. Initially focusing on programs offering a PhD in rhetoric and composition, the authors explored whether those programs required a course in techno pedagogy. The authors argue that "to develop functional, critical, and rhetorical literacies and to develop as teachers of digital writing, students need access to adequate instruction and mentoring by computers and writing specialists, as well as access to consistent and current digital technology" (49); most participants in their study, however, did not report graduate students having access to either. The two issues participants reported were lack of access and lack of "robust techno-pedagogy" (52). This second issue is long standing and ongoing in technology professional development: where training exists, it is often offered at a university level and is adisciplinary, acontextual, and offered as a quick immersion workshop. Similar to Mina's recommendations, Haumann, Kastner, and Witte also recommend that theory infuse practice and vice versa, and that although functional literacy is important, effective, engaged technology professional development must offer more than just functional skill.[2]

OUR DEPARTMENTAL AND INSTITUTIONAL CONTEXT

A bit of context regarding our department: we're a stand-alone writing program in a College of Arts and Letters (an oddity among our peers in that we're exclusively an arts- and humanities-based college, rather than a college including liberal arts and sciences). We host the university first-year writing program, an undergraduate major in professional and public writing, an undergraduate major in experience architecture, and a graduate program in rhetoric and writing. Our undergraduate programs are inherently multimodal in focus: students produce grant proposals with budget sheets and infographics; they produce community-anchored publications rich in visual content; they produce audio and video content for digital texts with and for community partners. We focus here, however, on our department's commitment to and delivery of first-year writing.

The majority of first-year students at Michigan State University take their first writing course with us (we see about six thousand students a year), although two of our three residential colleges offer students their own residential-focused first-year writing courses (specifically, James Madison, our political science residential college, and RCAH, our residential college in the arts and humanities). In the past, our first-year writing course curricula reflected faculty interest and expertise and were thematic and US anchored (due to the majority of our past faculty having PhDs in English studies, American studies, etc.): women in America, men in America, science and technology in America, radical thought in America. Several years ago, however, the writing program converted to a shared writing-focused and writing-anchored curriculum: WRA 101, Writing as Inquiry.

The majority of instructors of our first-year writing offerings are non-tenure-track faculty, typically hired on an annual-year contract to teach a 3/3 load, with opportunities for promotion to Designation B (a status that guarantees a renewable five-year contract) and to associate or full professor. Ten to fifteen graduate students, primarily in our department but sometimes coming to us from the Department of English or the graduate program in African American and African Studies, teach first-year writing any given semester. Graduate students are unionized, and one of the conditions of their contract is that they are never in a situation in which they must, technically, "pay for training." This means we are not allowed to require a credit-based course related to their teaching (such as a teaching practicum seminar).

FIRST-YEAR WRITING AND THE REMIX ASSIGNMENT

As mentioned above, we recently developed and launched a revised first-year writing curriculum, shifting from an incredibly variable topics-based curriculum, which was often more literature focused and centered around individual faculty research interests, to a shared, story-based curriculum that is rhetorical, inductive, inquiry-based, and deeply attuned to writing-as-process. The goal of our FYW courses is to prepare students to approach new writing situations with confidence and to teach them the uses of rhetorical concepts for making sense of their world—most immediately in the transition to college life and learning. Our first-year writing classes ask students to put their prior knowledge in relation to new and developing understandings of rhetoric, literacy, and culture via five sequenced assignments, one of which is a remix assignment.

> The Remix Project invites students to engage inquiry as a means to discover and communicate new knowledge about their audiences by way of working in a new mode, genre, or collaborative capacity. This project builds on the learning of the preceding projects by making rhetorical moves implicit in these projects the explicit focus of attention. It asks students to create a product that helps them be more aware of the purpose, audience, medium, mode, and/or genre of the rhetorical product they make. It invites students to experience and reflect further on processes of invention and arrangement and further develops inquiries into relationships between rhetorical purposes, audiences, and resources (material, conceptual, and ethical). While students often create outstanding rhetorical products (movies, podcasts, live presentations, etc.), the goals of this project are to invite students to take risks, to undertake new writing experiences, to negotiate new ways of working, to make the most of mistakes they make along the way, and to use these experiences to formulate goals for how to use problem-solving strategies to inform their ongoing development as writers.

Clearly there are nods here in this assignment to Jody Shipka (2011) and others, including our own alums (e.g., see Angela Haas's "Wampum as Hypertext" [2007]), who have argued productively for an expansive notion of multimodality—including tactile material objects, performances, and more and not necessarily inherently anchored to digital tools and productions.

That said, there are two types of instructor know-how required of this assignment: first is **rhetorical expertise**—including the ability to scaffold, frame, and situate this assignment for and to students and to productively guide students in making rhetorically powerful decisions as they compose. Second is technological expertise—because the assignment adopts such an expansive notion of remix and of multimodality, teachers may be attempting to address student questions about iMovie, for instance, at the same time they're offering support for producing a remix board mimicking a Pinterist interface.

SUPPORTING THE TEACHING OF MULTIMODAL COMPOSING

An appropriately multifaceted and rich teacher-training and ongoing teacher-support system is required to address the instructor know-how described above. At our institution, this support includes teaching groups, first-year writing workshops, and writing center support.[3]

Teaching Groups

All new first-year writing teachers participate in weekly mentor groups in fall and biweekly mentor groups in spring. These small groups (three to four teachers each) are facilitated by the program director, associate director, and graduate program assistant. *New* in this case means new to teaching in our program and department, so we have a broad group of participants in our mentor groups—sometimes including people who have taught ten or more years elsewhere along with second-year MA students teaching their first classes as instructors of record. Although sometimes constructed around a specific issues (e.g., assessment) or a particular project currently being taught through our shared curriculum, discussions also tend to be highly kairotic and most often reflect pedagogical concerns and challenges the teachers themselves raise, which their colleagues then problem solve together.

This mixed and diverse audience allows the groups to richly explore both the rhetorical and the technological contexts of teaching and supporting multimodal composition, especially in the case of the remix assignment. One of the key considerations we see in the mentor groups, sustained year after year, is that when supported well and nurtured thoughtfully, teachers can prioritize their rhetorical expertise and port it into new composing spaces. We're not saying here that technological expertise isn't an important part of supporting multimodal composing; in fact, below we discuss how tutors in our multimodal writing center can specifically highlight their own tech expertise; however, we often find teachers reflecting that, indeed, it is their ability to talk with students about audience, about context, about aspects of delivery of a composition—and other considerations that transcend a particular technological tool, app, or interface—that trumps attention to any one particular tool or technology. Our teaching groups allow us to reinforce this point with teachers hesitant about multimodal work.

Writing Center Support

Talking with students about the effects and affordances of rhetorical choices is something all writing centers, and writing teachers, excel at. Our writing center has leveraged this strength by creating a multimodal writing center. As a separate entity from our department, the writing center is a stand-alone unit that reports directly to the dean of our college, and it offers multiple graduate assistantships for students not just in rhetoric and writing or in the humanities broadly but also from across the university. A majority of these are filled by rhetoric and writing graduate students from our department, including Teresa and Wilfredo.

The writing center has a disciplinary commitment to helping writers succeed within their own literacy contexts and backdrops, their own majors or programs, and the writing skills they bring to their work. This commitment steers the daily, one-on-one, face-to-face consulting that happens at our main writing center, at our nine satellite centers (in the main library, in the residence hall "neighborhoods," in the Student Athlete Support Services complex, and elsewhere on campus), and in our online consulting; it also takes the form of workshops catered to FYW classes and other writing-intensive courses across the university. These workshops vary in foci, addressing, for instance, MLA and APA citation styles; conducting research through the physical and digital repositories of the MSU Libraries; and engaging in multimodal composing, including video editing, podcasting, and more generally how to approach the remix assignment.

Although our writing center has always been anchored by multimodal and multiliteracy approaches to composing (see, for instance, Thomas, DeVoss, and Hara 1998) and has embraced and worked with students on all writing-related projects—whether they be alphabetic-only essays, slideshow presentations, web pages, and more—the recently launched multimodal writing center (MWC, a space in which Wilfredo and Teresa, coauthors of this chapter, both work) offers specific consulting that engages both rhetorical and writerly and technological and instrumental composing concerns. Although all the writing center consultants have both broad and deep skill in working with writers on the development of their compositions, there are times when students are looking for a mix of rhetorical and technical expertise. To meet these needs, the MWC displays the unique and specific prior experiences, training, and skills of each individual consultant using the proprietary WCONLINE system. Consultants can showcase their technological and multimodal proficiencies so writers signing up for a session can seek out the specific assistance they need. For example, on WCONLINE, Wilfredo spotlights his interest and professional experience in document design and often works with students who are revising their resumes and developing curriculum vitae and have questions that span the written content to include formatting and design decisions. Specific to the remix assignment, he has also worked with students turning their alphabetic essays into presentations, carrying over considerations of color, design, typography, and audience, all of which come up in conversations about composer considerations like rhetorical effect and accessibility.

Similarly, Teresa has extensive website-development experience and knowledge of video production and advertises their expertise in these areas, often attracting students working on websites and composing videos for their FYW remix projects. For example, Teresa often navigates helping first-year writing students decide how to remix their previous papers into videos. Through the consultation, Teresa discusses potential software to use for video making based on student confidence and prior knowledge; how to collect and select the necessary components of a video, such as sound, music, and images; the ethical implications of copyright and an explanation of fair use and how it applies to them as students; and the importance of storyboarding and scripting prior to creating videos. It's clear in their work that both Wilfredo and Teresa toggle across both rhetorical and technological expertise to support student multimodal compositions, and this is precisely the kind of work a multimodal-specific writing center can do to support teachers and students in their work.

FIRST-YEAR WRITING INSTRUCTOR WORKSHOPS

We're a big department and a busy unit, as are, frankly, all writing programs we've worked with, observed, or studied. We're also a big department in a big, busy institution. As a department, we've created a commitment to offering courses four days a week (Monday–Thursday), protecting Fridays for committee meetings, department events, and pedagogy workshops. One of our regular department events, for instance, is a "Lightning Strikes" event coordinated by faculty in the department, in which faculty are invited to present their research or creative work in the form of a five-minute talk. We also host—in late fall and just before spring semester ends—a First-Year Writing Symposium, for which we take over the second and third floors of our classroom building and students share posters, presentations, videos, models, and other compositions.

Along with these regular offerings, the first-year writing program facilitates pedagogy workshops for teachers. Recent offerings included a workshop on working with the MSU Museum, specifically to support a cultural artifact project core to the FYW curriculum; a Career Services-hosted workshop, focused on how Career Services can be a resource in our disciplinary/professional literacy project, also key to our curriculum; and workshops on topics like responding to students in crisis, focused on student mental-health needs and resources available to them, and on work-life balance for teachers. To help instructors, first to acclimate to the remix assignment and the myriad student composition possibilities, and second to engage instructors in creating their own multimodal compositions, Teresa and Wilfredo hosted a "Let's Remix" workshop this past academic year.

This teacher-development workshop emerged after a separate workshop Teresa and Wilfredo attended in which their expertise conducting remix-focused workshops, working with multiple instructors and their approaches to the remix project, and working in the MWC was pointed out by the workshop coordinator. They were asked by the first-year writing program team to conduct a workshop after several faculty expressed concern about the remix project, particularly around (1) issues of assessing remix compositions and multimodal writing and (2) concerns about being able to support and assist students running into technological issues. Although the writing center has always supported all the work of our FYW curriculum, and has hosted a variety of multimodal composing workshops in the context of specific instructors and for specific courses, this instance marked the first time the WC—through the MWC—conducted a remix-focused workshop for all FYW instructors.

In the workshop, Teresa and Wilfredo reviewed multiple multimodal composition tools (including Canva, the GNU Image Manipulation Program, Adobe Spark, and Audacity), highlighting the features of each and describing how students might use them in their remixes. Teresa also reviewed assessment models for reviewing remix projects (drawing primarily from Teston, Previte, and Hashlamon [2019]), paying close attention to the inequalities that might affect students' technological proficiencies and how faculty might factor that into assessment. After, Wilfredo facilitated an in-class activity with faculty around remixing album art from popular musicians, offering faculty a chance to showcase their media knowledge within and through their individual remixes. Important, Teresa and Wilfredo designed the workshop so faculty were offered the space and provided the room to be students who, in a sense, created their own remix projects (though on, admittedly, a smaller scale). The pop-culture aspect and focus on music indirectly provided a bit of space for teachers to play—and to experiment across their pop-culture knowledge, music preferences, and multimodal composing abilities.

By actually engaging in hands-on practice at the workshop, faculty were able to anticipate some of the rhetorical concerns and considerations students would navigate working on the assignment, to play with new technologies their students might bring to the course or they might want to introduce students to in the context of the remix assignment, to experiment with and troubleshoot some of the technical issues that might arise during facilitation, and to tweak the program-shared assignment as needed for their own course.

SUPPORTING TEACHER MULTIMODAL TRAINING AND DEVELOPMENT

From what we've shared above, we want to highlight a few key points: first, a rich body of scholarship focuses on teacher training and development that merits a sustained and significant turn toward multimodal composing. Indeed, we could learn much if we ran research on teacher training and development perpendicular to research on multimodal composing. We might work to address questions like the ones we pose in the introduction of this chapter and others, including: What practices transcend particular technologies? What practices are perhaps anchored to particular types of technologies or spaces (e.g., word-processing software, social media sites)? What are effective models for and approaches to teacher training that port well to multimodal composing? Likewise, what philosophical and theoretical orientations toward multimodal composing lend themselves to developing effective teacher training? What support can be philosophical and theoretical and tap into the rhetorical skills and writing orientations of faculty (e.g., our best practices of talking about issues of audience transcend particular digital tools or spaces). What support must be hands-on and technically driven?

Graduate Student and Faculty Development in Multimodal Composing   37

This research could also happen locally, within a writing program, by engaging such work as technology audits, surveys, and/or focus groups. A technology audit provides a means by which a WPA (or a faculty member committed to and interested in technology professional development) can assess the means, modes, and materials individual faculty have access to in engaging their teaching. Surveys provide a wide-angle lens perspective and might be crafted to address two broad types of questions: (1) What do you know? (2) What do you want to know? Surveys asking these types of questions can be difficult, however, as they require survey takers to be able to articulate what they don't know, and—as Julie Lindquist, the WPA of our FYW program often quips—often we don't know what we don't know. Thus focus groups are another method through which technology professional development needs might be surfaced. A group of faculty engaged in a shared conversation might draw from each other's responses and bring to light issues a survey alone may not surface.

Second, one-time, adisciplinary workshops—although generally the norm at most larger institutions—are not enough to provide the rich, situated, contextual training and support faculty need in engaging multimodal composing in their writing classrooms. Admittedly, such training is important to reach broad faculty audiences across an institution and to connect faculty from different units to university-level resources available. Two ways to extend university-level general services are via student assistance and institutional partnerships. Richard Selfe (2004) has long championed students as technology assistants. One innovative method of engaging in faculty technology professional development might be to identify students whose work connects across writing studies and digital production and hire them to provide faculty support, which may include hands-on workshops and also one-on-one support to address specific questions. Students in our classes are the primary users of our course-management spaces and our computer labs, for instance, yet how often do we invite them into our development processes? Consult with them about how we use the digital and physical spaces to teach our classes, share our materials, and engage students in writing? Provide student-focused, student-centered analysis of the teaching content we produce and present?

Another model Selfe (2004) innovated was to engage teachers and students in learning together. What might it look like if we encouraged our departments or our colleges to host technology professional development sessions where each faculty member is required to invite a student to attend (with compensation)? What approaches might emerge if faculty consulted with undergraduate or graduate students as the faculty member learned new places, spaces, and tools for multi-modal composing?

Another way to extend adisciplinary, university-level approaches might be to partner *with* the university offices that host such workshops. Doing so would allow faculty, departments, and units to blend their local disciplinary practices with the university-level support and resources available. We've had good luck here at Michigan State University working with our institutional teaching and learning offices to leverage their experiences in providing all-university support and utilizing their broad networks and resources, and they've been engaged partners in helping us implement those resources at local levels. And, honestly, we've found they're more than engaged partners—they're exceptional collaborators, often mentioning to us that they realize the ways they're not often able to operate from a broad university-level perspective and that they enjoy opportunities to engage their work with department partners and within disciplinary contexts.

Third, and as other scholars have noted, any teacher training and development requires attention to both the rhetorical savvy and expertise of instructors and to the technical, instrumental specifics of composing using different tools, technologies, spaces, and places. If our work is to engage students in writing, writing more, writing well, and writing in contexts beyond our writing classrooms—whether that be in other courses, at their internships, in their jobs, in their civic lives, and so forth—we must lean into what we know and do well. We are writing studies scholars and teachers who engage our work from perspectives that transcend any one technology but who must always already be attentive to the spaces and places in which students compose. Concepts of audience, purpose, and context; rhetorical considerations including ethos, pathos, and logos; processes of writing including drafting, inventing, revising, and more—none of these practices are tied to a particular technology. In today's multimodal, digital, networked world, however, *all these considerations* happen in and across digital spaces, engaging a range of writerly tools. We can't teach principles of writing without attending to digital tools; likewise, we can't engage multimodal composing without prioritizing rhetorical moves and strategies and writerly engagement. Thus, and not surprisingly based on what we show and share in this chapter, all technology professional development and teacher training should be anchored to our writerly practices and our disciplinary values. Indeed, reviewing our department mission statements, our writing program promises, our writing center commitments, our disciplinary values, and our national frameworks and policy statements provides us much from which we can continue to build robust multimodal composing support for each other and for our writing programs.

Cultivating a multimodal writing-focused commitment requires, as we demonstrate here, a robust partnership between and across faculty, units, departments, writing centers, and other partners. Our first-year writing program is oriented toward not only the literacies students bring to our classrooms but also to engaging students in multimodal work as part of their inquiry processes and compositional repertoire. Delivering on this commitment requires an ongoing, deliberate commitment across mentoring practices for teachers, workshops and shared support, and relationships with other units. Committing to multimodal composing and delivering on that commitment can't be addressed by one conversation, one workshop, or by turning toward one affiliate or source of support (e.g., the writing center or the library). Supporting graduate students and faculty to deeply engage across the rhetorical and technological dimensions of multimodal composing requires a complex, connected, committed approach. It also requires a sustained scholarly commitment to developing rich mentorship and development networks across multiple units and mediums.

Although the content of this piece focuses on Michigan State University, it also brings attention to the ways departments and units are developing increasingly creative and collaborative approaches to multimodal pedagogies. Some prominent examples include the work of Cynthia Selfe; Hauman, Kastner, and Witte; Lilian Mina; and others. For other examples, we can turn toward our alums, who both came to our graduate program with interests in multimodal composing and have carried forward our multimodal composing commitment and brought it to their institutions and curricula (e.g., Doug Eyman, Angela Haas, Stacey Pigg, Jim Ridolfo, Doug Walls, and others). In conversation with these scholars, Michigan State University's model offers us new ways of situating faculty development in multimodal composing—as a core commitment in a writing program and as shared teacher-development activity. We also demonstrate a need for sustained rhetorical interventions on the role of faculty development in multimodal pedagogies and invite further conversations from the field. Our professional-development and institutional structures must foster the strengths of writing teachers, recognizing and cultivating their ability to teach rhetorical affordances, situations, and choices in modes beyond alphabetic text. At the same time, we cannot ignore the technological skill required for particular multimodal projects. Constellating and leveraging existing strengths both inside and outside one's home department open exciting possibilities for our multimodal futures, from engaging teacher professional development to supporting and sustaining a programmatic culture of multimodal composing.

NOTES

1. If we turn to education, a great deal of literature focuses on teachers' multimodal composing practices (e.g., Johnson and Smagorsinky 2013; Kajder and Parkes 2012) and on K–12 teacher preparation (e.g., Hicks 2009; Karchmer-Klein, Shinas, and Park 2014; Reed and Hicks 2015; Turner and Hicks 2017).

2. Other important work includes a piece by Dan Anderson, Anthony Atkins, Cheryl Ball, Krista Homicz Millar, Cynthia Selfe, and Richard Selfe (2006) reporting on a survey supported by a CCCC research grant; Kris Blair's ample work on technology and training, focused on engaging girls in computing and spanning to approaches for faculty development (e.g., Blair 2011, 2014; Blair et al. 2011; Blair, Deitel-McLaughlin, and Graupner 2010); and special issues of *Computers and Composition* (DeVoss et al. 2015) and *Computers and Composition Online* (Ball et al. 2015) focused on the practices and impact of DMAC, the Digital Media and Composition Institution held annually at The Ohio State, which began life as CIWIC, the Computers in Writing Intensive Classrooms summer institute led by Cynthia Selfe at Michigan Technological University.

3. Of course, though, there are a variety of less-formal teacher-support approaches: we have an email list to which all WRA 101 instructors are subscribed to surface questions and share ideas. We also have a centrally located faculty library with comfortable space to work—tall café tables so faculty can stand and chat and small tables to sit and work, along with ample coffee and a fairly regular supply of snacks people have brought from home or purchased on their way to work.

REFERENCES

Anderson, Dan, Anthony Atkins, Cheryl Ball, Krista Homicz Millar, Cynthia Selfe, and Richard Selfe. 2006. "Integrating Multimodality into Composition Curricula." *Composition Studies* 34 (2): 59–84.

Artze-Vega, Isis, Melody Bowdon, Kimberly Emmons, Michele Eodice, Susan K. Hess, Claire Coleman Lamonica, and Gerald Nelms. 2013. "Privileging Pedagogy: Composition, Rhetoric, and Faculty Development." *College Composition and Communication* 65 (1): 162–84.

Ball, Cheryl, Dànielle Nicole DeVoss, Cynthia L. Selfe, and Scott Lloyd DeWitt. 2015. In "CIWIC, DMAC, and Technology Professional Development in Rhetoric and Composition." Special issue, *Computers and Composition Online* (June). http://cconlinejournal .org/prodev.htm.

Blair, Kristine. 2011. "Preparing 21st-Century Faculty to Engage 21st-Century Learners: The Incentives and Rewards for Online Pedagogies." In *Higher Education, Emerging Technologies, and Community Partnerships: Concepts, Models and Practices*, edited by Melody A. Bowdon and Russell G. Carpenter, 141–61. Hershey, PA: IGI Global.

Blair, Kristine. 2014. "Composing Change: The Role of Graduate Education in Sustaining a Digital Scholarly Future." *Composition Studies* 42 (1): 103–6.

Blair, Kristine, Erin Dietel-McLaughlin, and Meredith Graupner. 2010. "Looking into the Digital Mirror: Reflections on a Computer Camp for Girls by Girls." In *Girl Wide Web 2.0*, edited by Sharon Mazzarella, 139–60. New York: Peter Lang.

Blair, Kristine, Katie Fredlund, Kerri Hauman, Em Hurford, Stacy Kastner, and Alison Witte. 2011. "Cyberfeminists at Play: Lessons on Literacy and Activism from a Girls' Computer Camp." *Feminist Teacher* 22 (1): 43–59.

Brunk-Chavez, Beth. 2010. "Embracing Our Expertise through Faculty and Instructional Development." *WPA: Writing Program Administration* 34 (1): 152–55.

Bullock, Richard. 1999. "In Pursuit of Competence: Preparing New Graduate Teaching Assistants for the Classroom." In *Administrative Problem Solving for Writing Programs and Writing Centers: Scenarios in Effective Program Management,* edited by Linda Myers-Breslin, 3–13. Urbana, IL: NCTE.

DeVoss, Dànielle Nicole, Cheryl Ball, Cynthia L. Selfe, and Scott Lloyd DeWitt, eds. 2015. In "CIWIC, DMAC, and Technology Professional Development in Rhetoric and Composition." Special issue, *Computers and Composition* 36.

Dobrin, Sidney. (2005). *Don't Call It That: The Composition Practicum.* Urbana, IL: NCTE.

Dryer, Dylan B., Darsie Bowden, Beth Brunk-Chavez, Susanmarie Harrington, Bump Halbritter, and Kathleen Blake Yancey. 2014. "Revising FYC Outcomes for a Multimodal, Digitally Composed World: The WPA Outcomes Statement for First-Year Composition (Version 3.0)." *WPA: Writing Program Administration* 38 (1): 129–43.

Fedukovich, Casey J., and Tracy Ann Morse. 2017. "Failures to Accommodate: GTA Preparation as a Site for a Transformative Culture of Access." *WPA: Writing Program Administration* 40 (3): 39–60.

Gouge, Catherine. 2009. "Conversations at a Crucial Moment: Hybrid Courses and the Future of Writing Programs." *College English* 71 (4): 338–62.

Griffin, June, and Deborah Mintner. 2013. "The Rise of the Online Writing Classroom: Reflecting on the Material Conditions of College Composition Teaching." *College Composition and Communication* 65 (1): 140–61.

Haas, Angela M. (2007). "Wampum as Hypertext: An American Indian Intellectual Tradition of Multimedia Theory and Practice." *Studies in American Indian Literature* 19 (4): 77–100.

Hauman, Kerri, Stacy Kastner, and Alison Witte. 2015. "Writing Teachers for Twenty-First-Century Writers." *Pedagogy: Critical Approaches to Teaching Literature, Language, Composition, and Culture* 15 (1): 45–57.

Hicks, Troy. 2009. *The Digital Writing Workshop.* Portsmouth, NH: Heinemann.

Johnson, Lindy L., and Peter Smagorinsky. 2013. "Writing Remixed: Mapping the Multimodal Composition of One Preservice English Education Teacher." In *Exploring Multimodal Composition and Digital Writing,* edited by Kristine Pytash and Richard Ferdig, 262–80. Hershey, PA: IGI Global.

Kajder, Sara, and Kelly A. Parkes. 2012. "Examining Preservice Teachers' Reflective Practice Within and Across Multimodal Writing Environments." *Journal of Information Technology for Teacher Education* 20 (3): 229–37.

Karchmer-Klein, Rachel, Valerie Harlow Shinas, and Sohee Park. 2014. "Framing K–12 Multimodal Digital Writing Instruction." In *Digital Tools for Writing Instruction in K–12 Settings: Student Perception and Experience,* edited by Rebecca S. Anderson and Clif Mims, 499–519. Hershey, PA: IGI Global.

Lauer, Claire. 2009. "Contending with Terms: 'Multimodal' and 'Multimedia' in the Academic and Public Spheres." *Computers and Composition* 26 (4): 225–39.

Marshall, Margaret J. 2008. "Teaching Circles: Supporting Shared Work and Professional Development." *Pedagogy: Critical Approaches to Teaching Literature, Language, Composition, and Culture* 8 (3): 413–31.

Meloncon, Lisa, and Peter England. 2011. The Current Status of Contingent Faculty in Technical and Professional Communication. *College English* 73 (4): 396–408.

Mina, Lilian W. 2019. "Analyzing and Theorizing Writing Teachers' Approaches to Using New Media Technologies." *Computers and Composition* 52, 1–16.

Mina, Lilian W. 2020. Technology Professional Development of Writing Faculty: The Expectations and the Needs. *Composition Forum* 43. https://compositionforum.com/issue/43/professional-development.php.

Reed, Dawn, and Troy Hicks. 2015. *Research Writing Rewired: Lessons That Ground Students' Digital Learning.* Thousand Oaks, CA: Corwin.

Reid, E. Shelley. 2018. "Beyond Satisfaction: Assessing the Goals and Impacts of Faculty Development." *WPA: Writing Program Administration* 41 (2): 122–34.

Restaino, Jessica. 2012. *First Semester: Graduate Students, Teaching Writing, and the Challenge of the Middle Ground.* Urbana, IL: NCTE.

Ritter, Kelly, and Paul Kei Matsuda, eds. 2010. *Exploring Composition Studies: Sites, Issues, and Perspectives.* Logan: Utah State University Press.

Selber, Stuart A. 2004. *Multiliteracies for a Digital Age.* Southern Illinois University Press.

Selfe, Cynthia L. 1999. *Technology and Literacy in the Twenty-First Century: The Importance of Paying Attention.* Carbondale: Southern Illinois University Press.

Selfe, Cynthia L. 2007. *Multimodal Composition: Resources for Teachers.* Hampton.

Selfe, Richard J. 2004. *Sustainable Computer Environments: Cultures of Support in English Studies and Language Arts.* New York: Hampton.

Sheppard, Jennifer. 2009. "The Rhetorical Work of Multimedia Production Practices: It's More Than Just Technical Skill." *Computers and Composition* 26, 122–31.

Shipka, Jody. 2011. *Toward a Composition Made Whole.* Pittsburgh, PA: University of Pittsburgh Press.

Teston, Christa, Brittany Previte, and Yanar Hashlamon. 2019. "The Grind of Multimodal Work in Professional Writing Pedagogies." *Computers and Composition* 52: 195–209.

Thomas, Sherry, Dánielle Nicole DeVoss, and Mark Hara. 1998. Toward a Critical Theory of Technology and Writing. *Writing Center Journal* 19 (1): 73–86.

Turner, Kristen Hawley, and Troy Hicks. 2017. *Argument in the Real World: Teaching Students to Read and Write Digital texts.* Portsmouth, NH: Heinemann.

Werner, Courtney L. 2015. "Speaking of Composing (Frameworks): New Media Discussions, 2000–2010." *Computers and Composition* 37: 55–72.

Willard-Traub, Margaret K. 2008. "Writing Program Administration and Faculty Professional Development." *Pedagogy: Critical Approaches to Teaching Literature, Language, Composition, and Culture* 8 (3): 433–45.

2

(E)MERGING EXPERTISE
Multivocal, Multimodal Preparation and Development of Graduate Teaching Assistants in Writing Programs

Kelly Moreland, Sarah Henderson Lee, and Kirsti Cole

This chapter showcases one institution's curricular revision[1] to merge and update three different writing programs in the same English department. Our institution has included composition and second language (L2) writing courses and has recently developed an online-only offering. As the program coordinators for these three curricula, we present our experiences implementing multimodal curriculum and provide an autoethnographic reflection on uniting them into one adaptable curriculum: a multivocal, multimodal curriculum. We define a multivocal, multimodal writing curriculum as one that provides a safe pedagogical space for experimentation with multiple modes and literacies that powerfully decenters standard academic English. While we recognize online writing courses are not inherently multimodal, we worked to forward multiple modes and literacies as inclusive, accessible, and supportive of our first-year writing students and the GTAs teaching them.

Our research indicates professionalization in our field has advanced in such a way that we have three lanes: composition, L2 writing, and multimodal writing. The professionalization of GTAs largely depends on the specific graduate program and program faculties' expertise. It is still the case that graduate students who come to MA and PhD programs in rhetoric and composition might only have experience with taking first-year composition. Our development and preparation of GTAs tends to focus on catching them up to the basics of the field and institutional contexts rather than the advancements of the field and the kinds of composing people do outside the academy in multiple languages and modes. The increased specialization in our field has provided a plethora of important scholarship but has also recreated the siloing compositionists bemoan in early articles. Our contribution in this chapter, and at

---

https://doi.org/10.7330/9781646424184.c002

our institution, is unique because the three of us purposely sought each other out to overcome that siloing and create an adaptable curriculum that can be used across our contexts. We recognized collaboration across our expertises could empower us to do more engaged work in these areas. In a way, it was serendipitous (Goggin and Goggin 2018) that the three of us were so invested in the progressive trends in composition and L2 pedagogy because it made the bringing together of our curriculum natural. This chapter includes a discussion of our institutional context, the revision work we are doing to our first-year writing curriculum, and how we work with graduate students in our individual contexts to prepare GTAs to teach and assess multimodal composition.

Our curricular revision began in fall 2019, followed shortly by talk of this chapter. What we didn't know then was that our first semester implementing the new curriculum would carry the weight of a global pandemic. Our university's response was to offer courses in a hybrid/flexible format, with a limited number of students attending the synchronous class meetings in person and the rest attending via Zoom. We found this response problematic for composition and for the GTA population that primarily staffs the course. In an effort to prioritize GTAs' and students' health and safety, and to acknowledge that graduate student assistantships at our university do not include health-insurance coverage, we made the decision to code all GTA sections of composition as hybrid in the course catalog. We encouraged GTAs to plan to teach their course fully online. If they were comfortable, they could offer to meet with students face to face, individually or in small groups, for conferences or office hours during the scheduled class time. This response ensured GTAs could choose how much, if any, in-person instruction to offer in their course, and it allowed us to focus on online writing instruction during the summer GTA workshop. Of course, preparing *all* first-year GTAs to teach online interrupted the distinction of our three roles: there was a group of GTAs who were meant to be teaching online, and then there were the groups of GTAs who unintentionally needed to be teaching online due to the pandemic.

We argue that, even in the context of the pandemic, our curriculum represents a best-practices model whether face to face, hybrid, or online and whether offered by experienced or novice teachers of writing. The core principle of our curriculum is adaptability, not just in the context of delivery but also in content. The principles that guided our curriculum development—the individual assignments, the assessment protocols, the goals of the first-year writing course—build a multivocal, multimodal curriculum flexible enough to meet not only students but also teachers where they are. As we set out to prepare new GTAs to teach first-year writing in August 2020, what became quite clear was that reasonable logistics shared across assignments, logistics that prop up creativity, kindness, equity, and adaptability on the part of the teacher and the student, shift the discourse of expertise to practitioner, fomenting a community of writers that can learn and work together.

PEDAGOGICAL REMIX

In this section we outline the areas of scholarship that guided our curricular revision, and we reference our reflective inquiry about doing that revision, including personal narratives and a follow-up conversation. To reconceptualize first-year writing on our campus, we realized that the most salient pedagogies we regularly engage in are writing about writing (WAW), multimodal and online writing best practices (OWI), and pluralization of academic writing (see chapter 1 of this collection for further discussion of remixing). In addition to these areas being current in rhetoric, composition, and writing studies scholarship, these areas represent our individual expertise based on our own current research and teaching practices. We see these three areas of scholarship as critical to better understanding a multivocal, multimodal curriculum. It wasn't until we collaborated that we realized how interdependent these areas of scholarship are, and, once they are brought together, how expansive the possibilities for first-year writing can be.

Writing about Writing

> One of the things I love most about the curriculum we designed is that we started with "students will investigate how writing works," and one of the ways students do that is by positioning multimodality as a core area of interest within writing studies. (Kelly, narrative)

Central to our three approaches and our curriculum is the idea that writing ought to be the *content* of our ENG 101 course. Taking cues from scholarship on writing transfer (Anson and Moore 2016; Driscoll and Wells 2012; Moore and Bass 2017; Reiff and Bawarshi 2011; Yancey, Robertson, and Taczak 2014) and specifically the writing-about-writing (WAW) approach (Downs and Wardle 2007; Wardle and Downs 2013), we envisioned a curriculum that would align with current best practices in first-year writing pedagogy while still offering flexibility for our diverse student and instructor populations. We also recognized a need within our particular university context for a strong focus on multimodal content within the first-year writing curriculum. Across contexts,

Table 2.1. Comparison of ENG 101 course description and learning outcomes

ENG 101 Description and outcomes precollaboration	Revised ENG 101 description and outcome

This course helps students develop a flexible writing process, practice rhetorical awareness, read critically to support their writing, research effectively, represent others ideas in multiple ways, reflect on their writing practices, and polish their work.
 	
By the end of this course, students should be able to
  a. generate ideas, draft, revise, and edit their work;
  b. write for various audiences, purposes, and genres;
  c. read critically to support their writing;
  d. research effectively to enrich their intellectual contributions in writing;
  e. integrate sources into their work, adhering to summary, paraphrase, quotation, and citation conventions;
  f. use reflection to advance their writing development;
  g. employ syntax and usage appropriate to academic disciplines and the professional world.
	First-Year Writing (ENG 101) or Foundations of Rhetoric and Writing is a process writing course. Students in this course approach writing as a subject of study by investigating how writing works across a variety of contexts. Most Minnesota State Mankato students take this course during their first two years of college. As a matter of best practice, we strongly encourage students to take ENG 101 during their first two semesters.
	
	In this course, students will investigate how writing works by
	  1. increasing genre awareness, rhetorical knowledge, and use of multimodalities;
	  2. exploring language variation and multiliteracies by context;
	  3. developing information literacy through primary and secondary research;
	  4. reflecting on writing processes and labor;
	  5. collaborating to create and revise texts.

our students are asked to compose texts beyond the alphabetic "paper," but up until this point, multimodal composition hadn't officially been a part of our university's composition curriculum.

As we synthesized our goals and assignments, we realized we'd all been teaching "how writing works":[2] genre, literacy, rhetoric, person- and community-based research, writing and research processes, reflection, language diversity, and multimodality. The content was already there in our approaches—what we needed to do was synthesize what we were already doing into an updated course description and outcomes we could share program wide. We made a concerted effort to include keywords from writing studies research in the revised language (see table 2.1). Clearly articulating that language in the learning outcomes, we hoped, would signal to students and their instructors that ENG 101 is a content-based course.

We recognized this curricular approach likely would be new for our GTA populations, who staffed 46 percent of our fall 2020 composition courses. As we discussed how to implement the new curriculum among cohorts of first-year GTAs, we had to acknowledge and account for their experience (see chapter 4 of this collection for further discussion of GTA expertise) with the content and thus design GTA education curricula that would help them feel comfortable and confident in their teaching.

During the pandemic, we also had to ensure TAs were prepared to teach the new curriculum in an online environment. There is a relationship between online writing instruction and multimodal writing, although the two are in no way dependent upon one another. Even a brief review of multimodality in the field of writing studies lends itself to the inherent complications in the term (Borgman 2019; Lutkewitte 2013; Palmeri 2012).

Online Writing Instruction

> *Many of my composition graduate students were involved in the process of identifying how online writing instruction, assignment scaffolding, and assessment practices can best function in an asynchronous environment. (Kirsti, narrative)*

A number of recent articles have presented arguments for the powerful intersectional writing spaces provided by multimodal engagement. Lillian Bridwell-Bowles, Karen Powell, and Tiffany Walter Choplin (2009) outline the ways multimodal communication united disparate and seemingly incommensurate disciplines across the university to provide an umbrella under which courses in writing, communication, and technology could convene. Angela Shetler, Susan E. Thomas, Francis di Lauro, and Benjamin Miller (2013) connect cross-cultural approaches to multimodal writing practices rooted in local contexts. We are certainly not the first to argue a multivocal, multimodal approach is the most beneficial for first-year writing and the GTAs and instructors who teach it. Traci Fraiberg (2010) traces multilingual and multimodal practices in order to argue for best practices in teaching writing now. He extends Suresh Canagarajah's work on code meshing to call attention to "the complex blending of multimodal and multilingual texts and literacy practices in our teaching and research" (102). Beyond arguments about how multimodal writing might function as a cornerstone in our writing and pedagogical practices, specific texts (Borgman and McArdle 2019; Hewitt and DePew 2015) extend this work one step further into praxis, which we used throughout our "GTA Development Workshop." We focused specifically on the concept of access in OWI and multimodal work for students and teachers. Our GTAs are always already both students and teachers. What might that dual role mean for the complexities of teaching first-year writing?

The notion of multimodal writing provided us with a way into thinking about novice teachers teaching writing (Conference on College Composition and Communication OWI Standing Group 2013). The possibilities of multiple modes like genre, and rhetoric before it, allowed

48 MORELAND, HENDERSON LEE, AND COLE

us to rethink what the professional-development experience for the GTAs could be. Our curriculum-and-development program responded to the print-digital paradigm shift Meredith Graupner and Lee Nikoson-Massey (2009) argue is relevant to all composition coursework (13–14).

Pluralization of Academic Writing

> *I believe in a curriculum that recognizes students as knowledgeable and reflective individuals and supports their exploration of how written, spoken, and visual language is contextually situated, as well as their experimentation with how modes, genres, and languages intersect. (Sarah, narrative)*

Grounded in a variety of sociocultural constructs and methodologies, research related to the pluralization of academic writing critiques the prescriptive history of writing instruction in the United States (e.g., Horner and Trimbur 2002; Matsuda 2006) and challenges writing instructors to understand students' varied language practices and lived experiences as sites of explorative learning (e.g., Canagarajah 2013; Young and Martinez 2011). To ensure linguistically and culturally diverse writers are met with ethical and equitable instruction, both writing curricula and instructors must make space for the languages and experiences of all students and the facilitation of a "global literacy" (Matsuda and Matsuda 2010, 373) that will serve students in the academy and beyond. Doing so provides students with opportunities to see themselves as knowledgeable writers and to gain a heightened sense of how language is contextually situated across multiple modes. The reconceptualization of writing instruction from a difference instead of deficit model also allows for more meaningful exploration and innovation in the writing classroom. Code meshing is one example of such innovation. As "a strategy for merging local varieties with Standard Written English in a move toward gradually pluralizing academic writing and developing multilingual competence for transnational relationships" (Canagarajah 2006, 586), code meshing is a communicative tool that can be effectively used in the writing classroom to emphasize the importance of a balanced responsibility between writer and reader. Prioritizing early conversations with our new GTAs (Gonzales 2015) about redefining reader and writer roles, and challenging what constitutes academic English, has sparked genuine curiosity, which, for many GTAs, has led to more pedagogical risk taking and innovation.

The collaborative curricular work showcased in this chapter answers recent calls (e.g., Inoue 2019a; Baker-Bell et al. 2020) for WPAs and writing instructors to move beyond tolerance of linguistic pluralism to active, meaningful change. By reconceptualizing our first-year writing curriculum as a multivocal, multimodal framework, we have designed activities, assignments, and assessments[3] that promote "flexibility across a wide range of discourses, genres, strategies, and practices that support and shape various forms of thinking and social action" (Skerrett and Bomer 2013, 334). This curricular shift requires a renewed commitment to preparing and developing GTAs from a dynamic and pluralistic perspective. Writing instructors need reflective, collaborative, and hands-on training and professional-development opportunities to become comfortable and confident in employing, for example, Aya Matsuda and Paul K. Matsuda's (2010) related principles: (1) teach the dominant language forms and functions, (2) teach the nondominant language forms and functions, (3) teach the boundary between what works and what does not, (4) teach the principles and strategies of discourse negotiation, and (5) teach the risks involved in using deviational features. Because this level of GTA professional development is time intensive, it is best incorporated into our semester-long workshop course taken by all new GTAs during their first semester. Our GTAs are able to explore each of the above principles and related ideas first through collaborative reflection (see chapter 5 of this collection for a strong model of collaboration between graduate students and faculty mentors) and discussion and then through material (re)development, teaching demonstrations, and mentor and peer feedback.

OUR REFLECTIVE INQUIRY PROCESS

The collaboration highlighted in this chapter represents a recent critical friendship of three colleagues and writing program coordinators. To bring together the curricula of our department's composition, L2 writing, and online writing programs, we focused our initial conversations and subsequent work on a multivocal, multimodal approach to teaching first-year writing. In this section, we detail the procedures of our related reflective inquiry. This inquiry is centered on personal narratives and collaborative discussions and focuses on our designing of a shared curriculum and the preparation and development of GTAs to implement such a curriculum. By utilizing collaborative autoethnography (Chang, Ngunjiri, and Hernandez 2016), we were able to achieve a deeper understanding of our individual and shared experiences across our varying contexts while being fully engaged throughout the collaborative process.

To start our reflective inquiry, we each responded in writing to the following guiding questions:

- What is your background teaching composition and training GTAs?
- How do you envision composition curriculum?
- What is the role of multimodalities in teaching composition (especially for your specific GTA population)?
- How does teaching multimodal comp impact your training of GTAs?
- What did your individual curriculum look like prior to collaboration?
- What were you most excited about in terms of collaboration?

We read each other's narratives and made notes of our initial responses in preparation for an online follow-up conversation via Zoom. We shared our reactions to each individual narrative before expanding the discussion to the threads connecting all three narratives, including more descriptive approaches to teaching academic writing and the critical role of both faculty and mentors. In addition to our initial narratives and the collaborative-discussion recording, we also accessed curriculum artifacts via our professional-development D2L Brightspace shell we created in spring and summer 2020.

Recursive content analysis was used with all data sources. The following themes were identified as critical to advancing our understanding of a multivocal, multimodal curricular framework and GTA training model and are discussed in the next section:

1. Developing teachers as writers
2. Developing teachers as collaborators
3. Developing teachers as researchers

We realized that in order for our curriculum to work, we needed to understand and treat our teachers (ourselves included) as functioning in the reciprocal space that demands practice in writing, research, and collaboration.

DISCUSSION

The major source of connection between our pedagogies and our work is multimodal writing because it powerfully decenters standard academic English while facilitating a focus on written expression in multiple, commonly used academic and nonacademic modes. These flexible modes serve not only the students in our first-year writing courses but also our teachers. Our curriculum is an offering to our teachers that asks them,

"How does this curriculum intersect with your interests and strengths?" The structure of the curriculum is meant to build confidence for novice teachers but also to provide plenty of room for experimentation and adaptability for those teachers who have spent more time in a writing classroom.

As we were discussing our individual sections, we noted each of us felt hopeful and forward thinking not only as we were planning the curriculum but also in that moment—during a pandemic, during uncertain teaching environments, during a budget crisis—because of the possibilities inherent in the curriculum. While many of our colleagues were navigating how to go online and how to navigate stringent teaching requirements, the nature of our curriculum allowed us to make space for our teachers and for ourselves. In other words, it centered on identity as a guiding principle within the threshold concepts that lead us as teachers of writing. Identity is the core component, the ways teachers do and do not identify themselves as writers, researchers, and collaborators. And while our professional organizations documents (Conference on College Composition and Communication 2015a, 2015b) the need for strong and equitable teaching of writing practices, they are mostly focused on training, labor compensation, and student needs. We focus here on the teachers.

Developing Teachers as Writers

One thread that emerged immediately from our conversations about the multivocal, multimodal curriculum and preparing GTAs to teach it was identity, specifically the extent to which, if at all, our GTAs identify as writers (and writing teachers). In our recorded conversation we noted differences we've encountered with our respective graduate student populations.

> Many [L2 writing TAs] come into the TA training with years' worth of language teaching. They identify as language teachers but not necessarily as writing teachers and definitely not as writers. (Sarah, recording)

> It's so interesting because I think that sometimes, especially the students who are in creative writing, think exactly the opposite. Like, they're terrified of teaching. They want to do it, but they're really scared to start and try to translate what they know. And they know so much about writing, but they've never had the opportunity to find the language to talk about writing as content. (Kelly, recording)

Does it matter whether GTAs identify as writers themselves? What or where is the intersection of writer and teacher identities? And, as people who prepare and support multiple GTA populations through their teaching, how should we account for their varied writing identities in our pedagogy? We know from prior research (Dryer 2012; Reid 2009, 2017; Zoch et al. 2016) that GTA education curricula ought to give (novice) graduate student writing teachers opportunities to explore their own (academic) writing, whether it be in a practicum course or professional-development space. We are to "reimagine writing instructional practices," Melody Zoch, Joy Myers, Claire Lambert, Amy Vetter, and Colleen Fairbanks (2016) write, by affording teachers "the space and support to try on new ways of being teachers and writers" (19). During our recorded conversation, Sarah echoed that goal for our GTA populations: "first and foremost, setting up a curriculum and a training program that recognizes our TAs as writers and gives them opportunities to develop as writers in this unique way that they're going to be teaching."

Our conversation made it clear that we work with an array of writers, some of whom see themselves almost exclusively as teachers (of language if not specifically writing) and others who see themselves as writers from the perspective of craft (i.e., creative writing). Shelley Reid (2009) writes about the disillusionment the latter group of GTAs might encounter when their prior knowledge about writing, from their experience as "naturally" good writers, doesn't line up with their newfound knowledge of composition. "Current composition pedagogy is based on the premise that writing well is difficult," Reid writes. "People who do not believe that premise themselves may only go through the motions as writing teachers" (W202). As GTA educators, (part of) our job is to, as Kelly wrote in her narrative, "orient the TA Workshop course in praxis: As we're discussing the *whys* of composition pedagogy we must also do the *hows*—practice composing in multiple modes, practice assessing multimodal texts, etc." When we engage TAs in the work of "learn[ing] *how to learn to write*" (Reid 2009)—especially from the standpoint of the multivocal, multimodal framework we present here—perhaps we're also moving toward the opening of borders between creative writing and composition, as called for by Doug Hesse (2010). The multivocal, multimodal approach we're developing across GTA development in our program opens the door for the possibilities of what they and we all can learn from each other.

Developing Teachers as Collaborators

Critical friendship, according to Neville Hatton and David Smith (1995), is "to engage with another person in a way which encourages talking with, questioning, and even confronting, the trusted other, in order to examine planning for teaching, implementation, and its evaluation" (41). Such collaboration highlights teachers' voices while providing a safe and constructive space for positive, critical change. As Thomas Farrell (2001) notes, the "critical" component of this collegial relationship "refers to separating teaching into its parts, and discerning how those parts work together (if they do), and how teaching is related to other areas of life" (369). A critical friendship is the foundation of the collaborative curriculum work represented in this chapter. It is how we envision strengthening collaboration with and between our first-year writing GTAs to continue developing our multivocal, multimodal framework.

Prior to this collaboration, the three of us reported regular collaboration related to writing curriculum with graduate students and GTAs. During our recorded conversation, Kirsti reflected,

> Part of the reason my curriculum became what it was, is because I sat down with my graduate students who are teachers and said, How do we do this thing? How do we think about multimodality in your context?, and that included wildly different contexts and accesses to technology. (Kirsti, recording)

While such faculty-student collaboration proved effective on a local level (i.e., for a particular graduate class or population-specific GTA training), Sarah and Kirsti noted the limitations of having students participate in collaborative dialogues led by one faculty member. In bringing our three expertise areas together for this curriculum update and moving forward as a collective writing program, we see potential for our collaboration serving as a model for GTAs. Such a model would provide GTAs with an opportunity to observe how multiple teacher perspectives can both come together and challenge each other for positive pedagogical change and, as Kelly pointed out in our discussion, "help them to find the flexibility in the curriculum." An additional benefit to faculty consistently modeling effective collaboration is increased mentorship between GTAs, which removes the power dynamics often evident in faculty-led mentorship of GTAs (Barr Ebest 2002).

All three of us referenced the excitement surrounding our new collaborative efforts.

> I'm excited to now be in a collaboration with two colleagues who value context in writing curriculum and recognize multimodality as critical. In our curriculum work so far, we were able to identify where our previous curriculums intersected and then build a new curriculum from those shared points. . . . this collaboration also allows us as TA directors to more

easily bring the three TA populations together to learn from and collaborate with each other. (Sarah, narrative)

For Sarah and Kirsti, this excitement stemmed from a long-held desire to update the department's first-year writing curriculum. With the addition of Kelly as a new colleague and GTA director, we seized the opportunity to reconceptualize both the curriculum and GTA development. The possibilities for GTA growth under the new model continue to fuel our excitement. In addition to modeling collaboration through a critical friendship, we provide GTAs with a safe space to practice collaboration themselves. In the workshop courses and through ongoing mentoring, GTAs are able to observe teacher collaboration through our critical friendship and are also encouraged to participate in a variety of collaborative tasks. These include opportunities to reflect and to receive peer feedback on their new teaching experiences, as well as more focused collaborations like material and assessment (re)design. As GTAs gain confidence in their ability to teach writing through a multivocal, multimodal framework, the expectation is that they will begin to explore pedagogical possibilities together. We want to challenge GTAs as new teachers to explore "how genre conventions and language variation might be taught in innovative ways with multimodal writing" (Sarah, narrative). As Wanda Martin and Charles Paine (2002) emphasize, "There's nothing like new people with new ideas and experiences to keep the writing program moving forward, fostering new projects, still more new ideas, and new relationships, not only among GTAs but also among undergraduates and the faculty" (231). Encouraging GTAs to innovate and prioritizing reflective collaboration in writing-teacher preparation and development ensures both mentors and GTAs have a voice at the curriculum table and, in turn, strengthens the community of practice (Wenger 1998). It also supports curriculum development as cyclical and; in our recorded conversation, Kelly shared with us, "I can't wait to get their feedback so we can keep the curricular conversation going. It's never really finished."

Developing Teachers as Researchers

In order to keep the curricular conversation going, and expand the participants in the conversation, we must engage in research and reflective practice together. The work the three of us did to develop the curriculum can only evolve and grow with the addition of new voices, but it requires a step beyond collaboration; it requires informed practice. Ruth Ray (1993) reflects on teacher research saying, "Something is missing in the way we create and disseminate knowledge in schools and universities. This is the primary message of teacher research" (49). A good working definition of teacher research is "systematic and intentional inquiry carried out by teachers" (Cochran-Smith and Lytle 1990, 2). Teacher research is also called "action research" (Stenhouse 1985, 3), or scholarship of teaching and learning (SOTL) (Boyer 1990; Hutchings and Shulman 1999; Hutchings et al. 2011), and these titles reinforce the idea that there is a distinct demarcation between teaching and research. This dichotomy is false, but it is still relevant. As recently as 2006, Kathleen McKinney asserted that "the scholarship of teaching and learning . . . involves systematic study of teaching and/or learning and the public sharing and review of such work through presentations, performance, or publications" (39). This work is not new to composition, rhetoric, and writing studies teachers, but there are still hierarchies throughout our research, often because of who has time to do and publish research in our field.

In order to teach well, teachers do research. We research our content, we research our assigned readings, we research how to adapt to the teaching environments in which we find ourselves and with the students with whom we work. Teachers are researchers, but they don't think about themselves this way, in part because of the dichotomy outlined above.

> Graduate students in our programs don't consider themselves writers. They don't consider themselves researchers. They are teachers. So, we can talk about pedagogy easily. But their own praxis is all about teaching, not about interacting with writing or research themselves. (Kirsti, recording)

It makes sense that graduate students and GTAs would struggle to see themselves as researchers when veteran teachers might not. As a part of our GTA workshop preparation we made it transparent that we were pulling from multiple sources. We had to find answers in front of them, we had to troubleshoot technology in front of them, and we referred to other people, other pieces of scholarship, repeatedly. We modelled productively not knowing things and working together to find out what the answers were.

During our conversation, we identified the ways we want GTAs to explore how multimodality can bridge written, spoken, visual texts and better support L2 writers. Part of this exploration comes from collecting data on how the GTAs' students are developing under this curriculum and their related teaching practices. Each of us embraces the recursivity of teaching and research; we recognize they fundamentally and deeply inform one another.

NEXT STEPS FOR OUR MULTIVOCAL, MULTIMODAL CURRICULUM AND TRAINING

Two of the key questions that have continually surfaced for us since completing the curriculum revision are

- What else can we be doing to support the development of our GTAs/instructors as writers, collaborators, and researchers?
- In what ways can we use our multivocal, multimodal curriculum to build a culture of writing in our department and across our campus that is engaging for both faculty and students and makes connections to our local community?

A number of strategies and future plans have presented themselves as we've discussed our work during the writing of this chapter. By far the most important aspect is openness and goodwill among our colleagues. Without an explicit willingness to divest ourselves of curricular "territory," this curriculum would never have happened. As Hesse (2005) points out, when we think about who owns writing, the concept of "ownership has the double sense of controlling use and assuming responsibility" (337).

We agreed tacitly that the three of us would assume responsibility, and we rejected the notion of ownership of the conditions of writing wholesale. Instead, we were and continue to be interested more in how we might collectively work with our graduate and undergraduate students to reimagine a polyvocal, polymodal writing practice. As we modeled collaborative practices for and with our graduate students, we initiated a discussion around teaching pedagogy that also relied on collaborative practice.

We wanted most of all to create a safe but also exciting and exploratory space for GTAs, and for our writing students. This endeavor is deeply local and contextualized; the populations of GTAs, our department, and our institution will change, which means our curriculum will have to as well. Our multivocal, multimodal curriculum thrives on change because in multimodal projects, it is incumbent upon the instructor to talk about what counts as writing, and what counts is not the simple academic essay of old. Even if a teacher chooses to do something like a literary analysis of a novel, they must still think about and talk about how writing theory plays into creating a multimodal analysis.

This reevaluating of ownership and the fielding of flexibility as core to this curriculum might get at the imposter syndrome many early-career teachers report experiencing. But even more than genre, this kind of curriculum is cyclical. We make the case that our multivocal, multimodal framework can bridge the gap between writing as content and writing as process/craft. With the focus on writing and the modes of writing as the content of the course, and with and assessment practices grounded in labor-based grading (see chapter 3 of this collection on antiracist, anti-ableist teaching practices), GTAs and students have room to explore, to play, without getting caught up in the nerves and defensiveness of the novice writer, or teacher.

To paraphrase Kelly, our work is never done, and that is a good thing. So far, we see seven potential sites for expanding our exploration of what an adaptable writing curriculum might mean.

1. When faculty, instructors, and GTAs identify themselves as writers, collaborators, and researchers, they are modeling those roles for their students. But how can we best showcase this? We want to explore an onsite, online conference and publication that exhibits together undergraduate, graduate, GTA, instructor, and faculty writing on campus and in the community.

2. Because all incoming students at our university take our first-year writing course, it is imperative to have continuing conversations across campus about writing and writing practices in the disciplines. Our campus writing-across-the-curriculum initiative is currently disconnected from our department's first-year writing initiative. In order to best serve our students, it is necessary to explore and develop a robust writing program. This program could be the site of more interactive professional development, teacher engagement, and collaborative curriculum development.

3. As we collaborate across campus, we must continually acknowledge that our students, faculty, and staff live and participate in a local community that is diverse, vibrant, and deeply connected to the university. We have already started the process of collaborating with faculty in our department who do a great deal of work with local community members, and we plan to pursue a grant to set up a community writing center. Sites like this could present additional opportunities for our GTAs and students to facilitate multivocal, multimodal writing initiatives in our local community.

4. We plan to reevaluate our graduate programs in rhetoric and composition, all of which are offered online only, to ensure our graduate coursework models this multimodal framework comprehensively and that graduate students have multiple opportunities as teachers and as students to engage in multivocal, multimodal, and digital teaching, research, and writing.

5. As we were discussing the *why*s of composition pedagogy, we realized we must also do the *how*s. As writing-teacher educators we must ourselves practice composing in multiple modes, practice assessing multimodal texts, practice engaging multilingual voices, and practice crafting multivocal texts.

6. We must engage in a persistent and planned discussion of professionalism and duties around GTA development and mentoring in the context of our department and our institution, including our own roles respective to the GTA populations we supervise, our university's lack of a traditional WPA role, and the potentiality for growth in GTA peer mentorship.

7. As we continue to engage in the recursive processes of curriculum development, program assessment, and GTA education, we must focus additionally on the role labor-based writing assessment plays in our work. We see this as a twofold next step, both for our continued collaborative scholarship and for our multivocal, multimodal curriculum.

NOTES

1. Our curriculum can be found here: https://sites.google.com/view/multivocalmulti modal/home.
2. This language comes from the first line of our state transfer curriculum: "The goal is to provide students with . . . a rich understanding of how writing works." We borrowed the same phrase for our revised ENG 101 course description (see table 2.1).
3. The curriculum we introduced to GTAs included a labor-based grading contract, borrowed and closely adapted from Asao Inoue's work (2019b). While exploring the significance of this part of our multivocal, multimodal curriculum was beyond the scope of this project, we see labor-based grading an avenue for our continued research and curricular development.

REFERENCES

Anson, Chris, and Jessie L. Moore, eds. 2016. *Critical Transitions: Writing and the Question of Transfer*. Fort Collins, CO: University Press of Colorado. https://wac.colostate.edu/books/perspectives/ansonmoore.

Baker-Bell, April, Bonnie J. Williams-Farrier, Davena Jackson, Lamar Johnson, Carmen Kynard, and Teaira McMurtry. 2020. "This Ain't Another Statement! This Is a DEMAND for Black Linguistic Justice!" CCCC. https://cccc.ncte.org/cccc/demand-for -black-linguistic-justice.

Barr Ebest, Sally. 2002. "Mentoring: Past, Present, and Future." In *Preparing College Teachers of Writing: Histories, Theories, Programs, and Practices*, edited by Betty P. Pytlik and Sarah Liggett, 211–21. Oxford: Oxford University Press.

Borgman, Jessie. 2019. "Dissipating Hesitation: Why Online Instructors Fear Multimodal Assignments and How to Overcome the Fear." In *Bridging the Multimodal Gap: From Theory to Practice*, edited by Antosh Khadka and J. C. Lee, 43–68. Fort Collins, CO: WAC Clearinghouse.

Borgman, Jessie, and Casey McArdle. 2019. *Personal, Accessible, Responsive, Strategic: Resources and Strategies for Online Writing Instructors*. Fort Collins, CO: WAC Clearinghouse. https://wac.colostate.edu/books/practice/pars/.

Boyer, Ernest. 1990. *Scholarship Reconsidered: Priorities of the Professoriate*. San Francisco: Jossey-Bass.

Bridwell-Bowles, Lillian, Karen Powell, and Tiffany Walter Choplin. 2009. "Not Just Words Any More: Multimodal Communication Across the Curriculum." In "Writing Technologies and Writing Across the Curriculum." Special issue, *Across the Disciplines*, 6. https://wac.colostate.edu/docs/atd/technologies/bridwellbowlesetal.pdf.

Canagarajah, A. Suresh. 2006. "The Place of World Englishes in Composition: Pluralization Continued." *College Composition and Communication* 57 (4): 586–619.

Canagarajah, Suresh. 2013. *Translingual Practice: Global Englishes and Cosmopolitan Relations.* New York: Routledge.

Cochran-Smith, Marilyn, and Susan L. Lytle. 1990. "Research on Teaching and Teacher Research: The Issues That Divide." *Educational Researcher* 19 (2): 2–11.

Conference on College Composition and Communication. 2015a. "Principles for the Postsecondary Teaching of Writing." Position statement. https://cccc.ncte.org/cccc/resources/positions/postsecondarywriting.

Conference on College Composition and Communication. 2015b. "Statement on Preparing Teachers of College Writing." Position statement. https://cccc.ncte.org/cccc/resources/positions/statementonprep.

Conference on College Composition and Communication OWI Standing Group. 2013. https://sites.google.com/view/owistandinggroup/home?authuser=0.

Chang, Heewon, Faith Wambura Ngunjiri, and Kathy-Ann C. Hernandez. 2016. *Collaborative Autoethnography.* New York: Routledge.

Downs, Doug, and Elizabeth Wardle. 2007. "Teaching about Writing, Righting Misconceptions: (Re)envisioning 'First-Year Composition' as 'Introduction to Writing Studies.' " *College Composition and Communication* 58 (4): 552–84.

Driscoll, Dana Lynn, and Jennifer Wells. 2012. "Beyond Knowledge and Skills: Writing Transfer and the Role of Student Dispositions." *Composition Forum*, 26. https://compositionforum.com/issue/26/beyond-knowledge-skills.php.

Dryer, Dylan B. 2012. "At a Mirror, Darkly: The Imagined Undergraduate Writers of Ten Novice Composition Instructors." *College Composition and Communication* 63 (3): 420–52.

Farrell, Thomas. 2001. "Critical Friendships: Colleagues Helping Each Other Develop." *ELT Journal* 55 (4): 368–74.

Fraiberg, Steven. 2010. "Composition 2.0: Toward a Multilingual and Multimodal Framework." *College Composition and Communication* 62 (1): 100–26.

Goggin, Maureen, and Peter Goggin, eds. 2018. *Serendipity in Rhetoric, Writing, and Literacy Research.* Logan: Utah State University Press.

Gonzales, Laura. 2015. "Multimodality, Translingualism, and Rhetorical Genre Studies." *Composition Forum* 31. https://compositionforum.com/issue/31/multimodality.php.

Graupner, Meredith, and Lee Nikoson-Massey. 2009. "Remediating Knowledge-Making Spaces in the Graduate Curriculum: Developing and Sustaining Multimodal Teaching and Research." *Computers and Composition* 26 (1): 13–23.

Hatton, Neville, and David Smith. 1995. "Reflection in Teacher Education: Towards Definition and Implementation." *Teaching and Teacher Education* 11 (1): 33–49.

Hesse, Doug. 2005. "2005 CCCC Chair's Address: Who Owns Writing?" *College Composition and Communication* 57 (2): 335–57.

Hesse, Doug. 2010. "The Place of Creative Writing in Composition Studies." *College Composition and Communication* 62 (1): 31–52.

Hewitt, Beth L., and Keven E. DePew, eds. 2015. *Foundational Practices of Online Writing Instruction.* Anderson, SC: Parlor. https://wac.colostate.edu/books/perspectives/owi/.

Horner, Bruce, and John Trimbur. 2002. "English Only and US College Composition." *College Composition and Communication* 53 (4): 594–630.

Hutchings, Pat, Mary Huber, and Anthony Ciccone. 2011. *The Scholarship of Teaching and Learning Reconsidered.* San Francisco: Jossey-Bass.

Hutchings, Pat, and Lee E. Shulman. 1999. "The Scholarship of Teaching: New Elaborations, New Developments." *Change* 31 (5): 10–15.

Inoue, Asao B. 2019a. "How Do We Language So People Stop Killing Each Other, or What Do We Do About White Language Supremacy?" Keynote address at the Conference on College Composition and Communication, Pittsburgh, March 14.

Inoue, Asao B. 2019b. *Labor-Based Grading Contracts: Building Equity and Inclusion in the Compassionate Writing Classroom.* Fort Collins, CO: WAC Clearinghouse https://wac.colostate.edu/books/perspectives/labor/.

Martin, Wanda, and Charles Paine. 2002. "Mentors, Models, and Agents of Change: Veteran TAs Preparing Teachers of Writing." In *Preparing College Teachers of Writing: Histories, Theories, Programs, and Practices,* edited by Betty P. Pytlik and Sarah Liggett, 222–32. Oxford: Oxford University Press.

Matsuda, Aya, and Paul K. Matsuda. 2010. "World Englishes and the Teaching of Writing." *TESOL Quarterly* 44 (2): 369–74.

Matsuda, Paul K. 2006. "The Myth of Linguistic Homogeneity in U.S. College Composition." *College English* 68 (6): 637–51.

McKinney, Kathleen. 2006. "Attitudinal and Structural Factors Contributing to Challenges in the Work of the Scholarship of Teaching and Learning." *New Directions for Institutional Research* 129 (Summer): 37–50.

Moore, Jessie L., and Randall Bass, eds. 2017. *Understanding Writing Transfer: Implications for Transformative Student Learning in Higher Education.* Sterling, VA: Stylus.

Palmeri, Jason. 2012. *Remixing Composition: A History of Multimodal Writing Pedagogy.* Carbondale: Southern Illinois University Press.

Ray, Ruth E. 1993. *The Practice of Theory: Teacher Research in Composition.* Urbana, IL: National Council of Teachers of English.

Reid, E. Shelley. 2009. "Teaching Writing Teachers Writing: Difficulty, Exploration, and Critical Reflection." *College Composition and Communication* 61 (2): W197–W221.

Reid, E. Shelley. 2017. "On Learning to Teach: Letter to a New TA." *WPA: Writing Program Administration* 40 (2): 129–45.

Reiff, Mary Jo, and Anis Bawarshi. 2011. "Tracing Discursive Resources: How Students Use Prior Genre Knowledge to Negotiate New Writing Contexts in First-Year Composition." *Written Communication* 28 (3): 312–37. https://doi.org/10.1177/0741088311410183.

Shetler Angela, Susan E. Thomas, Francis di Lauro, and Benjamin Miller. 2013. "Multimodal Writing Instruction in a Global World." *Kairos: A Journal of Rhetoric, Technology, and Pedagogy* 17 (3). http://kairos.technorhetoric.net/17.3/praxis/shetler-et-al/index.html.

Skerrett, Allison. and Randy Bomer. 2013. "Recruiting Languages and Lifeworlds for Border-Crossing Compositions." *Research in the Teaching of English* 47 (3): 313–37.

Wardle, Elizabeth, and Doug Downs. 2013. "Reflecting Back and Looking Forward: Revisiting 'Teaching about Writing, Righting Misconceptions' Five Years On." *Composition Forum,* 27. https://compositionforum.com/issue/27/reflecting-back.php.

Wenger, Etienne. 1998. *Communities of Practice: Learning, Meaning, and Identity.* Cambridge: Cambridge University Press.

Yancey, Kathleen Blake, Liane Robertson, and Kara Taczak. 2014. *Writing across Contexts: Transfer, Composition, and Sites of Writing.* Logan: Utah State University Press.

Young, Vershawn Ashanti, and Aja Y. Martinez, eds. 2011. *Code-Meshing as World English: Pedagogy, Policy, Performance.* Urbana, IL: NCTE.

Zoch, Melody, Joy Myers, Claire Lambert, Amy Vetter, and Colleen Fairbanks. 2016. "Reimagining Instructional Practices: Exploring the Identity Work of Teachers of Writing." *Teaching/Writing: The Journal of Writing Teacher Education* 5 (1): 1–23.

3

PRACTICING (ANTIRACIST AND ANTI-ABLEIST) MULTIMODALITY
TA Training and Student Responses to Implementing a Multimodal Curriculum in First-Year Writing

Megan McIntyre and Jennifer Lanatti Shen

INTRODUCTION

> *I feel like the most important skill I developed over the course of my ENGL 100B class was storytelling and just building confidence in my writing.—A first-year student in Jennifer's first-year writing course*

Faculty choose to assign multimodal projects in writing classes for many reasons: these projects give students opportunities to use composing skills they already have; they echo the ways students create and communicate outside class; they reflect, as Christina Cedillo (2018) reminds us, an embodied approach to writing. For many, though, we suspect, the decision to assign multimodal projects also boils down to this: these projects are more creative, more engaging, and just more fun for teachers and for student-composers. In what follows, we outline the literature, particularly in antiracist and anti-ableist pedagogy, that informs our ways of thinking about multimodal writing pedagogy, review the process that led to Jennifer's creation of a multimodal first-year writing course as a graduate teaching associate, and discuss the results of a brief survey of Jennifer's students that offers insight into how students view such an approach. We conclude by offering a few takeaways for teachers considering a similar critical, antiracist/anti-ableist, multimodal approach.

LITERATURE REVIEW

Writing studies has been grappling with how to teach students to compose multimodally for at least twenty-five years, from the New London Group's (1996) early work on multiliteracies to Cynthia Selfe's (2004) call for our profession to recognize how changing technologies have made multimodality even more necessary. Among first-year writing faculty, multimodality has been a popular way to engage often-reluctant students in required first-year composition courses (Yancey 2004). Beyond

https://doi.org/10.7330/9781646424184.c003

these broader calls for attention to the affordances of multimodality, scholars, particularly Black scholars, Indigenous scholars, and other scholars of color, have articulated important links between multimodal composition and antiracist (Turner, Hayes, and Way 2013), community-based (Turner 2012), culturally responsive (Castagno and Brayboy 2008; Cedillo 2017), Indigenous knowledge-based (Mills et al. 2015), translingual (Gonzales 2015), and anti-ableist (Butler 2016; Cedillo 2017, 2018; Yurgeau, et al. 2013) pedagogies. Multimodal pedagogies are also postpedagogies (McIntyre 2016, 2018): they can encourage creativity, reflection, making, and remaking while also empowering students to make and articulate a wider variety of rhetorical choices. Multimodality, then, is not just a vehicle for building technical capacity or for encouraging creative thinking, though it does both; it is also a vehicle for creative antiracist and anti-ableist teaching practices.

ANTIRACIST PEDAGOGY AND MULTIMODALITY

Antiracist composition pedagogy offers important correctives to the whitestream approaches that litter our disciplinary history. As Asao Inoue (2019), April Baker-Bell (2019), and H. Samy Alim and Geneva Smitherman (2012) have convincingly argued, composition's emphasis on a supposedly colorblind "academic writing" serves only to reinforce the white default of our discipline: "It is the language and communicative norms of those in power, in any society, that tend to be labeled as 'standard,' 'official,' 'normal,' 'appropriate,' 'respectful.' . . . In our case, White Mainstream English and White ways of speaking become the invisible—or better, inaudible—norms of what educators and uncritical scholars like to call academic English, the language of school, the language of power, or communicating in academic settings" (171). Similarly, Inoue (2015), in his book *Antiracist Writing Assessment Ecologies*, argues, "As a habitus that is practiced in language, expected in classroom behaviors, and marked on the bodies of students and teachers, whiteness, then, is a set of structuring structures, durable, transposable, and flexible . . . these structures construct whiteness as invisible and appealing to fairness through objectivity. . . . They are set up as apolitical" (48). Academic writing, then, with its claims of objectivity and invisibility, instead perpetuates white ways of speaking and writing while excluding the ways of speaking, writing, and making meaning that invigorate Black, Indigenous, Asian/ Asian-Pacific Islander, and Chicanx communities and discourses.

Antiracist multimodal pedagogies, on the other hand, offer concrete ways of inviting and supporting diverse ways of thinking, writing, speaking, and creating. In her discussion of rhetorical genre studies, multimodal composition, and translingualism, Laura Gonzales (2015) notes multimodal approaches are one way of achieving antiracist, translingual ends: "By moving away from the linear, container-bound approach to writing, we might continue unbinding genres from rigid forms, languages, and classrooms, seeing and teaching them as ways of meaning-making across contexts." In particular, specific multimodal approaches like K. C. Nat Turner, Nini Hayes, and Kate Way's (2013) critical multimodal hip-hop pedagogy explicitly emphasize the home languages, values, and interests of students and their communities. And, they argue, centering students' lived experiences and home languages leads to increased engagement and learning: "When students' lived experiences and popular culture become the texts for discussion and analysis, students become more engaged and develop literacy skills that connect to other disciplines" (352). Multimodal pedagogies can be antiracist in that they allow us to eschew whitestream academic language and instead center the lived experiences and literacies of students from diverse backgrounds.

ANTI-ABLEIST PEDAGOGY AND MULTIMODALITY

Multimodal pedagogy, though, doesn't just serve antiracist ends; it also supports anti-ableist ones. Let us begin by first defining what we mean by anti-ableist pedagogy. Cody Jackson's (2020) description is operative here: "Anti-ableist composition is . . . about gesturing toward the possibility of agential composing through and with negation. It . . . doesn't cede ground to essentialist arguments about what disability is or isn't. It is a politics of accountability that finds itself dreaming for something more than words." As Jackson's description makes clear, anti-ableism emphasizes fulsome, embodied participation across ability and difference. It is also an activist stance: it demands full access and participation for disabled students, faculty, and scholars and accountability from the wider composition community. Full access necessitates a multiplicity of approaches, bodily responses, and, particularly relevant to the current discussion, modes.

Unlike static, monomodal notions of academic writing and the pedagogies that support such classroom and teaching approaches, multimodality calls for the multiplication of voices and modes to represent a fuller spectrum of communicative and writing practices. In her article on dynamic captioning, multimodality, and accessibility, Janine Butler (2018) argues that anti-ableist, embodied multimodal composition pedagogies "make students conscious of the experience of multimodal and multisensory communication." This emphasis on embodiment is a particularly important feature of an anti-ableist multimodal pedagogy because it also allows us to recognize and support students' and teachers' complex, intersecting identities, as Cedillo (2018) argues: "From my intersectional positionality of racialized disability, I argue that we must strive for critical embodiment pedagogies, or approaches that recognize and foreground bodily diversity so that students learn to compose for accessibility and inclusivity." More specifically, Cedillo argues embodied, multimodal approaches to language and literacy "make room for bodily diversity in composition by highlighting race and disability as critical means of embodied invention that gainfully unsettle habituated expectations."

Furthermore, as Butler (2016) argues in her webtext, "Where Access Meets Multimodality," multiple modes are necessary if we aim to make our classrooms and our pedagogies accessible for all our students. In her conclusion, Butler also lays out a series of questions about the intersections between multimodality and access: "What other multimodal conventions can we reshape to communicate our differences or communicate to different audiences? Which excluded audience members can we include to broaden the reach of our message and benefit both designer and audiences?" These questions are vital to thinking about equitable access and to the instantiation of a critical multimodal pedagogy that is both antiracist and anti-ableist. As we note in the institutional context section that follows, Megan's goal was to anchor the coursework for graduate teaching associates in antiracism and anti-ableism. Multimodal approaches to teaching composition, especially first-year composition, allowed her to do just that because multimodal approaches of all stripes are interested in expanding our sense of what counts as literacy.

Multimodal approaches are flexible and polyvocal; they encourage agency, engagement, and creativity. Cedillo's (2017) notion of multimodal homeplace "centers the importance of those norms, values, and attitudes that are homegrown while drawing attention to overlapping geographies that students traverse and the technological conventions associated with each space." Picking up on Jacqueline Jones Royster's work on voice, identity, and disciplinarity, Cedillo notes that multimodal homeplaces are "composed principally of students' community-determined perspectives that inform their rhetorical aims and intent and that complement and/or contest the ethics and attitudes of the dominant culture and those represented by the media and modalities they engage." Culturally relevant and sustaining literacy classes invite students to center community-based, experiential literacies rather than participating solely in academic discourses that rely on whitestream notions of literacy and language. What Cedillo (2017, 2018) calls for (what we argue is possible in the sections that follow) is a critical multimodal pedagogy both antiracist and anti-ableist, one that encourages agency and reflection.

INSTITUTIONAL CONTEXT

At this point, it seems useful to offer some context about the university in which we both work. Sonoma State is a regional public university and part of the California State University system; we are also a Hispanic-serving institution, a designation we received in the spring of 2017, as well as a public liberal arts school. In the academic year 2019–2020, our first-year class was the most diverse ever: 46 percent of incoming students were Hispanic self-identifying, first-generation, and Pell Grant eligible, with more than 70 percent of the incoming class falling into at least one of those groups.

Prior to teaching in the first-year writing program, graduate teaching associates must complete a course on the history and pedagogy of rhetoric and composition, work through an application process that includes composing and reflecting on their prospective teaching philosophy and practices, and attend orientation. (Megan also offers optional syllabus and teaching workshops over the summer before they begin teaching.) During their first semester teaching, graduate teaching associates also participate in a teaching practicum, which asks them to reflect on their experiences in the classroom, engage with additional literature about teaching and learning, compose and workshop writing assignments, and practice giving feedback on sample student work.

Early on, Megan decided (in part because of her own investment in new media and postpedagogy and in part because of the research affirming the value of multimodal approaches to literacy development) that along with antiracist and culturally responsive pedagogies, multimodal composition would be an important part of TA training. In the history and pedagogy course, this meant Megan assigned work on multimodality from Jody Shipka, Angela Haas, Adam Banks, and Christina Cedillo, among others; she also assigned multimodal texts (including Asao B. Inoue's 2019 CCCC address; Shipka's and Cedillo's work are also themselves multimodal texts) so students had the opportunity to read multimodal texts while also reading about them.

JENNIFER'S EXPERIENCE AS A NEW TA

Megan's class introduced Jennifer to a wide variety of scholars and pedagogies that shaped her view on teaching writing multimodally. As Jennifer worked her way through Megan's syllabus, which covered everything from ancient rhetorical tradition to emerging and radical rhetoricians, Jennifer's view of what literacy and composition *should be* was completely abolished and restructured with new, unfamiliar, but exciting possibilities of what her first syllabus could look like.

Each unit of English 587 was dedicated to a different branch of pedagogy. One of the earlier readings was Paolo Freire's (1978) *Pedagogy of the Oppressed*; his words made Jennifer completely reexamine traditional pedagogy and think more deeply about not only what educators were choosing to teach but also who that teaching was really serving. Freire explains, "Liberation is a praxis . . . liberating education consists in acts of cognition, not transferrals of information" (79). After reading Freire's text, Jennifer felt excited about offering a pedagogy that values students' preexisting knowledge, but she was left wondering what could be the best way to implement this style of curriculum in the twenty-first-century composition classroom.

When our class moved from critical pedagogy to multimodal pedagogy, Jennifer first read Kathleen Blake Yancey's (2004) words, "How is it that what we teach and what we test can be so different from what our students know as writing?" (298). Yancey's work was published fifteen years prior to Jennifer reading it, and her question was as relevant as ever. We then read chapters from Shipka's text, *Toward a Composition Made Whole*. Shipka (2011) interrogates the concept of traditional academic rigor and explains how multimodal creation involves complex decision-making processes just as useful to student development as existing models requiring students to adhere to measures such as grammatical correctness or essay structuring (1–17). Jennifer found multimodal pedagogy blended well with Freire's theories. Yancey, Shipka, and Freire alike are asking educators to value the lived knowledge their students already possess upon entering the classroom and encourage students to continue to hone their skills rather than force them into conforming to arbitrary guidelines.

When our class moved into the section focusing on antiracist pedagogy, and we studied the work of scholars such as Vershawn Ashanti Young, Jennifer was again struck by how well Young's vision for a pedagogy equitable for a diverse group of students fit in with the methods put forth by multimodal pedagogy. Young (2010) points out that students' home languages and dialects aren't inferior by any measurable standard, but rather by the guidelines pushed by white supremacy—because of this, we must reexamine what successful communication looks like. At this juncture in English 587, it was clear to Jennifer she needed to create a syllabus that was not only receptive to students with diverse literacies but that uplifted their ways of knowing. The work of anti-ableist pedagogues, then, such as Cedillo (2018), continued to contribute to the methods Jennifer could use that would implement multimodal pedagogy in a way that was critical, antiracist, and anti-ableist for any student who might enter her classroom. Cedillo offers this: "Writing *is* political"—and we must recognize this and be upfront about it in the classroom to create an accessible rather than hostile space.

Equipped with all the knowledge offered in English 587 and the support of her advisor (Megan), Jennifer was ready to begin creating the syllabus for her first first-year composition class. Megan suggested Jennifer first decide on a class theme and what she wanted her students' end-of-the-year culminating project to be. Since Jennifer knew she wanted students to write about work that was meaningful to them, she easily landed on the theme of advocacy, which would allow students to explore and compose on topics of their choosing. Jennifer had written a multigenre project in her undergrad work and wanted to use that project as inspiration for her student's culminating project. However, given her thinking throughout ENGL 587, Jennifer decided that instead of students focusing solely on written genres, she should ask them to create genres that covered different modalities. They would work on these varying genres throughout the year and have a final portfolio consisting of all their multimodal projects: this portfolio would be their culminating project.

We reiterate that the first-year composition class Jennifer teaches is a two-semester "stretch" course for students who choose to lengthen out their composition requirements[1] over the course of a full academic year. The primary focus of this chapter is on the curriculum implemented in the 100B section (the second semester) of Jennifer's course, but in 100A, students chose their topic of advocacy and built the skills, practices, and habits they needed to write and compose about that topic thoughtfully and effectively.

During Jennifer's first semester of teaching, she worked on creating the 100B syllabus with Megan. Over the course of multiple meetings, Jennifer and Megan discussed how to best achieve Jennifer's vision of the culminating project. Megan suggested she create loose guidelines for each genre project in order to provide students with some sort of structure. This outline is what they landed on for the major assignments (in order of due date):

Genre 1: Written Genre (exploratory/informational genre)

> **Genre 1 Constraints:** (1) must utilize at least three of the sources from your annotated bibliography, (2) must be mostly written work (no more than five pages and at least one thousand words).

Genre 2: Visual Genre (tell a story that gives the human side of the problem)

> **Genre 2 Constraints:** (1) must utilize knowledge from your sources but no specific citation is required, (2) must be mostly visual work (i.e., pictures, drawings, etc.), (3) must be the equivalent of at least four pages, but fewer than five hundred words.[2]

Genre 3: Auditory Genre (advocate for a specific way to address the problem)

> **Genre 3 Constraints:** (1) must utilize at least one source from your annotated bibliography, (2) must be primarily an auditory genre (podcast, speech, PSA, etc.), (3) must be at least three minutes of content.

Culminating Project: Final Portfolio and Reflective Cover Letter

Before each project was due, the preceding unit focused on students exploring and practicing composing in various genres that utilized the modality assigned. Examples of the kinds of homework assigned are Ta-Nehisi Coates's (2015) memoir *Between the World and Me* (preceding the written project), Alison Bechdel's (2006) graphic novel *Fun Home* (preceding the visual project), and Rudy Francisco's (2017) spoken word poem "Rifle" (preceding the auditory project). Students were introduced to many different genres, and during class time they analyzed what made a certain piece effective and how that quality could transfer to a new medium.

Planning all these units, with their foundational lessons and homework building to each corresponding Genre Project, was an exciting way to offer composition to students; however, Jennifer knew much of what she was asking of students would be unfamiliar, and therefore uncomfortable, to them. It is difficult to ask students to trust us and commit themselves to creative work when they have been conditioned to believe writing and literacy can only be one thing. Because of this disconnect, labor-based grading contracts (Inoue 2019) became useful. Jennifer decided her students would be graded solely on participating in the process and doing their best work. This approach took away the pressure of arbitrary perfection and allowed students to try new things and invest in themselves creatively.

METHODS

The Google Forms survey was sent to students who provided their informed consent at the conclusion of the spring 2020 semester. (This study, including the survey instrument, was approved by Sonoma State University's IRB in December 2019.) The survey's main purpose was to gather and assess student's feelings about the curriculum; more specifically, the survey asked students to consider the relationship between their work in first-year composition and their writing/composing outside our writing class. Questions of engagement, interest, and utility were all important to judging the relative success of Jennifer's curricular choices because the structure of the class was specifically designed to value students' various literacies and their personal and academic interests.

Focusing on qualitative responses and allowing students to use their own language[3] in providing feedback, we analyzed the linguistic data for emerging themes using grounded theory (Glaser and Strauss 2017). Since multimodality is a widespread but a highly context dependent and variable practice, grounded theory was the best way for us to hypothesize and learn about teaching in this constantly shifting field (Denscome 2003; Fernandez 2004; Tan 2010). Furthermore, by letting the data tell us what themes emerged, we were in the best position to thoughtfully assess the success of the pedagogy. Utilizing Barney Glaser's (2018) approach to grounded theory, we acknowledge our prior influence and theoretical sensitivity regarding the field of composition (Heath and Cowley 2004; Kelle 2011); in particular, as our literature review suggests, we are sensitive to connections between multimodality and critical, antiracist, and anti-ableist pedagogical goals.

The questions were designed for students to reflect on their 100B classroom experiences by comparing them to their expectations, their interests, and their academic major in order to encourage informed category building (Kelle 2011) while avoiding the "preconceived emergence of data" (Glaser 2018, 3). After collecting the survey results, we individually assessed the responses to search for emerging trends. We then compared our answers and categorized connected themes. We sorted the most connected themes, created subcategories, and discussed areas of divergence.

COMMON THEMES IN STUDENT SURVEY RESULTS

Across the students' responses, we identified seven themes or codes: (1) *confidence*, (2) *enjoyment*, (3) *creativity*, (4) *storytelling*, (5) *transfer*, (6) *grading*, and (7) *content- or genre-informed decision-making*. (This final category refers to answers that suggest students considered either the genre conventions or needs/requirements of the topic they addressed as they made decisions about which genres to compose for various projects.)

Confidence: Students mentioned they had built confidence in their writing, felt more self-assured about their abilities, or had become a better writer in general. As one student noted, "The [projects] really helped me develop new skills." Another wrote, "I ended up . . . getting better results.'" Both these responses, as well as others that referenced "growth" or "talent," were coded as *confidence*.

Enjoyment: Students also wrote that they enjoyed the class and their ability to work in a multimodal framework. Some examples of student responses that reference enjoyment included, "The work was hard but I liked doing the research and putting the projects together" and "I ended up putting much more passion into my assignments." All these responses were coded *enjoyment,* as were responses that referenced "fun" or "care."

Creativity: The most common trend among student responses was the word *creativity*. Many believed the loose guidelines for their projects allowed them more creative freedom than they expected or were used to having in the classroom. Other comments we felt were evidence of their creativity were, "In high school, there is always a list of guidelines we had to follow and really no creativity, and it was cool to just get away from that" and "[I had to] push myself outside of my comfort zone." Responses expressing surprise about getting to create particular genres (like comic books) and/or trying new things were also coded as *creativity*.

Storytelling: Another notable theme was storytelling. Multiple students mentioned they learned how to tell or to develop a good and/or effective story while creating their projects. Evidence of this can be found in the following responses: "I feel like the most important skill I developed over the course of my ENGL 100B class was storytelling" and "All the projects I did helped me learn how to tell a good story."

Transfer: Students also noticed the skills they developed while creating their projects had the potential to be transferred to other areas. Students stated, "I learned [how] to get my point across in different ways effectively" and "[I can] get my ideas across using different methods." Most notably, one student stated, "[There were] objectives I can apply to other courses, not just English ones."

Grading/Assessment: Some students also mentioned how feedback and/or assessment influenced their class experiences. A student stated, "The one on one conferences throughout the semester, as well as the feedback I got from you and my classmates, it was just super helpful and just built up my confidence." Another wrote, "I was able to play around with ideas I was interested in rather [than] what I thought my teacher wanted to see."

Content/Genre-Informed Decision-Making: The last trend among the survey responses was students making decisions about mode, genre, or approach based on the content/genre project they were working on at the time. Students realized they had to write/compose in different ways based upon the assigned modality and the target audience for that project. As one student noted, "I learned how to write a script for a podcast in a way where if people were listening to me speak that it would flow easily." Another student stated, "[I] had to find a [different] way to explain things . . . in order for the audience to understand everything I was saying which is something I have never done before."

RESULTS AND ANALYSIS/STUDENT RESPONSES

Seven students (half the students who completed their first-year writing course with Jennifer) responded to the survey. As noted above, we identified seven codes from our initial examination. We applied the same seven codes to all three open-ended questions. Table 3.1 below lists the frequency of each code for each question.

Question 1: What is the most important skill (if any) you feel you have developed over the course of your English 100B class?

The purpose of this question was to gauge both what skills students felt they developed and what skills they felt were important for them to learn. We found that in response to this question, the most common theme among student answers was creativity. Students noticed the way their projects challenged them to work in new and creative ways, to explore their unique interests and talents, and to use their creative judgment to determine the best way to structure their projects. This trend of students finding the curriculum creative and easily adaptable to their own interests fit in with our goal of an antiracist multimodal curriculum that emphasizes students' values, interests, and lived experiences (Turner, Hayes, and Way 2013), as well as the anti-ableist multimodal curriculum that centers inclusivity and accessibility (Cedillo 2018). The second most common theme among student responses to this question was the idea of transfer; students mentioned they found it important that they learned how to get their point across in different ways by composing in different genres for various audiences.

Table 3.1. Code Frequencies by Question

Code	Question: What is the most important skill (if any) you feel you have developed over the course of your ENGL 100B class?	Question: What thing(s) did you compose that helped you learn the skill you listed above?	Question: How is the work you did in English 100B similar to what you expected it to be like? How is it different?
Confidence	2	2	2
Enjoyment	2	1	4
Creativity	4	3	5
Storytelling	1	1	0
Transfer	3	2	1
Grading/assessment	1	1	0
Content/ genre-informed decision-making	2	3	1

Question 2: What thing(s) did you compose that helped you learn the skill you listed above?

We felt it was important to understand how students correlated the skills they learned to the specific projects they created. Out of the three major projects students created (the written, the visual, and the auditory), the answers were fairly evenly distributed, with the auditory/visual projects trending only slightly higher than the written. It seemed students found that creating all the projects together was what helped them build their skills. Similar to the previous question, the most repeated theme was creativity. Students thought that challenging themselves to get creative was an important aspect of the class. The other trending theme in response to this question was content/genre-informed decision-making. This theme fits in with the second-highest trending skill in question 1, transfer; students correlated their decision-making processes with their genres with their adaptability to new composing situations.

Question 3: How was the work you did in English 100B similar to what you expected it to be like? How was it different?

We also wanted to determine whether the course met the students' expectations. Most students said the class was much different from what they anticipated. We found again that the most common theme was creativity. Many students compared it to their high-school experiences, in which they usually had to adhere to strict writing rules and prompts, stating this course challenged them to think differently. The second theme that strongly emerged was enjoyment. Students stated they enjoyed it much more than they thought they would, primarily because they had agency in their choices. These results support research in antiracist writing pedagogy—students expressed that in their prior experiences in the writing classroom, White Mainstream English was presented to them as what was "normal" (Alim and Smitherman 2012; Baker-Bell 2020; Inoue 2019). As a consequence, a diverse group of students had not found their writing classrooms to be places where they could work on what interested them. The curriculum presented in Jennifer's class left them feeling valued and invigorated to do their work.

ANALYSIS

The questions from Jennifer's survey can be roughly categorized in two ways: students were asked, on the one hand, what they enjoyed, and on the other hand, what they thought would be useful for the writing/composing they expect to do beyond their first-year writing class. Perhaps not surprisingly, students enjoyed the auditory and visual projects more than the written project, but they believed the work they did to create the written text would be more useful for the future. Here we come to our first somewhat contradictory finding: out of the seven survey responses, five students indicated they believed the written project was the most useful project for them academically. However, out of the seven survey responses, five students indicated that either the auditory or the visual project (or both) helped them develop the most important skills they learned in the class, namely, creativity and transferability. In other words, while students who responded to the survey asserted their experiences with written text would be more useful in the future, the skills they enumerated as most useful for future writing/composing were the ones they gained from their multimodal work. This finding is again consistent with the assertion that White English disguises itself as academic writing and is labeled as *standard, official,* and *normal* (Alim and Smitherman 2012). The students' default belief was that their written project was academic and therefore the most useful.

Despite this seeming disconnect, we actually see this finding as a confirmation of the value of Jennifer's approach: by asking students to work across modes, students were able to compose in the genres they expect to see in future academic and professional settings, and they were able to practice the skills (creativity, decision-making, flexibility) that will serve them well across various writing situations. Specifically, the multimodal projects helped them tap into the habits and dispositions postpedagogy, antiracist pedagogy, and multimodal pedagogy all value, which rest on confidence, enjoyment, and creativity.

CONCLUSION

The experiences of reexamining multimodal, antiracist, and anti-ableist pedagogical theories, building Jennifer's ENGL100A-B classroom curriculum, and developing and analyzing the student survey responses to the curriculum reaffirmed Megan and Jennifer's beliefs that language, literacy, and composition practices should be political and embodied and that educators must recognize this and encourage students to challenge themselves creatively in the classroom. Students enter college with many preconceived notions about what composition should look like and how that view already corresponds to their own abilities to write and create. The findings of this study suggest a multimodal approach that centers the lived experiences, literacies, and creativity of students from diverse backgrounds can help build student confidence while making composition more approachable and enjoyable for them; most important, the skills students develop in a multimodal context can be reapplied to a variety of different academic, professional, and personal encounters.

Given these findings, we'd like, to offer some specific suggestions for faculty interested in taking a similar approach in their own classrooms.

- *Talk to students about why you're giving them freedom to make choices they haven't had to make before*: transparency about the course goals may help alleviate some of the confusion and anxiety engendered by the approach we discuss above.
- *Be as clear as possible about the goals of each project*: almost unanimously, students named creativity/creative freedom as their primary takeaway from the class. While it is important to encourage and develop student creativity, there were other objectives with this curriculum—and while many of these objectives still trended in student responses, their frequency was much less than that of creativity. Specifically, it may be useful to differentiate the goals of the written project and the visual and auditory projects. Student responses indicated they believed the written project was the "academic" project, while the visual/auditory projects were the "fun" projects. It is important for students to realize the skills they learned in their "fun" projects are also useful to them academically.
- *Use reflective assignments (both large and small) frequently throughout the course*: students had a final reflective-letter assignment; however, more ongoing and consistent reflection may have helped students

better engage in the metacognitive work needed to connect their projects to the skills they developed.

Finally, we'd like to leave you with the words of one of the students who replied to Jennifer's survey: "I learned a lot about myself as a writer/composer because during these genres I became more confident in my work. In all of my genres, I was really proud of the work that I did. I think that I also learned a lot of different skills and different ways of writing and getting your idea across and that I could do it well if I tried." There is no perfect approach to a writing class, but these responses from students suggest to us that an explicitly reflective, multimodal, antiracist, and anti-ableist approach to teaching composition offers students real opportunities for growth, discovery, and increasing confidence in themselves and their abilities.

NOTES

1. At SSU, students are required to fulfill a general education writing requirement in their first year. Students can fulfill this requirement via the one-semester ENGL 101 class or the two-semester "stretch" class, ENGL 100A-B.
2. Because the project requires the students to use images, the word count for each page is below what a fully textual page would be.
3. We're referring here to the 1974 Conference on College Composition and Communication resolution, Students' Right to their Own Language, in which the members of CCCC "affirm the students' right to their own patterns and varieties of language—the dialects of their nurture or whatever dialects in which they find their own identity and style."

REFERENCES

Alim, H. Samy, and Geneva Smitherman. 2012. "Change the Game: Language, Education, and the Cruel Fallout of Racism." In *Articulate While Black: Barack Obama, Language, and Race in the U.S.*, 167–98. Oxford: Oxford University Press.

Baker-Bell, April. 2019. "Dismantling Anti-Black Linguistic Racism in English Language Arts Classrooms: Toward an Anti-Racist Black Language Pedagogy." *Theory into Practice* 59 (1): 8–21. https://www.tandfonline.com/doi/abs/10.1080/00405841.2019.1665415.

Butler, Janine. 2016. "Where Access Meets Multimodality: The Case of ASL Music Videos." *Kairos: A Journal of Rhetoric, Technology, and Pedagogy* 21 (1). http://kairos.technorhetoric.net/21.1/topoi/butler/index.html.

Butler, Janine. 2018. "Embodied Captions in Multimodal Pedagogies." *Composition Forum* 39. https://compositionforum.com/issue/39/to-move.php.

Castagno, Angelina, and Brian McKinley Jones Brayboy. 2008. "Culturally Responsive Schooling for Indigenous Youth: A Review of the Literature." *Review of Educational Research* 78 (4): 941–93. https://journals.sagepub.com/doi/abs/10.3102/0034654308323036.

Cedillo, Christina V. 2017. "Diversity, Technology, and Composition: Honoring Students' Multimodal Home Places." *Present Tense: A Journal of Rhetoric in Society* 6 (2). https://

www.presenttensejournal.org/volume-6/diversity-technology-and-composition-honoring-students-multimodal-home-places/.

Cedillo, Christina V. 2018. "What Does It Mean to Move? Race, Disability, and Critical Embodiment Pedagogy." *Composition Forum* 39. https://compositionforum.com/issue/39/to-move.php.

Denscombe, Martyn. 2003. *The Good Research Guide for Small-Scale Social Research Projects.* Berkshire: Open University Press.

Fernández, Walter D. "The Grounded Theory Method and Case Study Data in IS Research: Issues and Design." In *Information Systems Foundations: Constructing and Criticising.* Canberra: Australian National University Press.

Freire, Paulo. 1978. *Pedagogy of the Oppressed.* New York: Seabury.

Glaser, Barney. 2018. "Getting Started." *The Grounded Theory Review* 17 (1): 3–5. http://groundedtheoryreview.com/2018/12/27/getting-started/.

Glaser, Barney, and Anselm L. Strauss. 2017. *The Discovery of Grounded Theory: Strategies for Qualitative Research.* New York: Routledge.

Gonzales, Laura. 2015. "Multimodality, Translingualism, and Rhetorical Genre Studies." *Composition Forum* 31. https://compositionforum.com/issue/31/multimodality.php.

Heath, Helen, and Sarah Cowley. 2004. "Developing a Grounded Theory Approach: A Comparison of Glaser and Strauss." *International Journal of Nursing Studies* 41 (2): 141–50. https://www.sciencedirect.com/science/article/abs/pii/S0020748903001135.

Inoue, Asao B. 2015. *Antiracist Writing Assessment Ecologies: Teaching and Assessing Writing for a Socially Just Future.* Fort Collins, CO: WAC Clearinghouse.

Inoue, Asao B. 2019. "2019 CCCC Chair's Address: How Do We Language So People Stop Killing Each Other, or What Do We Do about White Language Supremacy?" *College Composition and Communication* 71 (2): 352–369. https://library.ncte.org/journals/CCC/issues/v71-2/30427.

Inoue, Asao. 2019. *Labor-Based Grading Contracts: Building Equity and Inclusion in the Compassionate Writing Classroom.* Fort Collins, CO: WAC Clearinghouse.

Jackson, Cody. 2020. "The Urgency of an Anti-ableist Composition Studies." Paper presented at the Conference on College Composition and Communication, Milwaukee, WI.

Kelle, Udo. 2007. "The Development of Categories: Different Approaches in Grounded Theory." In *The SAGE Handbook of Grounded Theory*, 191–213. Thousand Oaks, CA: SAGE.

McIntyre, Megan. 2016. "Reflection, Detours, and Postpedagogical Practice." *Textshop Experiments* 2 (1). http://textshopexperiments.org/textshop02/reflection-detours-and-postpedagogical-practice.

McIntyre, Megan. 2018. "Productive Uncertainty and Postpedagogical Practice in First-Year Writing." *Prompt* 2 (2). https://thepromptjournal.com/index.php/prompt/article/view/26/53.

Mills, Kathy A., John Davis-Warra, Marlene Sewell, and Mikayla Anderson. 2016. "Indigenous Ways with Literacies: Transgenerational, Multimodal, Placed, and Collective." *Language and Education* 30 (1): 1–21. https://www.tandfonline.com/doi/full/10.1080/09500782.2015.1069836.

New London Group. 1996. "A Pedagogy of Multiliteracies: Designing Social Futures." *Harvard Educational Review* 66 (1): 60–93. https://doi.org/10.17763/haer.66.1.17370n67v22j16ou.

Selfe, Cynthia L. 2004. "Toward New Media Texts: Taking Up the Challenges of Visual Literacy." In *Writing New Media: Theory and Applications for Expanding the Teaching of Composition*, edited by Ann Francis Wysocki, Johndan Johnson-Eilola, Cynthia L. Selfe, and Jeffrey Sirc, 67–110. Logan: Utah University Press.

Shipka, Jody. 2011. *Toward a Composition Made Whole.* Pittsburgh: University of Pittsburgh Press.

Tan, Jin. 2010. "Grounded Theory in Practice: Issues and Discussion for New Qualitative Researchers." *Journal of Documentation* 66 (1): 93–112. https://www.emerald.com/insight/content/doi/10.1108/00220411011016380/full/html.

Turner, K. C. Nat. "Multimodal Hip Hop Productions as Media Literacies." *Educational Forum* 76 (4): 497–509. https://www.tandfonline.com/doi/abs/10.1080/00131725.2012.708617.

Turner, K. C. Nat, Nini V. Hayes, and Kate Way. 2013. "Critical Multimodal Hip Hop Production: A Social Justice Approach to African American Language and Literacy Practices." *Equity and Excellence in Education* 46 (3): 342–54. https://www.tandfonline.com/doi/abs/10.1080/10665684.2013.809235.

Yancey, Kathleen Blake. 2004. "Made Not Only in Words: Composition in a New Key." *College Composition and Communication* 56 (2): 297–328. https://www.jstor.org/stable/4140651?seq=1.

Yergeau, Melanie, Elizabeth Brewer, Stephanie Kerschbaum, Sushil K. Oswal, Margaret Price, Cynthia L. Selfe, Michael J. Salvo, and Franny Howes. 2013. "Multimodality in Motion: Disability and Kairotic Spaces." *Kairos: A Journal of Rhetoric, Technology, and Pedagogy* 18 (1). http://kairos.technorhetoric.net/18.1/coverweb/yergeau-et-al/.

Young, Vershawn A. 2010. "Should Writers Use They Own English?" *Iowa Journal of Cultural Studies* 12 (1): 110–17. https://ir.uiowa.edu/cgi/viewcontent.cgi?article=1095&context=ijcs.

4

PROFESSIONAL DEVELOPMENT FOR MULTIMODAL COMPOSITION
Preparing Graduate Teaching Assistants for the Twenty-First Century

Tiffany Bourelle

INTRODUCTION

Because of multimodality's steadfast place in composition, graduate teaching assistants (GTAs), as the future instructors of tomorrow, must receive training in teaching a multimodal pedagogy. Such training starts with GTAs first learning the theory, reading the scholarship that will inform their pedagogy. As I suggest in this chapter, training should begin with rhetoric, as much of the scholarship surrounding multimodal composition focuses on rhetorical considerations of audience, purpose, and context (Ball 2012; DePalma and Alexander 2018; Hawisher and Selfe 2013; Lauer 2009; Selber 2004; Sheppard 2009; VanKooten 2013). As I illustrate, rhetoric can be interwoven throughout this training, specifically in regard to teaching GTAs to effectively create assignments, integrate technology into their curriculum, and teach reflection, while simultaneously reflecting on their own practices. Based on my own experiences as an administrator and teacher at the University of New Mexico (UNM), this chapter details training approaches and offers suggestions for WPAs and other teacher trainers when implementing such training, especially when resources are scarce. This chapter may be read best in conjunction with Kelly Moreland, Sarah Henderson Lee, and Kirsti Cole's chapter 2 in this collection, "Emerging Expertise."

TRAINING GRADUATE STUDENTS AS A UNIQUE POPULATION

While scholars have argued composition has always been multimodal (see Palmeri 2012; Shipka 2009), in the 1980s, technology began slowly making its way into the classroom, with instructors using computers to

https://doi.org/10.7330/9781646424184.c004

teach writing concepts like revision (Bean 1983). Around the same time, scholarship surrounding GTA teacher training began to surface, indicating this specific population needed a strong background in theory (Haring-Smith 1985) and rhetoric (Bridges 1986) within a practicum course. The curriculum within these courses has often changed with paradigm shifts and the demands of the job market. Recently, the job market's demands have included necessary knowledge of teaching both *about* and *with* technology. With the rise of widely accessible technology, Stuart Selber's *Multiliteracies for a Digital Age* (2004), for example, became an important reader often used in practica to encourage instructors to approach "computer literacy" in their classrooms, helping writing students develop technological skills while enhancing their rhetorical judgments when selecting media for communication (30).

The integration of the computer into the classroom and practica has not been without challenges. Barbara Duffelmyer (2003) notes that the new teaching role of GTAs "is both enriched and problematized by the integration of computers in our composition pedagogy" (296). With the rise of multimodal composition, GTAs may feel the strain of having to learn technology alongside learning theory and taking their own courses. Sibylle Gruber (2010) discusses the practicum course at Northern Arizona University, noting how the GTAs felt teaching multimodal composition was an "additional responsibility, as they saw it, [that] interfered with their own studies in the various English Department master's programs. How could they teach writing successfully, learn new software and teach it, and get a degree on the side?" (138). While this article was published in 2010, these GTAs' questions ring true today: many GTAs may not think multimodal composition will be beneficial to their futures as teachers of disciplines outside composition, and the burden of learning new technology can be too great for them, if not for their first-year writing students (see chapter 5 of this collection for more firsthand accounts of teaching a multiliteracies curriculum).

Joe Moxley and Ryan Meehan (2007) indicate graduate students may be more inclined to focus on work they assume will provide them with jobs rather than learning new technology, leading them to potentially resist multimodal composition. Ironically, a focus on multimodal composition *is* providing them with marketable skills, but this benefit may need to be conveyed to GTAs at the onset of training. As Claire Lauer (2014) indicates in "Expertise with New/Multi/Modal/Visual/Digital/Media Technologies Desired," more jobs than ever require knowledge of multimodality in some capacity. Lauer argues that the rising trend of these terms in job advertisements indicates what we should be doing to prepare graduate students to teach, be successful on the job market, and sustain pedagogy in the field at large (as future administrators of writing programs, for instance). In a recent study of instructors teaching with digital resources, including using technology to teach multimodal projects in the classroom, Joy Robinson, Lisa Dusenberry, Liz Hutter, Halcyon Lawrence, Andy Frazee, and Rebecca E. Burnett (2019) found that "over one-third of teachers either teach themselves or use their own knowledge to support their digital pedagogy" (2). If we are to move forward and sustain multimodal composition as an integral part of our field, we must focus on providing GTAs with more support in terms of training, including guiding them in reading multimodal theory and applying it to successful practices. Such training should be grounded in the idea that learning multimodal composition can be beneficial for GTAs in their careers.

Perhaps the fear or resistance stems from the definition (or lack of a unified one) or what may be presumed when teaching multimodal composition. Even in Lauer's article mentioned above, the terms found on the Modern Language Association Job List vary widely. Cheryl Ball and Ryan Moeller (2007) suggest *new media* "relies more on meaning-making strategies from all modes of communication rather than being stiffly situated within the domain and logistics of written texts." The terms *new media* and *multimodality* are often used interchangeably but maybe to a fault. According to Ball and Moeller, new media does not rely heavily on the written word or text as the main mode of communication; instead, such texts incorporate video, sound, and animation and may not use text at all (or use it very little). Arguably, the assumptions surrounding multimodal composition may cause resistance—for one, the assumption that to be multimodal, a project must incorporate semiotic modes that require knowledge of software programs such as video or sound editing. In *Teaching Writing in the Twenty-First Century*, however, Beth Hewett, Tiffany Bourelle, and Scott Warnock (2022) suggest that image and spoken or written word work in conjunction, where "imagery makes creating textual meaning possible." They urge their readers to consider these ties and not discount alphabetic text as a mode, suggesting alphabetic composing already naturally has a multimodal element tied with imagery. While Ball and Moeller (2007) are not necessarily trying to discount text as a mode, they do acknowledge instructors' fear of new-media design based on lack of knowledge and resources available to them. Indeed, what follows in this chapter aligns with Moreland, Henderson Lee, and Cole's approach in chapter 2, with the intent that such training in multimodality will ensure GTAs are confident and comfortable teaching such a curriculum within their first-year courses.

I argue for starting multimodal training with what we already know: rhetoric and composition. Many of the WPAs (or readers who want more guidance) should start with a background knowledge of rhetoric and principles that inform teaching the written word and build from there. By starting GTA training with Jason Palmeri's (2012) argument of multimodality's historical roots (see *Remixing Composition: A History of Multimodal Writing Pedagogy*) combined with Hewett, Bourelle, and Warnock's (2022) insistence on alphabetic text as a viable multimodal mode, teacher trainers can hopefully assuage fear and gain GTA buy-in from the onset, especially within departments where GTAs come from a variety of backgrounds, including rhetoric, creative writing, and literature. After establishing this comfort level, teacher trainers can then start the multimodal training by discussing what these instructors already know about writing instruction, moving forward with discussions of multimodal scholarship and newer practices.

THE TRAINING: FIVE PRINCIPLES AND PRACTICES

In this section, I break down five principles and practices for training GTAs:

1. Understanding rhetoric and composition
2. Developing their pedagogies
3. Creating assignments and evaluating projects
4. Scaffolding curriculum
5. Crafting ePortfolios and reflections

These elements of training are relevant for other instructors as well, depending on the format and time constraints of the training. Ideally, the training for GTAs should come in the form of a teaching practicum in which there is time to deconstruct and critically reflect on theory and praxis. Many institutions across the country already have a mandatory practicum course, including UNM, where I currently serve as an administrator of an online writing program. Where a practicum is required, multimodality should be blended throughout the course and not contained in just one unit. This establishes the pedagogy's importance from the onset; students can see it is not just an "add-on." Such a blending can filter down to the courses GTAs teach, where first-year students recognize multimodal composition in all aspects of their writing or composing process. I suggest that such a practicum course is paired with an orientation that prepares the GTAs *before* they start teaching their own classes, supplemented by readings, discussions, and course-design activities throughout the semester. Where practicum courses are not possible, WPAs can implement a shortened version of the practices described below within a workshop that helps GTAs alter one previously designed assignment; GTAs would read scholarship before the workshop and participate in discussions that will inform this new assignment design, including the scaffolding exercises they will incorporate in their classes. The following section highlights where to start with ideas that can be expanded upon or shortened depending on which training model the WPA chooses and the local context.

UNDERSTANDING RHETORIC AND COMPOSITION

Many graduate students will not be studying rhetoric and composition in their coursework and will need some background within the practicum, including learning and understanding rhetorical concepts (see Bourelle, Hewett, and Warnock's [2022] *Administering Writing Programs in the Twenty-First Century* for ways to incorporate such rhetoric concepts into teacher training). At UNM, the vast majority of GTAs entering the English department come from creative writing and literature programs, not rhetoric and composition, and typically need such grounding. Even GTAs with a solid understanding of rhetoric may need to reconsider how rhetorical principles affect an author's choice of medium when communicating for different contexts. Pamela Takayoshi and Cynthia Selfe (2007) posit, "Conventional rhetorical principles such as audience awareness, exigence, organization, correctness, arrangement, and rhetorical appeals are necessary considerations for authors of successful audio and visual compositions" (6); guiding GTAs to understand how rhetoric informs composition provide them a foundation from which to build their assignments and structure their curriculum. As Claire Lauer (2009) suggests, multimodal composition must focus on the process of developing a project for the audience, purpose, and context; using readings such as Lauer's not only sets up a conversation on how rhetoric informs multimodal composition but also paves the way for more in-depth conversations regarding composition principles that inform pedagogy, including process, collaboration, and technological literacy. Additionally, GTAs may also benefit from designing a multimodal curriculum after they have read *Writer/Designer: A Guide to Making Multimodal Projects* (2018) by Cheryl E. Ball, Jennifer Sheppard, and Kristin L. Arola.

Many teaching for the first time will also find an overview of composition helpful to realize where we have been, where we are now, and where we are headed. Palmeri (2012) states overtly that his tracing of multimodality's history is his way of attempting to dispel fear about and resistance to multimodal composition; his book may be a useful way to start the practicum to illustrate to GTAs the history of multimodality and ease their worries about teaching a "new" pedagogy. Specifically, teacher trainers should trace for GTAs how the field has taken a multimodal turn and why this turn is important for students' futures, for both social and academic success. Questions for discussions regarding this turn could include:

1. How did the field of composition arrive at this moment?
2. Why are we teaching multimodal composition?
3. Is this actual writing?
4. What skills transfer from multimodal projects to written text?
5. What is lost when teaching multimodal composition? What is gained[1]?

Those leading workshops or practica must be prepared to answer these questions, or better yet, scaffold the readings to prompt GTAs to consider the questions and potential answers while reading. Beyond Palmeri, other beginning readings include Cynthia Selfe's (2009) "The Movement of Air, the Breath of Meaning" and the edited collection *Multimodal Composition: Resources for Teaching* (2007). While both are key pieces to ground the discussion, there are newer essays and books to incorporate that can illustrate the whys of teaching multimodal composition, and I have included these throughout this chapter for easy reference.

Course topics can be threaded together—for instance, the WPA or teacher of the practicum can ask GTAs to read foundational process scholarship such as Kenneth Bruffee's "Collaboration and the Conversation of Mankind" (1984) paired with scholarship on collaboration in multimodality, such as Molly J. Scanlon's (2015) "The Work of Comics Collaborations: Considerations of Multimodal Composition for Writing Scholarship and Pedagogy." Susan Jarratt's (2001) foundational chapter "Feminist Pedagogy" in Gary Tate, Amy Rupiper, and Kurt Schick's *A Guide to Composition Pedagogies* can be assigned in conjunction with "I Never Know What to Expect: Aleatory Identity Play in Fortnite and Its Implications for Multimodal Composition," in which Jialei Jiang (2020) discusses identity formation through multimodality. Articles with similar themes can be juxtaposed first to model the intertwining of foundational ideas with newer practices and then to guide GTAs in critically considering how foundational and newer scholarship can inform their practices. Where themes do not obviously overlap in the scholarship, GTAs can be prompted to think about how multimodality could enter the conversation.

84 BOURELLE

DEVELOPING THEIR PEDAGOGIES

Writing program administrators and departments as a whole may have their own ideas that influence pedagogy or what is taught in first-year writing courses; however, GTAs should be prompted to think through their own approaches to multimodal composition. In *Toward a Composition Made Whole*, Jody Shipka (2009) famously provides her readers a picture of a pair of ballet shoes with handwritten text using different colors of ink, urging us to rethink multimodal composition and to push beyond digitality. Throughout her book, Shipka suggests that focusing only on the digital offers students a narrow definition of literacy. As WPAs, teacher trainers, and educators, we all have our own biases about multimodal pedagogy; however, we must present a variety of scholarship and practices to let GTAs craft their own. In my own practicum courses and workshops, GTAs read Shipka in conjunction with Stuart Selber's (2004) *Multiliteracies for a Digital Age* in an effort to recognize the influence of technology on the development of their multimodal pedagogies. Selber names three approaches to digital literacy GTAs must consider:

1. *Functional literacy*: students learn how computers and software programs work. This could include the basics of learning how to manipulate templates or following "how-to" guides when learning new software.

2. *Critical literacy*: students consider who makes the software, who has access, and how the software has affected society (i.e., social media privacy rules and the use of algorithms for advertisements based on searches and preferences). Students can problematize certain software programs based on this investigation.

3. *Rhetorical literacy*: students uncover why, for what audiences, and in what context they might use mediums[2] and programs to communicate.

After they read Selber and Shipka, I encourage GTAs to use a mix of digital and nondigital multimodal assignments to see students' reactions and to better understand how rhetoric influences the multimodal process regardless of medium.

In regard to Selber's literacies, some practical discovery must occur because campus resources might influence the GTAs' approaches to functional literacy; they must find the resources (and the WPA should as well) available to them and their students either through their organization or via open-source platforms. For instance, many universities offer software applications and packages free for students and instructors. A scavenger hunt of software can be an engaging way to get GTAs involved in that they search for such technology and report back. in addition, they can be prompted to find the best tutorials that will help their students learn the programs; the GTAs can then share tutorials with one another. As part of this exploration, GTAs can find campus resources that will also guide students to use such software, such as free training or tutoring from multiliteracy centers (Bancroft 2016; Sabatino 2019).

Even with university-wide free software and campus resources, students (and GTAs) may have access challenges for different reasons: they could be taking online classes and unable to physically come to campus to utilize computer labs or other resources such as the writing center; they might live in a rural area with limited access to the internet at home or in their community; or they might be using mobile technology to complete course assignments. GTAs should be prompted to consider these challenges as they design their courses, specifically their multimodal assignments and scaffolding exercises. To begin a critical exploration of accessibility, teacher trainers should ask GTAs to research their own communities and the student demographics to learn, for example, how many students live in rural areas with dial-up or how many access the internet through resources such as local libraries. Trainers can prompt GTAs to create technology surveys to be sent privately to their students in an effort to design their curriculum to accommodate *all* students. Such surveys can ask questions regarding students' access to the internet, but wording on such assessments must be carefully considered to avoid establishing a deficit model from the onset of class. Students need to know that while they are creating multimodal projects, they can succeed in the course, so alongside such technological surveys, GTAs must assure their students they can succeed as long as they can learn and articulate their rhetorical choices.

In teacher training, GTAs should consider using what Daniel Anderson (2008) calls "low-bridge" software, such as Microsoft Word and open-source web platforms that have similar layouts, encouraging students to understand that while design concepts of multimodal composition are important, the focus of the class will be on rhetorical concepts, not the students' use of technology (see Arola 2010; Wysocki 2005). Students can use templates to create rhetorically effective projects. In an effort to combine design instruction, GTAs can integrate smaller-stakes writing assignments that ask students to complete a rhetorical analysis of the template, considering the design of a template they wish to use and including its affordances and challenges. GTAs can conduct similar template analysis within their training to better understand what templates they can offer to their students; utilizing such low-bridge software and encouraging rhetorical analysis may offer comfort to first-year students who recognize they do not have to be graphic designers or know the

86   BOURELLE

most current software to succeed in the class. Similarly, encouraging GTAs to use low-bridge software in their course curriculum helps them understand they also do not have to be technologically savvy to teach multimodal composition. The following sections describe how GTAs can create assignments that allow students low- and high-bridge choices in multimodality while also considering how to attend to functional, critical, and rhetorical literacies in the practices leading up to the students' finished projects.

CREATING ASSIGNMENTS AND EVALUATING PROJECTS

The best way for GTAs to build successful assignment prompts is to draft them and create them from the student seat. To begin, teacher trainers should ask GTAs to do an analysis of the genre they hope to teach for their first assignment. They can discover the conventions of that genre, the audience expectations, and the purpose, but they should also uncover the mediums in which this genre occurs. For instance, the review genre is a popular one that often generates interest in first-year students because they have most likely read reviews of their favorite movies, books, or restaurants. When developing the assignment prompt, GTAs can write an authentic rhetorical situation in which students create a review they could submit to their local paper, post on a social media blog, or provide to organizations in their community to boost the profile of the thing they are reviewing (i.e., for a play review, they might contact the local theater and ask to write a review the theater can post in its yearly bulletin). They should do a genre analysis to understand what mediums work best for a particular genre and incorporate those mediums into their assignments as choices for students.

After they have drafted their assignment, they should go back to the prompt and discover how many choices they make for the students. Can these rhetorical choices be opened up more? I suggest drafting an assignment that offers choices within parameters for the first assignment; in other words, instructors can choose two or three mediums for students and give them the parameters (length, word count, number of images that must be used) so students become familiar with composing multimodally. The assignments in the semester can then build up to a sort of "free for all" in which students choose their own audience, purpose, and medium based on the lessons they have learned leading up to this open-ended assignment.

In the practicum course I teach, in addition to reading Shipka's "Negotiating Rhetorical, Material, and Methodological, and Technological

Difference" (2009), GTAs also read Elizabeth Murray, Hailey Sheets, and Nicole Williams' (2009) "The New Work of Assessment," which suggests instructors can evaluate multimodal projects the same way they would a text-based project. I acknowledge Kathleen Blake Yancey's (2004) argument against using text-based values when adopting a multimodal pedagogy. Yancey clearly argues for a new way to approach multimodal composition, stating, "Without a new language, we will be held hostage to the values informing print, values worth preserving for that medium, to be sure, but values incongruent with those informing the digital" (89–90). I agree to a certain extent—many graduate students I have worked with have the basis to evaluate written texts but resist asking students to create multimodal texts because of their fear of not being able to adequately provide feedback. Asking GTAs what they value in written texts and how that overlaps with multimodal texts may provide the bridge they need to continue working through the challenges of a multimodal pedagogy, prompting them to think through the pedagogy's unique values upon conclusion of the practicum.

After they have read the above-mentioned scholarship, I ask GTAs to collaboratively draft a generic rubric they might use to evaluate any multimodal project. They each shout out a criterion they think is important, and after they are finished, I guide them to consider the overlaps with rhetorical concepts from the readings in the course. Together, we decide on a rhetorically focused rubric we ultimately use to evaluate one text-heavy low-bridge multimodal project and one high-bridge project, the idea being to illustrate how one rubric can potentially be used to evaluate projects no matter what the medium or technology used. This same type of exercise can be implemented in their classes in which they collaboratively design rubrics with students; similarly, this collaborative rubric exercise can also be used in conferences with their students when labor-based grading is part of the pedagogy (Inoue 2019).

Reflection is a key component to multimodal composition and can be tied to labor-based grading. Much of the scholarship in the field already champions reflection (Yancey 1988, 2016) and can easily be paired with Shipka's (2011) work on evaluation using students' statements of goals and choices (SOGCs), in which students think through what their goals are for the assignment in prereflections before getting to work. These SOGCs can also be informative for labor-based grading practices, for which students can set their own goals for a project and then conference with the instructor upon completion to determine the points the student will receive for the project or the overall grade for the course. On a broader level, teacher trainers can model this practice for GTAs

88   BOURELLE

by asking them to establish their goals for the course and then conferencing with them after to discuss how their teaching philosophy and practices have changed.

When evaluating projects, Sonya Borton and Brian Huot (2007) suggests a mix of summative versus formative feedback in which instructors give feedback during the process and at the end for final revision of an ePortfolio. To teach the concepts of summative and formative feedback, for a second exercise, I ask GTAs to swap their second assignment prompt with a peer. They talk through the assignment with the peer, and the peer completes a draft of the project. At this point, the GTA who designed the original prompt gives feedback to the "student" (peer) who completed the assignment. This feedback on the project itself allows the GTAs to gain experience in giving student feedback. I also encourage the GTAs to talk to each other about what scaffolding would be needed to teach the concepts required by the prompt. Together, this exercise allows GTAs to not only practice giving formative feedback but also to receive ideas from their peer regarding small-stakes assignments leading up to the project that might further students' success. These discussions lead to the principle of scaffolding, which I discuss in the next section.

SCAFFOLDING CURRICULUM

By creating their own projects, GTAs naturally gain a sense of what needs to be taught leading up to the final draft. For example, they may realize they need to establish exercises that focus on students' understanding of genre conventions and the mediums in which the genre is often communicated, not to mention those that focus on process work. By completing the assignment, GTAs can recognize how long a project will take from the brainstorming phase, to drafting and peer review, to reflection. After they create their project, I often ask them to complete a timeline they think their students can successfully work through from inception of the assignment to final draft, and they scaffold their assignment unit accordingly.

Part of this scaffolding inherently must address time for Selber's (2004) idea of functional literacy. I encourage GTAs to develop low-stakes assignments called *media labs* that allow for scaffolding of the assignment by asking students to experiment with technology. These media labs ask first-year students to play with technology they might use to create their final projects while doing some drafting or brainstorming of ideas. For instance, for a proposal assignment that gives them the option of a video or sound public service announcement, students might be asked to use sound or video software to pitch their idea to the instructor in the media lab; thus, the media lab both scaffolds the assignment and allows for technology play while simultaneously taking the pressure off the instructor to "teach technology" in a traditional way. Bourelle and Hewett (2017) discuss media labs for training of online faculty where computer labs may not be readily available; in these media labs, trainees themselves (instructors) test out the software they plan to implement in the classroom. As Bourelle and Hewett claim, instructors themselves need to create media labs from the student seat, and these types of exercises are beneficial in understanding the learning curve associated with multimodal composing. Subsequently, GTAs can develop their own media-lab assignments that model this exercise.

GTAs can design curriculum that builds to multimodality concepts, starting with assignments that make choices for students (such as audience and medium) and then ask students to make decisions in a final project. Alternatively, GTAs can assign a creative revision toward the end of the semester in which students reconsider a traditional essay they wrote for a different medium, thereby encouraging transfer (DePalma 2015). GTAs can build multimodality into the onset of the course with the free-for-all assignment in which students are given a rhetorical situation and must choose the audience, purpose, and medium. Teacher trainers must encourage GTAs to design their curriculum around their comfort levels or pedagogical goals, but regardless, they will also need to include scaffolding exercises for student success no matter what the assignment. For instance, if GTAs decide they want to start with an assignment that asks students to choose their own audience and medium, an exercise on audience awareness must occur. Similarly, if students are given choices between two mediums, GTAs should build in smaller assignments that ask students to rhetorically analyze projects created using such mediums so they learn what is rhetorically effective and for what context the project might have been created. These scaffolding exercises should work in conjunction with the clear assignments GTAs build first in the training course. Finally, GTAs should build in some exercises that allow for reflection, culminating in a final ePortfolio, which I discuss further in the next section.

CRAFTING EPORTFOLIOS AND REFLECTIONS

Within a practicum course, GTAs need time to reflect on their learning, and they can showcase this learning by creating a portfolio complete

90   BOURELLE

with curriculum they have developed and critical reflections on theory and practice. Their own portfolios should model the project their first-year students will create. More than likely, the WPA or program will have a standard portfolio for the first-year program (as we do at UNM), and the same assignment can be written for the GTA training course. In many first-year writing courses, students write in-depth reflection letters regarding the student learning outcomes for first-year composition as developed by the department. To design a similar learning experience, the WPA should craft outcomes for a practicum course in which GTAs are required to reflect on their learning of the outcomes, making arguments for their learning and using evidence of this learning in the form of the projects they've created, the readings they've read, the conversations they've had with other GTAs and the instructor, peer review, and so on.

First-year students often need assistance in writing these reflections, specifically making an argument for their multimodal learning using evidence to support these arguments. Evidence is actually the work they have done in the course, the conversations they have had with peers and the instructor, readings from the textbook—the list goes on as to what evidence they can use. Within the training ePortfolio, GTAs should reflect in the same manner and connect their own work to the course outcomes in order to adequately guide their first-year students in developing their ePortfolios.

The GTAs' ePortfolios should be created using the same software platform (or one similar) they require their students to use so they can not only provide a model for students but also critically consider the technology they are using (see the section above for critical consideration of technology). This practice not only ensures GTAs are experiencing the technology from the student seat but also allows them to give their first-year students guidance when using the technology from a functional standpoint.

FINAL SUGGESTIONS

This chapter assumes WPAs will be leading the training; where that isn't possible, there are other avenues, such as designating trainers who have been through the training themselves or have appropriate knowledge of multimodal composition through prior coursework, research, or reflective practice (indeed, someone with all three makes an ideal trainer). In addition, GTAs who have taken the training might also lead subsequent training workshops that provide them with professional-development practices before entering the job market. Indeed, the training I have outlined in this chapter can be done in a practicum class *but should also be ongoing*. After GTAs test the curriculum, they should be prompted to come back and discuss what worked and what didn't. A departmental conference is a good way for all instructors to showcase and discuss new ideas, assignments, and student projects (with human-subject approval).

An area of research that needs further development in the field is the interweaving of multimodal pedagogy with antiracist pedagogy, and there is perhaps no better place to start the conversation than in practicum courses. As Megan McIntyre and Jennifer L. Shen suggest in chapter 3 of this collection, "Antiracist multimodal pedagogies . . . offer concrete ways of inviting and supporting diverse ways of thinking, writing, speaking, and creating." Wendy Cui (2019) suggests that, when developing an antiracist multimodal pedagogy, instructors can use multimedia to cultivate understanding of various underserved populations and marginalized groups in our society. Similarly, GTAs can consider using media in their classes to not only model multimodality but to also guide students to question their biases and assumptions. They can develop assignments from an antiracist standpoint that ask students to create authentic videos, podcasts, or radio PSAs for real contexts in their community. Such activism should be explored more in the scholarship, especially regarding how to effectively make a change through media and digital spaces. As a starting point, I suggest teacher trainers and WPAs read Frankie Condon and Vershawn Young's (2016) *Performing Antiracist Pedagogy in Rhetoric, Writing, and Communication* alongside McIntyre and Shen's "Practicing Antiracist and Anti-ableist Multimodality" (chapter 3 in this collection) and search for ways to juxtapose or layer multimodal pedagogy with an antiracist approach.

As mentioned in a previous section, GTAs should consider how foundational scholarship can inform new practices, and they should also be encouraged to contribute their own ideas regarding such newer practices in the field. The final project, as part of the ePortfolio, could be an article in which GTAs connect theory to their practice that could be appropriate for digital scholarship venues such as *Kairos, ROLE,* or *Computers and Composition Online*. A final project like this allows GTAs to establish their arguments and create media themselves, thereby also contributing to their technological literacy. As part of this project, they could also research which venue and what category might be best (theory or practice, etc.) for showcasing their work; this exercise also encourages them to be more prepared for the job market and for success in publishing when in future roles as academics.

CONCLUSION

While all the above-mentioned practices can help GTAs understand multimodal pedagogy and prepare them to teach their curriculum accordingly, WPAs or teacher trainers themselves may have trepidation when it comes to teaching multimodal composition, let alone training other instructors to do it. However, as I have hopefully shown, WPAs do not need to be experts in technology; more than likely they have the background in rhetoric and composition and can build from there with the lessons I provide. I acknowledge not all WPAs are rhetoric and composition scholars, and I encourage my audience in this camp to seek out assistance from other instructors. I also encourage all my readers to read the scholarship I offer throughout this chapter and attend conferences where multimodality is at the forefront, such as Computers and Writing; many venues offer special-interest groups and research network forums where newer WPAs can share ideas.

In addition to fear and nervousness, other issues may arise: lack of time and resources. It is best practice for teacher trainers to look for ways to involve GTAs in the training, as this takes the pressure off of overworked WPAs as teacher trainers while giving GTAs more professional-development opportunities. GTAs can create video or written tutorials for software that can be used in future training sessions, they can give small workshops within a practicum, or they can lead a breakout group in workshop format. In smaller workshops, "homework" can guide GTAs to test out new technology and report back to the larger group. Other ideas include creating fellowships (preferably paid) or research assistantships that allow GTAs to hold office hours and work with other GTAs one on one. These same research GTAs can work with the WPA to improve future training practices, thus gaining experience with WPA work necessary for success on the job market and within many academic appointments. There are multiple ways to get GTAs involved and interested in the training, all while simultaneously preparing them to lead similar training practices at their future institutions. The future is wide open for such training to be continued, thereby further establishing the values and successful practices of multimodal composition.

NOTES

1. Adapted from Pamela Takayoshi and Cynthia Selfe's (2007) "Thinking about Multimodality" in *Multimodal Composition: Resources for Teachers*.
2. I use the term *mediums* with the plural *s* to denote the vehicles for communication and the plural *media* to indicate finished products for public consumption (video, podcast, etc.).

REFERENCES

Anderson, Daniel. 2008. "The Low Bridge to High Benefits: Entry-Level Multimedia, Literacies, and Motivation." *Computers and Composition* 25 (1): 40–60.

Arola, Kristin. 2010. "The Design of Web 2.0: The Rise of the Template, the Fall of Design." *Computers and Composition* 27 (1): 4–14.

Ball, Cheryl, Jennifer Sheppard, and Kristin L. Arola. 2018. *Writer/Designer: A Guide to Making Multimodal Projects*, 2nd ed. Boston: Bedford.

Ball, Cheryl. 2012. "Assessing Scholarly Multimedia: A Rhetorical Genre Studies Approach." *Technical Communication Quarterly* 21 (1): 61–77.

Ball, Cheryl, and Ryan Moeller. 2007. "Reinventing the Possibilities: Academic Literacy and New Media." *Fibreculture Journal* 10. http://ten.fibreculturejournal.org/wp-content/dynmed/ball_moeller/home.html.

Bancroft, Joy. 2016. "Multiliteracy Centers Spanning the Digital Divide: Providing a Full Spectrum of Support." *Computers and Composition* 41: 46–55.

Bean, John C. 1983. "Computerized Word-Processing as an Aid to Revision." *College Composition and Communication* 34 (2): 146–48.

Borton, Sonya, and Brian Huot. 2007. "Responding and Assessing." In *Multimodal Composition: Resources for Teachers*, edited by Cynthia Selfe, 99–112. Cresskill, NJ: Hampton.

Bourelle, Tiffany, and Beth Hewett. 2017. "Training Instructors to Teach Multimodal Composition in Online Courses." In *Handbook of Research on Writing and Composing in the Age of MOOCs*, edited by Elizabeth Monske and Kristine Blair, 348–69. Hershey, PA: IGI Global.

Bourelle, Tiffany, Beth L. Hewett, and Scott Warnock. 2022. *Administering Writing Programs in the Twenty-First Century*. New York: Modern Language Association.

Bridges, Charles, ed. 1986. *Training the New Teacher of College Composition*. Urbana, IL: National Council of Teachers of English.

Bruffee, Kenneth, A. 1984. "Collaborative Learning and the 'Conversation of Mankind.' " *College English* 46 (7): 635–52.

Condon, Frankie, and Vershawn Young (eds.). 2016. *Performing Antiracist Pedagogy in Rhetoric, Writing, and Communication*. Fort Collins, CO: WAC Clearinghouse.

Cui, Wenqi. 2019. "Rhetorical Listening Pedagogy: Promoting Communication Across Cultural and Societal Groups with Video Narrative." *Computers and Composition* 54: 1–14.

DePalma, Michael-John. 2015. "Tracing Transfer across Media: Investigating Writers' Perceptions of Cross-Contextual and Rhetorical Reshaping in Processes of Remediation." *College Composition and Communication* 66 (4): 615–42.

DePalma, Michael-John, and Kara Poe Alexander. 2018. "Harnessing Writers' Potential through Distributed Collaboration: A Pedagogical Approach for Supporting Student Learning in Multimodal Composition." *System* 77: 39–49.

Duffelmeyer, Barbara. 2003. Learning to Learn: New TA Preparation in Computer Pedagogy. *Computers and Composition* 20 (3): 295–311.

Gruber, Sibylle. 2010. "Technological Literacy in First-Year Composition: Implementing a Module Approach." *Journal of Literacy and Technology* 11 (1–2): 132–63.

Haring-Smith, Tori. 1985. "The Importance of Theory in the Training of Teaching Assistants." *ADE Bulletin* 82: 33–39.

Hawisher, Gail, and Cynthia Selfe. 2013. "Studying Literacy in Digital Environments." In *Exploring Composition Studies*, edited by Kelly Ritter and Paul Kei Matsuda, 189–98. Logan: Utah State University Press.

Hewett, Beth, Tiffany Bourelle, and Scott Warnock. 2022. *Teaching Writing in the Twenty-First Century*. New York: Modern Language Association.

Inoue, Asao. 2019. *Labor-Based Grading Contracts: Building Equity and Inclusion in the Compassionate Writing Classroom*. Fort Collins, CO: WAC Clearinghouse.

Jarratt, Susan. 2001. "Feminist pedagogy." In *A Guide to Composition Pedagogies*, edited by Gary Tate, Amy Rupiper, and Kurt Schick. 113–31. Oxford University Press.

Jiang, Jailei. 2020. "I Never Know What to Expect": Aleatory Identity Play in Fortnite and Its Implications for Multimodal Composition. *Computers and Composition* 55: 1–14.

Lauer, Claire. 2009. "Contending with Terms: 'Multimodal' and 'Multimedia' in the Academic and Public Spheres." *Computers and Composition* 26 (4): 225–39.

Lauer, Claire. 2014. "Expertise with New/Multi/Modal/Visual/Digital/Media Technologies Desired: Tracing Composition's Evolving Relationship with Technology through the MLA JIL." *Computers and Composition* 34: 60–75.

Moxley, Joseph M., and Ryan Meehan. 2007. "Collaboration, Literacy, Authorship: Using Social Networking Tools to Engage the Wisdom of Teachers." *Kairos: A Journal of Rhetoric, Technology, and Pedagogy* 12 (1). http://kairos.technorhetoric.net/12.1/binder.html ?praxis/moxley_meehan/index.html.

Murray, Elizabeth, Hailey Sheets, and Nicole Williams. 2009. "The New Work of Assessment: Evaluating Multimodal Compositions." *Computers and Composition Online.* http:// cconlinejournal.org/murray_etal/index.html.

Palmeri, Jason. 2012. *Remixing Composition: A History of Multimodal Writing Pedagogy.* Carbondale: Southern Illinois University Press.

Robinson, Joy, Lisa Dusenberry, Liz Hutter, Halcyon Lawrence, Andy Frazee, and Rebecca E. Burnett. 2019. "State of the Field: Teaching with Digital Tools in the Writing and Communication Classroom." *Computers and Composition* 54: 1–19.

Sabatino, Lindsay. 2019. Introduction to *Multimodal Composing: Strategies for Twenty-First-Century Writing Consultations,* edited by Lindsay Sabatino and Brian Fallon. Logan: Utah State University Press.

Scanlon, Molly. 2015. "The Work of Comics Collaborations: Considerations of Multimodal Composition for Writing Scholarship and Pedagogy." *Composition Studies* 43 (1):105–30.

Selber, Stuart. 2004. *Multiliteracies for a Digital Age.* Southern Illinois University Press.

Selfe, Cynthia, ed. 2007. *Multimodal Composition: Resources for Teachers.* Cresskill, NJ: Hampton.

Selfe, Cynthia 2009. "The Movement of Air, the Breath of Meaning: Aurality and Multimodal Composing." *College Composition and Communication* 6 (4): 616–63.

Sheppard, Jennifer. 2009. "The Rhetorical Work of Multimedia Production Practices: It's More Than Just Technical Skill." *Computers and Composition* 26 (2): 122–31.

Shipka, Jody. 2009. "Negotiating Rhetorical, Material, Methodological, and Technological Difference: Evaluating Multimodal Designs." *College Composition and Communication* 61 (1): W343–W366.

Shipka, Jody. 2011. *Toward a Composition Made Whole.* Pittsburgh: University of Pittsburgh Press.

Takayoshi, Pamela, and Cynthia Selfe. 2007. Thinking about Multimodality. In *Multimodal Composition: Resources for Teachers,* edited by Cynthia L. Selfe, 1–12. Cresskill, NJ: Hampton.

VanKooten, Crystal. 2013. "Toward a Rhetorically Sensitive Assessment Model for New Media Composition." In *Digital Writing Assessment and Evaluation,* edited by Heidi A. McKee and Dànielle Nicole DeVoss. Logan, UT: Computers and Composition Digital Press. http://ccdigitalpress. org/dwae/09_vankooten. html.

Wysocki, Ann Frances. (2005). "awaywithwords: On the Possibilities in Unavailable Designs." *Computers and Composition* 22 (1): 55–62.

Yancey, Kathleen Blake. 1998. *Reflection in the Writing Classroom.* Logan: Utah State University Press.

Yancey, Kathleen Blake. 2004. "Looking for Sources of Coherence in a Fragmented World: Notes Toward a New Assessment Design." *Computers and Composition* 21(1): 89–102.

Yancey, Kathleen Blake, ed. 2016. *A Rhetoric of Reflection.* Logan: Utah State University Press.

5

INCORPORATING MULTIMODAL LITERACIES ACROSS AN FYW PROGRAM
Graduate Instructors' Preparation and Experiences

Lauren Brawley, Morgan Connor, Meghalee Das,
Aliethia Dean, Claudia Diaz, Michael J. Faris,
Michelle Flahive, Maeve Kirk, Max Kirschenbaum,
Joshua Kulseth, Alfonsina Lago, Kristina Lewis,
Lance Lomax, Brook McClurg, Zachary Ostraff,
Anthony Ranieri, Sierra Sinor, Rebekah Smith, and Yifan Zhang

Despite arguments that composition courses should meaningfully incorporate multimodal literacies, doing so at the programmatic level has remained a challenge for writing programs, especially those relying on graduate students unprepared or inexperienced in multimodal literacies and composition. As Carrie Leverenz (2008, 41) observes, multimodality continues to be treated as the purview of individual teachers and rarely receives attention as a program-wide endeavor. While a few scholars have tackled preparing new teachers to critically consider technology and teach multimodal composition (e.g., Graban, Charlton, and Charlton 2013), there are relatively few models of meaningfully and effectively preparing graduate instructors to teach multimodal composition. (See chapter 1 in this collection for a thorough literature review of multimodality and teacher preparation.)

This chapter, coauthored by the writing program administrator (WPA) and eighteen graduate instructors (seven at the MA level and eleven at the PhD level during the 2019–20 academic year), shares and reflects on our experiences teaching multimodal literacies in Texas Tech's first-year writing (FYW) program. We first provide institutional context and discuss our methodology for collaboratively writing this chapter. We then turn to reflections written by graduate instructors to frame discussion around three themes: (1) preparation for teaching multimodal literacies through the practicum course and teaching

https://doi.org/10.7330/9781646424184.c005

96   BRAWLEY ET AL.

mentoring programs; (2) how new graduate instructors turned to peer learning and scaffolding in part as a response to their own teaching anxieties; and (3) teachers' conceptions of multimodal literacies. We conclude with implications for teacher preparation in writing programs that incorporate multimodal literacies.

INSTITUTIONAL CONTEXT

In 2017, Texas Tech's FYW program began a rapid one-year overhaul that radically reimagined the program. There were many exigencies for this overhaul, but two are particularly important for our discussion here. First, among the many issues with the curriculum was that every assignment was solely text based. The new curriculum incorporated a podcast episode in English 1301 designed to give students practice in engaging in composition and rhetoric as inquiry and designing a project in a mode other than alphabetic text. (This project was modeled after Jeremy Cushman and Shannon Kelly's 2018 podcast assignment at Western Washington University.) In English 1302, the new final project asks students to enter a conversation they've been researching all term by selecting the genre, medium, and purpose for persuading a stakeholder of their perspective. Some students write more traditional alphabet-based essays or reports, but many students create videos, posters, social media campaigns, podcasts, and more. Some students have been particularly innovative, creating new-media artifacts like board games or clothing designs. These two assignments are accompanied by a Statement of Goals and Choices—modeled after Jody Shipka's (2011, 110–39) assignment in *Toward a Composition Made Whole* in which students explain their rhetorical and personal goals, choices, and risks in composing the project.

While these two assignments are the focus of our reflections in this chapter, multimodality is also woven throughout the curriculum. As students practice critical reading, summary, synthesis, and rhetorical analysis in English 1301, they engage with both traditional and multimodal texts, and in 1302, students are encouraged to find texts by and about stakeholders delivered in a variety of media. Students in 1302 also deliver a speech to their classmates for which they're encouraged to consider visuals, material objects, and oral delivery (here, our curriculum is informed by "The Mt. Oread Manifesto" [2014]).

Second, there was inadequate teacher preparation in the old program. The redesigned teacher-preparation model includes a one-week orientation for incoming teachers, a required practicum course, and a mentorship program. Graduate instructors in the program are now required to take a one-credit practicum (English 5067) each of their first three semesters of teaching. This practicum is designed to promote what Shari Stenberg and Amy Lee (2002, 328) call "pedagogical inquiry," or studying our own teaching critically and reflecting on our pedagogical practices, goals, and theories. Graduate instructors in English 5067 discuss assignment rationales, lesson planning, feedback and assessment, and research and theory in the field. Graduate instructors teaching English 1301 for the first time read practical teaching advice, foundational composition theory, and recent work on teaching podcasts and accessibility (Buckner and Daley 2018; Cushman and Kelly 2018). Graduate instructors teaching English 1302 for the first time read and discuss "The Mt. Oread Manifesto" (2014) and theory on teaching researched writing and public discourse.

Additionally, the program developed a multipronged mentorship program. First-year PhD-level graduate instructors are matched with a peer mentor (an advanced PhD student) in groups of three to four. These peer-mentoring teams meet biweekly in the fall semester and then monthly in the spring semester. First-year PhD students also observe each other and their mentor teaching early in the semester and are observed by their peer mentor midsemester.

This mentoring program is different for first-year MA-level graduate instructors. To provide new MA students scaffolding into teaching, we designed a large FYW lecture course that meets once a week with accompanying discussion sections that meet twice a week. Experienced FYW instructors teach the lecture and serve as mentors to MA students, who each teach two discussion sections. In addition to engaging in activities similar to PhD student activities, MA students and their lead teacher meet weekly for collaborative lesson planning and problem solving. Also, lead teachers serve as models for teaching, as MA students observe and reflect on their practices during the lecture meetings. (This lecture-discussion section model is similar to the one at Michigan Tech described by Marika Seigel, Josh Case, William De Herder, Silke Feltz, Karla Saari Kitalong, Abraham Romney, and Kimberly Tweedale [2020].) We provide this institutional context to help situate our discussion, which focuses on graduate students' experiences as they teach multimodal literacies, many of them for the first time.

A NOTE ON METHODS AND COLLABORATION

Most studies of graduate instructors' experiences in FYW programs are written solely by the researcher who collects data—often from interviews, written reflections, surveys, teaching documents, classroom observations, and observations of practica. This is true of many excellent studies that have shaped how the field understands teacher preparation and development (e.g., Brewer 2020; Ebest 2005; Rankin 1994; Reid, Estrem, and Belcheir 2012; Restaino 2012). Rather than provide a study written by a single researcher, we have chosen to collaborate on this chapter for two important reasons.

First, a single-authored study of graduate instructors by the WPA has some ethical concerns. As with any study with power differentials between researcher and participants, graduate instructors might have felt compelled to participate in the study because Michael was simultaneously the researcher and instructors' supervisor. Further, Michael was concerned about interpreting and representing graduate instructors' experiences through his own lens rather than centering how graduate instructors might interpret their own preparation and experiences.

Second, as many feminist researchers remind us, researchers benefit (through publications and prestige) from the time and labor of their research participants, and these participants often receive little or no reward for their time and labor (Powell and Takayoshi 2003, 396). Many feminist researchers have addressed this inequity by inviting participants to coauthor publications with them. It seemed most responsible to provide graduate instructors with a publishing opportunity. Further, collaborating on this chapter affords graduate instructors the opportunity to see teaching as a site of research and scholarship and to see how teaching, service (including administration and mentorship), and research can be tightly intertwined.

Our process involved the following stages: Michael asked graduate instructors whether they would be interested in collaborating by writing and reflecting on their experiences. (We provide a list of graduate instructor collaborators in an appendix, with information about degree programs, prior teaching experience, and prior experiences with multimodal literacies.) Each collaborator wrote a reflection, resulting in over forty-six thousand words. Michael then read these reflections, developed tentative codes to organize the data, and developed more formal coding through iterative coding. Codes were developed in part through grounded theory (listening to the reflections for themes and ideas that arose naturally; see Farkas and Haas [2012]; Thornberg and Charmaz [2011]) and in part through preconceived analytic frames (we predicted, for instance, a discussion of the practicum). Michael then drew from the coded reflections to compose an initial draft of this chapter, which was then shared via Google Docs with collaborators. Collaborators then refined or revised their contributions, reframed discussions for accuracy or clarity, and suggested sources that could help situate our contribution to the conversation.

While writing this chapter collaboratively mitigates some issues we mention above, it does not erase power differentials. Michael is still the WPA and thus the supervisor of the collaborators on this chapter (except those who have graduated or now teach sophomore-level courses). It's possible some coauthors weren't comfortable objecting to how we framed portions of this chapter or suggesting revisions. It's also possible some valuable or insightful ideas don't appear here—perhaps because they were counternarratives that rarely surfaced in the reflections or because our initial reflections and brainstorming were done individually rather than collaboratively. We raise these limitations to admit our discussion here is still partial and fraught with power differentials, but we hope our discussion is helpful to WPAs as they consider integrating technology across a program and preparing teachers to teach multimodal literacies.

TEACHER PREPARATION: THE PRACTICUM COURSE AND MENTORSHIP PROGRAMS

As teachers commented in their reflections, the practicum and their mentoring groups helped them reconceptualize teaching and multimodal literacies away from notions of *mastery* and toward practices of what Stenberg and Lee (2002) call *pedagogical inquiry*. As Barb Blakely Duffelmeyer (2003, 296) writes, teaching with computers is a challenge for new teachers because they must perform before they feel competent. While new graduate instructors might desire concrete technological training, Duffelmeyer suggests such training risks separating pedagogy from technology and reducing composing to "formulaic, prescriptive, and regularized" technology use (301). Instead of trying to develop "expert use of a specific technology, the latest software update, or the most cutting-edge gadget" (Graban, Charlton, and Charlton 2013, 255), our program tries to develop "the kinds of intellectual habits of mind that would lead [teachers and students] to their own grounded and cohesive practices" (249) that focus on invention and practice, including habits of play, inquiry, and problem solving. By deemphasizing mastery, the program helped teachers feel less anxious about their limited experiences with multimodal literacies and new technologies and instead focus on their teaching practices as sites of inquiry. Lauren, for instance, observed, "[The practicum] helped me teach the podcast unit through reassuring me that I did not have to be a technological wizard to teach the podcast." This perspective was echoed in many teachers' reflections.

Further, the practicum and mentoring teams helped first-year teachers develop rationales for the projects (both for themselves and for students) and be reflective about lesson planning. They provided spaces for teachers to grapple with pedagogical questions rather than arrive at a "correct" way to approach teaching multimodal literacies. Because many undergraduates perceive English classes as literature classes or writing classes as solely about alphabetic writing, the practicum helped teachers like Meghalee understand the justification behind the podcast assignment and consequently explain it to students. Morgan observed, "The lesson planning workshops in 5067 pushed me to be more creative with lesson planning. Hearing what other instructors were doing . . . allowed me to come up with my own unique solutions for the specific set of problems that this assignment presented." And Max described his mentoring team meetings this way: "It was in my mentoring group that I was able to have honest discussions about my expectations for students." Mentoring teams also provided space "to hear and participate in complicated conversations that demand multiple voices and perspectives."

What MA students learned from their mentoring team was similar to what PhD students learned, but MA students also had the opportunity to see the teaching of multimodal literacies modeled by an experienced teacher. Alfonsina, for example, remarked that her lead teacher, Callie Kostelich, engaged students in multimodal literacies early in the semester of 1301, as the lecture portion of the course involved rhetorical analyses of visuals and videos, which planted seeds for exploring rhetorical practice as multimodal later in the semester. Further, teaching teams for first-year MA students provided a space to collaborate on lesson planning and developing resources. Yifan, for instance, appreciated her teaching team's collaboration on creating guidelines for options for the final 1302 project. This teaching collaboratively also provided graduate instructors the space to confidently take risks. Rebekah wrote, "Most of all, because of my teaching team, I felt confident giving my students leeway in experimenting with the ways they used technology for the final assignment" in 1302.

The practicum and the mentorship programs also facilitated creating communities of practice. Meghalee observed that as an international student, the practicum helped her "navigate the teaching aspects and provided a community boost through discussion" about articles, multimodal composing, and mental health for teachers. Such support systems help alleviate the isolation many first-time teachers might feel. Claudia noted, "The practicum was very helpful as it let me realize that I was not alone in my confusion," and as we discussed shared problems, she developed models for how to approach problems in her class. Maeve too remarked that the practicum revealed that "most other instructors were also feeling a bit out of water with the multimodal assignments." Kristina noted this community helped her feel "supported in being transparent, encouraging, patient, and active in helping students through what we both seemed to see as an unfamiliar and daunting medium."

NAVIGATING TEACHER ANXIETY: TURNING TO MODELING PRACTICES, IDENTIFYING WITH STUDENTS, AND PEER LEARNING

Many graduate instructors—especially those who identify as less tech savvy—experienced anxiety around teaching a technology-based project. While some graduate instructors had familiarity with podcasts as a medium (Morgan, for instance, was quite familiar with podcasts and had a variety of examples at hand to help her students explore producers' rhetorical and research goals) or with audio-recording hardware and audio-editing software (Brook had extensive experience with these materials), others, like Sierra, turned to online research once she learned she'd have to teach podcasts. Even those who have experience with the technologies and media can experience anxiety. Lauren, for example, created a podcast episode as an undergraduate—an experience that contributed to her anxiety for her students because she knew the process could be time consuming and overwhelming. Indeed, this anxiety or apprehension around teaching multimodal literacies and with technology was perhaps the most dominant theme in teachers' reflections. As other researchers have shown, new teachers experience anxiety and lack of self-confidence (Ebest 2005, 136–73; Rankin 1994, 92; Restaino 2012, 72), especially when it comes to teaching with unfamiliar technologies, which can lead to resistance or conservative teaching approaches (Duffelmeyer 2003). However, for our graduate instructor coauthors, this anxiety or lack of confidence often challenged them to develop more progressive pedagogies like peer-learning practices.

Often these anxieties led to a lack of confidence and fear students would view them as imposters or as incompetent. As Meghalee wrote, "It was hard not to think about all the technicalities of podcast creating software, and the anxiety was exacerbated by the fact that this was all happening in my first semester as an instructor." She expressed concern she wouldn't appear confident and knowledgeable when answering students' questions. Meghalee's concerns were echoed throughout teachers' reflections. Aliethia, for instance, was "convinced that students would see right through [her] and realize that [she] had no idea what [she] was doing." Teachers turned to three practices to navigate this anxiety: (1) learning along with students and making their uncertainty transparent; (2) identifying with their students; and (3) designing peer-learning activities.

Modeling learning practices and learning alongside students became a common practice for graduate instructors. Aliethia created a podcast episode along with students "to address some of the challenges students might encounter." As she did so, she realized her previous teaching approach was not ideal for a podcast assignment. She had been spending roughly half of class time lecturing and half on in-class discussion or student practice. She quickly realized she would need to provide students with more in-class time to plan and practice composing their podcasts. In one class period, Aliethia shared her experiences trying to edit audio, and students then shared their experiences, leading to fruitful discussions of both audio-editing software and anxieties around recording one's own voice. As Aliethia concluded in her reflection, "In part it was my willingness to expose myself as not being the expert" that led to students being more open about their experiences, anxieties, and struggles. Likewise, Yifan took a modeling and scaffolding approach by devoting a class period to creating a minipodcast in which students recorded themselves reading a humorous sentence, selected background music and sound effects as a class, and put those sounds together in audio-editing software.

For some, these practices of transparency and learning alongside students was partially motivated by identification with their students. New graduate instructors of FYW and their students are in similar spaces, entering new discourse communities with new norms, practices, and genres (Hesse 1993, 227). This similarity can lead to identification with students, which "compels an experientially immediate sensitivity to the process of learning" (Recchio 1992, 58). Kristina sensed students shared her anxiety about the podcast episode, which led her to share her process in audio recording an interview. She played the audio recording in class—bloopers, voice cracks, and "umms" included. She wrote, "I wanted them to see me making myself vulnerable in this way, even if only to create a 'you're not alone' feeling in the class." During a later in-class audio-editing workshop, Kristina practiced editing audio in front of the class. Though she was concerned students would see her as unqualified, students engaged in the workshop and helped her follow instructions and problem solve.

Additionally, teachers turned to peer learning to teach the podcast assignment. For a variety of reasons (including the desire to seem knowledgeable and competent), new instructors often lecture and discuss texts, even as they may be ambivalent about the role of a teacher as disseminator of knowledge (Restaino 2012, 40). However, the required podcast assignment almost "naturally" forced instructors to turn away from lecturing and to peer-learning activities. Anthony wrote he expected to teach the same way he had been taught (text-based analysis): "Show the students an argument, break down the rhetorical facets of that argument, then evaluate and analyze." However, as his class began the podcasting unit, he recognized an opportunity to shift his approach. Previously, Anthony, like Aliethia above, had spent about half the class time lecturing and half the class time in discussion. His approach quickly changed to spending most of the class period on peer-learning activities, workshops, and modeling practices.

In closing this section, we want to turn to Max's insights about this fear of being seen as an imposter or fraud by students. In his reflection, he wrote, "I began to see that what this fear actually represented was a misunderstanding of the role of the composition teacher in general." Max further explained,

> It now seems to me that this fear only makes sense if one maintains a very narrow view of what a composition teacher should be doing in the classroom. If one believes that the primary goal of a composition teacher is to merely transfer knowledge about various genres from their brain to the brains of their students, then of course this fear will be inevitable any time one is forced to lead instruction on a genre with which they are less familiar. On the other hand, if one is willing to accept that our primary role as compositions teachers is as *facilitators*, and if one begins to see the composition classroom as a place in which knowledge is *created together* with the students—rather than *transferred to* the students—this fear becomes illogical.

This insight—that teaching is not, in Paulo Freire's (2003, 72) terms, about "depositing" knowledge, but rather about "creating" knowledge—is difficult for new teachers to grasp and put into practice. The graduate instructors' experiences teaching multimodal literacies showed that anxieties caused by new technologies and literacy practices can lead teachers to take risks—to realize lectures alone don't work—and to identify with their students' learning, to model their own learning practices, and to develop peer-learning activities. In short, to give up on the myths of mastery that drive the fears of many early-career teachers.

But mastery is also a powerful lure, even pulling in teachers who resist it. For instance, Zachary attempted to focus on the rhetorical aspects of the podcast episode—exigence, audience, organization, incorporating research—but after encountering so much student anxiety around technologies, he turned to spending class time focusing on technologies. He was disappointed to find that many of his students' final podcast episodes showed technological proficiency but lacked rhetorical sophistication. When he taught 1302 the following semester, he backed off on the technological preparation in class, and his students submitted "quite successful and creative" projects. While Zachary rightfully attributed part of his 1302 students' success to their semester-long familiarity with their research, there's also a lesson: students' anxieties around technologies can lure teachers into teaching toward technological mastery, even when teachers are determined to focus on rhetorical aspects of multimodal literacies.

Many of these practices—modeling, showing vulnerability, workshops, and peer learning—were driven by graduate instructors' understanding that students, like them, were encountering a new rhetorical situation for the first time. Many teachers prioritized developing student confidence. Sierra, for instance, stressed she wanted "students to be comfortable being uncomfortable with composing in different genres. I want them to have the confidence to say, 'I don't know how to do this, but I can figure it out.'" Modeling problem solving, workshops, and peer learning assisted teachers in encouraging students to navigate their lack of confidence and approach invention and new multimodal literacies as experimentation and with a problem-solving mentality.

CONCEPTIONS OF MULTIMODAL LITERACIES

In her study of first-year graduate instructors, Meaghan Brewer (2020) offers the term "conception of literacy," defining it as "attitudes and beliefs about literacy" (6) or "a set of values and beliefs about literacy that colors one's way of viewing language and, consequently, the world" (15). Here we want to identify two shifts in teachers' conceptions of multimodal literacy as they reflected on their teaching: first, instructors began to realize multimodal literacies are not simply a matter of a teacher using multimedia to deliver content. Second, some teachers reconceptualized literacies from a cultural-literacy model to a more multiliteracies model.

A prominent thread in graduate instructors' reflections was the realization that a multimodal-literacies approach is not simply delivering multimedia content but rather an active engagement with multimodality. In this way, they resemble Max in Brewer's (2020) study, who understood all literacy to be multimodal and "invited his students into considerations of why some modes might be chosen (or privileged) above others and how academic writing can be and is multimodal" (113). For instance, Claudia's previous experiences with teaching with technology was working with smart boards as a substitute elementary-school teacher. Through teaching at Texas Tech for two years, she realized multimodal literacies are about interacting with the world, using multiple modes to "comprehend and interpret the world" and consequently to respond in multiple modes. Claudia observed she shifted her focus from assignment expectations early in her teaching to helping students understand the impact of their rhetorical choices on the world and how the practices taught in the class were transferable to future literacy practices. Others, like Aliethia and Anthony (whom we discuss above), transitioned from delivering content through multimedia to focusing on students' practice with multimedia.

One benefit of this redefinition of multimodal literacies was that it helped some graduate instructors move beyond being concerned about solely functional literacies. By reconceptualizing multimodal literacies from the purely functional to the critical and rhetorical, Morgan was better able to frame her approach in teaching multimodal literacies in FYW. As she defined multimodal literacies in her reflection, "What lies at the core of this term is the idea that students should be able to take the communication and rhetorical tools we teach them in composition and adapt them to different kinds of media." Morgan brought in a variety of media for students to analyze and consider as rhetorical, which helped her students understand how common technological choices within particular genres and media accomplish rhetorical goals. Her goal as a teacher was that students would see these examples as models for making choices in their own projects. If students struggled with putting those choices into effect, they could discuss them in the accompanying statement of goals and choices; the most important aspect of the assignment for Morgan was understanding how these choices helped accomplish rhetorical goals, even if students were not the best at navigating technologies.

This rhetorical approach to multimodal literacies was echoed in many reflections. Maeve's reflection stressed that multimodal literacies is not merely about teaching skills but rather about helping students be "capable of building effective messages" in a variety of modes. Rebekah too stressed that multimodal literacies is much more than "just the how-to": she further tied multimodal literacies to the larger goals of the course (and of college, we think): "We would be doing our students

106   BRAWLEY ET AL.

a disservice if we don't take risks as instructors, model inquiry and problem-solving, or ask our students to practice curiosity and composition in a variety of settings."

A second shift in conceptions of multimodal literacies was exemplified in Joshua's reflection, where he narrated his shift in valuing cultural literacy to valuing multimodal practices. Brewer (2020, 20) defines cultural literacy as a belief in stable texts that import cultural values to help a culture cohere. This conception of literacy, Brewer explains, creates a hierarchy of literacy practices that privileges elite texts and sees other texts as indulgent and can lead teachers to focus on close readings and textual interpretation at the expense of student writing practices (69, 80–89). Joshua's reflection is worth quoting at length:

> Skeptical as always of the over-reliance on technology, . . . it required a powerful adjustment to familiarize myself with even the more basic technological realities of life as an instructor. But what I realized was that my skepticism wasn't necessarily based on the convictions I thought I possessed—that Google is making us stupid, that books should be read on good old fashioned paper, etc.—but rather, upon a fear of the unknown, a fear that I wouldn't be able to keep pace with the advancements of a bygone, idyllic humanities department, and for the sake of my students, to limit as much as possible the encroaching influence of smartphones. . . . Now, while I wouldn't go so far as to say that I've been won over entirely to the large-scale multimodal diversifications within the humanities, having now taught two semesters' worth of technologically diverse assignments, I see how, as we advance in the direction of a more ubiquitous societal engagement with technology, it is important to wed the rhetorical and compositional concepts with technical literacy.

Like the graduate students in Brewer's (91) study, whose conceptions of literacy were shaped and reinforced by their undergraduate and graduate coursework in literature, Joshua's conception of literacy was shaped by his experiences and perspectives as a humanities scholar. In this reflection, Joshua initially (and to a lesser degree, still does) privileges print literacies for the deep reflection and slow engagement they afford.

For many graduate instructors, trained in close reading of alphabetic texts, teaching multimodal literacies is a new and anxiety-ridden challenge. While there are certainly drawbacks to a standardized curriculum, Joshua's experiences point to one of the benefits: it can challenge graduate instructors to confront their conceptions of literacy and perhaps revise them without necessarily requiring graduate instructors to adopt the literacy ideologies of the writing program itself. As Ronda Leathers Dively (2010) writes, a standardized assignment sequence can "[drive] inexperienced instructors beyond their comfort zones, *compelling* (rather than merely encouraging) them to experiment with models and strategies." As we show above, many novice teachers felt such compulsion, turning to experimenting with peer-learning and modeling strategies in order to teach multimodal literacies that felt uncomfortable or new to them.

CONCLUSIONS: IMPLICATIONS FOR TEACHER PREPARATION FOR MULTIMODAL LITERACIES

While this chapter only touches on some of the themes and ideas presented in graduate instructors' reflections, we close with a few implications for preparing new teachers to teach multimodal literacies. First, we call attention to a notably absent aspect of our discussion above: concerns of inclusion, difference, and equity. In their reflections, Meghalee and Michelle recognized the potential for pedagogies of multimodal literacies to challenge normative linguistic practices in FYW. Meghalee observed that "multimodal assignments . . . are one way of creating an inclusive experience for first-year writing students and a growing multicultural student population" because "they give students a chance to express their identities in non-Eurocentric academic genres and explore 'World English' in online spaces and modes" (see Fraiberg 2010). She further explained that because of the wide range of possibilities for tone, style, and approach in multimodal literacies, multilingual students have "more composition options" (see also chapters 2 and 12 in this collection on the relationship between multilingualism and multimodality). But students in FYW are not the only populace WPAs should consider when it comes to multimodality and difference. Most WPA scholarship on mentorship ignores issues of racial, ethnic, linguistic, and national backgrounds. The field must seriously address how the mentoring needs of underrepresented minority graduate students differ from more "traditional" graduate instructors and how "mentoring can often seem bent on shaping the scholar [or teacher] to the white dominant academy and not on transforming the institution into a space that values minoritized ways of knowing and being in the world" (Ribero and Arellano 2019, 337; see also Okawa 2002).

Second, graduate instructor preparation must include theories and practices of multimodal and new-media composing. While the first-semester 5067 section Michael taught included readings on multimodal literacies, this approach to reading and discussing has its limitations, perhaps most notably that teachers are not practicing with new-media composing. Some graduate instructors took the initiative to create podcast episodes their first semester of teaching, and Michael made creating a podcast episode a project option in the third-semester 5067 course. However, some graduate instructors, like Maeve and Meghalee, wrote in their reflections that they wished they had created a podcast episode in their first-semester 5067 course. Though there are certainly risks associated with asking graduate instructors to *do more* for professional development, gaining practice with new-media composition in a practicum can help them develop confidence and identify with students regarding anxieties about new-media composing and multimodal literacies—including functional and rhetorical literacies—and help new instructors consider the medial logics of new-media composition.

The inclusion of multimodal literacies will likely lead to some resistance from graduate instructors. While we have not focused on resistance in this chapter, it is worth noting that this resistance is *productive* rather than an impediment to teacher development. Brewer (2020) writes that graduate instructor resistance to theories of literacy and pedagogy might be understood productively as "moments when graduate instructors were confronting their own tacit beliefs about literacy," having them challenged "as a precursor to learning" (12). Joshua's conceptions of literacy provide one such example of a teacher who encountered such a tension, and Max's realization that conceptions of literacy instruction based in lecturing are grounded in fears or anxieties provides another. We want to echo Brewer's call to consider seriously the pedagogical benefits of resistance for graduate instructors as they reconcile (through conflict) various conceptions of literacy.

Last, we suggest teacher preparation for multimodal literacies is not solely within the purview of FYW programs, perhaps necessitating a broader cultural change. Brewer (2020) suggests that, given how graduate instructors' conceptions of literacy are shaped in part by their experiences in graduate courses, teacher preparation "must happen in conjunction with broader changes to the culture of English studies so it is more inclusive of diverse literate practices" (91). A broader cultural change across a department can help better facilitate pedagogies of multimodal literacies in FYW. In *Cultivating Ecologies for Digital Media Work*, Catherine Braun (2014) makes the case for departments that integrate new-media technologies across curricula and research. Texas Tech's English department, which houses undergraduate and graduate programs in technical communication and rhetoric and in English (comprising literature, film and media, creative writing, and linguistics), is becoming more "integrated," in Braun's taxonomy, with faculty integrating multimodal literacies across programs. Integrating multimodal literacies in the FYW program would be more challenging without departmental buy-in, and we suggest such departmental integration is important for graduate instructors who might be exploring teaching multimodal literacies.

Because FYW is likely the first teaching experience for many graduate students, we believe meaningfully incorporating multimodal literacies in FYW programs (especially those staffed largely by graduate instructors) is a benefit not only for FYW students but also for graduate students. We'd like to close with Lance's reflection, which suggested teaching multimodal literacies in FYW prepared him to teach multimodal projects in film courses, like having students create short films or audio essays. He wrote, "Composition courses seem to be an ideal space for both early students and instructors to acquire skills in multimodal pedagogy while also encouraging scholarly transference of concepts and ideas." FYW provides an opportunity and space to not only meaningfully teach undergraduates multimodal literacies but also to shape the future of the profession of all of English studies through the professional development of graduate instructors.

APPENDIX 5.A

Overview of Contributors' Experiences before Teaching at Texas Tech

Name	Status in program (2019–20 academic year)	Teaching experience before TTU	Experiences with multimodal composing or teaching before TTU
Lauren Brawley	1st-year MA, technical communication	Undergraduate writing center tutor	Undergraduate projects (creating podcast, using Wix to create websites)
Morgan Connor	1st-year PhD, literature	Undergraduate writing center tutor	None
Meghalee Das	1st-year PhD, technical communication and rhetoric	TA in British literature courses during MA	Using technology for interviews as a journalist
Aliethia Dean	1st-year PhD, technical communication and rhetoric	FYW during MA and as an adjunct	None
Claudia Diaz	2nd-year MA, creative writing	Elementary school substitute teacher	Using presentation technologies as substitute elementary teacher

continued on next page

APPENDIX 5.A—*continued*

Name	Status in program (2019–20 academic year)	Teaching experience before TTU	Experiences with multimodal composing or teaching before TTU
Michelle Flahive	2nd-year PhD, technical communication and rhetoric	K–2nd ESL; ESL for adult newcomers during MA; educational specialist for educational research center working with K–12 teachers	Worked with teachers to incorporate iPads, apps, and software into teaching; used Audacity
Maeve Kirk	1st-year PhD, creative writing (also taught as MA student in 2018–2019)	FYW during MFA	Taught e-magazines and websites in FYW
Max Kirschenbaum	1st-year PhD, creative writing	FYW during MA	Taught assignments that incorporated audio and video in essays
Joshua Kulseth	1st-year PhD, creative writing	FYW during MFA; Montessori elementary school	None
Alfonsina Lago	2nd-year MA, literature	None	None
Kristina Lewis	2nd-year PhD, literature	TA for undergraduate literature courses	TA'd for an online class and assigned many smaller multimodal assignments (videos in discussion boards, ekphrastic drawings of characters)
Lance Lomax	2nd-year PhD, literature	FYW during MA at TTU (in old program)	None
Brook McClurg	2nd-year PhD, creative writing	Tutored at a reading and writing center; FYW during MA	Audio recording for previous jobs; taught audio essay in FYW
Zachary Ostraff	1st-year PhD, creative writing	Middle school and high school; TA for Introduction to Literature during MFA; adjunct writing and creative writing	None
Anthony Ranieri	1st-year MA, literature	Middle school and high school; tutored high-school students	None

continued on next page

APPENDIX 5.A—*continued*

Name	Status in program (2019–20 academic year)	Teaching experience before TTU	Experiences with multimodal composing or teaching before TTU
Sierra Sinor	2nd-year MA, technical communication	Peer tutor in writing center; horseback-riding lessons and teaching dog owners during dog training	None
Rebekah Smith	1st-year MA, technical communication	Undergraduate assistant in writing program; undergraduate student director of writing center	Tutored students on multimodal projects
Yifan Zhang	2nd-year MA, literature	English in China middle school; tutored writing in study abroad preparation center	Created personal videos; assigned video and poster remediation projects in middle-school classes

REFERENCES

Braun, Catherine C. 2014. *Cultivating Ecologies for Digital Media Work: The Case of English Studies.* Carbondale: Southern Illinois University Press.

Brewer, Meaghan. 2020. *Conceptions of Literacy: Graduate Instructors and the Teaching of First-Year Composition.* Logan: Utah State University Press.

Buckner, Jennifer J., and Kirsten Daley. 2018. "Do You Hear What I Hear? A Hearing Teacher and a Deaf Student Negotiate Sound." In *Soundwriting Pedagogies*, edited by Courtney S. Danforth, Kyle D. Stedman, and Michael J. Faris. Logan, UT: Computers and Composition Digital Press. https://ccdigitalpress.org/book/soundwriting/buckner-daley/index.html.

Cushman, Jeremy, and Shannon Kelly. 2018. "Recasting Writing, Voicing Bodies: Podcasts Across a Writing Program." In *Soundwriting Pedagogies*, edited by Courtney S. Danforth, Kyle D. Stedman, and Michael J. Faris. Logan, UT: Computers and Composition Digital Press. https://ccdigitalpress.org/book/soundwriting/cushman-kelly/index.html.

Dively, Ronda Leathers. 2010. "Standardizing English 101 at Southern Illinois University Carbondale: Reflections on the Promise of Improved GTA Preparation and More Effective Writing Instruction." *Composition Forum* 22. http://compositionforum.com/issue/22/siuc.php.

Duffelmeyer, Barb Blakely. 2003. "Learning to Learn: New TA Preparation in Computer Pedagogy." *Computers and Composition* 20 (3): 295–311. https://doi.org/10.1016/S8755-4615(03)00037-9.

Ebest, Sally Barr. 2005. *Changing the Way We Teach: Writing and Resistance in the Training of Teaching Assistants.* Carbondale: Southern Illinois University Press.

Farkas, Kerrie R. H., and Christina Haas. 2012. "A Grounded Theory Approach for Studying Writing and Literacy." In *Practicing Research in Writing Studies: Reflexive and Ethically Responsible Research*, edited by Katrina M. Powell and Pamela Takayoski, 81–95. New York: Hampton.

Fraiberg, Steven. 2010. "Composition 2.0: Toward a Multilingual and Multimodal Framework." *College Composition and Communication* 62 (1): 100–26.

Freire, Paulo. 2003. *Pedagogy of the Oppressed*. Translated by Myra Bergman Ramos. 30th anniversary ed. New York: Continuum.

Graban, Tarez Samra, Colin Charlton, and Jonikka Charlton. 2013. "Multivalent Composition and the Reinvention of Expertise." In *Multimodal Literacies and Emerging Genres*, edited by Tracey Bowen and Carl Whithaus, 248–81. Pittsburgh: University of Pittsburgh Press.

Hesse, Douglas. 1993. "Teachers as Students, Reflecting Resistance." *College Composition and Communication* 44 (2): 224–31.

Leverenz, Carrie. 2008. "Remediating Writing Program Administration." *WPA: Writing Program Administration* 32 (1): 37–56. http://www.wpacouncil.org/aws/CWPA/pt/sp/journal-archives.

"The Mt. Oread Manifesto on Rhetorical Education 2013." 2014. *Rhetoric Society Quarterly* 44 (1): 1–5. http://dx.doi.org/10.1080/02773945.2014.874871.

Okawa, Gail Y. 2002. "Diving for Pearls: Mentoring as Cultural and Activist Practice among Academics of Color." *College Composition and Communication* 53 (3): 507–32.

Powell, Katrina M., and Pamela Takayoshi. 2003. "Accepting Roles Created for Us: The Ethics of Reciprocity." *College Composition and Communication* 54 (3): 394–422.

Rankin, Elizabeth. 1994. *Seeing Yourself as a Teacher: Conversations with Five New Teachers in a University Writing Program*. Urbana, IL: NCTE.

Recchio, Thomas E. 1992. "Parallel Academic Lives: Affinities of Teaching Assistants and Freshman Writers." *WPA: Writing Program Administration* 16 (3): 57–61. http://www.wpacouncil.org/aws/CWPA/pt/sp/journal-archives.

Reid, E. Shelley, Heidi Estrem, and Marcia Belcheir. 2012. "The Effects of Writing Pedagogy Education on Graduate Teaching Assistants' Approaches to Teaching Composition." *WPA: Writing Program Administration* 36 (1): 32–73. http://www.wpacouncil.org/aws/CWPA/pt/sp/journal-archives.

Restaino, Jessica. 2012. *First Semester: Graduate Students, Teaching Writing, and the Challenge of the Middle Ground*. Carbondale: Southern Illinois University Press.

Ribero, Ana Milena, and Sonia C. Arellano. 2019. "Advocating Comadrismo: A Feminist Mentoring Approach for Latinas in Rhetoric and Composition." *Peitho* 21 (2): 334–56. https://cfshrc.org/article/advocating-comadrismo-a-feminist-mentoring-approach-for-latinas-in-rhetoric-and-composition/.

Seigel, Marika, Josh Case, William De Herder, Silke Feltz, Karla Saari Kitalong, Abraham Romney, and Kimberly Tweedale. 2020. "Monstrous Composition: Reanimating the Lecture in First-Year Writing Instruction." *College Composition and Communication* 71 (4): 643–71.

Shipka, Jody. 2011. *Toward a Composition Made Whole*. Pittsburgh: University of Pittsburgh Press.

Stenberg, Shari, and Amy Lee. 2002. "Developing Pedagogies: Learning the Teaching of English." *College English* 64 (3): 326–47.

Thornberg, Robert, and Kathy Charmaz. 2011. "Grounded Theory." In *Qualitative Research: An Introduction to Methods and Design*, edited by Stephen D. Lapan, Marylynn T. Quartaroli, and Frances Julia Riemer, 41–66. San Francisco: Jossey-Bass.

PART II

Institutional Initiatives and Support

No two institutions are the same in terms of infrastructures, demographics, funding resources, and their missions and visions. The same is the case with departments and programs within and across diverse institutions. Since institutions, departments, and programs are situated in their own specific contexts, their recognition, preparation, and implementation of multimodal composition in their research and teaching practices vary drastically. Therefore, it is important to learn how each institution or academic unit has responded to the call for adopting multimodality and prepares their faculty to integrate it in their writing curricula.

The authors in this section recount and draw our attention to the initiatives taken in their own academic units or institutions. Therefore, these initiatives are diverse, unique, and situated to the authors' own local contexts. For instance, Scott Lloyd DeWitt and John Jones, in their chapter, discuss how the Digital Media and Composition Institute (DMAC) has become an excellent model of an institutional initiative that was started by Professors Cynthia Selfe and Scott Lloyd DeWitt himself back in 2006 at The Ohio State University. They highlight how a residential workshop has evolved into a national phenomenon in mentoring scores of faculty participants from diverse academic institutions to make effective use of digital tools and teach multimodal composing in college composition classrooms. Similarly, another chapter in the section talks about multimodal initiatives taken at six different institutions awarded the CCCC Writing Program of Excellence designation (Marquette, The Ohio State University, Purdue, Salt Lake Community College, the University of Texas–El Paso, and the University of North Carolina–Charlotte). Yet another chapter discusses how the authors laid the groundwork for developing a model built around internship-based courses at McDaniel College, in which multimodal composition is vitally important, and claims this model can be implemented at any college or university.

https://doi.org/10.7330/9781646424184.p002

6

DMAC AT FIFTEEN
Professionalizing Digital Media and Composition

Scott Lloyd DeWitt and John Jones

INTRODUCTION

In 2006, Professors Cynthia Selfe and Scott Lloyd DeWitt launched the Digital Media and Composition Institute (DMAC), a residential workshop on the effective use of digital media in college composition classrooms held annually in the Department of English at The Ohio State University.[1] Participants explore a range of contemporary digital-literacy practices—alphabetic, visual, auditory, and multimodal—and apply what they learn to the design of meaningful assignments, syllabi, curricula, programs, and community-engaged projects. The goal of DMAC is to suggest and encourage innovative approaches to composing students and faculty can use as they employ digital media in support of their own educational, professional, civic, and creative goals, in light of the specific contexts at their home institutions and within their local communities. In its last four years, the institute's curriculum has emphasized action, access, accessibility, activism, and social justice in digital contexts.

Since DMAC's inception, 446 scholars, instructors, graduate students, workplace professionals, and community activists have completed the institute as a significant component of their professional development, with attendees coming from a range of institutions across the country, including large universities, liberal arts colleges, two-year community colleges, and HBCUs, as well as the public and private sectors. DMAC attracts people interested in writing and communication from a range of disciplines and interests. Whereas most of its attendees come from English studies, the institute has hosted participants from the arts, nursing, education, and library science. Ohio State graduate students who enroll in DMAC take their experiences to new tenure-track positions or nonacademic opportunities, including for-profits and nonprofits, community organizations, or consulting.

https://doi.org/10.7330/9781646424184.c006

As a technology professional-development enterprise, DMAC has run continuously for fourteen years (thirty-four if one includes its predecessor at Michigan Technological University, Computers in Writing Intensive Classrooms [CIWIC]). Admittedly, despite our sustained success, we have been less than rigorous in measuring DMAC's impact on the field of multimodal composition, as well as how DMAC has facilitated community engagement and how its instruction has assisted individuals in nonacademic workplace contexts. To address this gap, we conducted a survey in the summer of 2020 that asked DMAC attendees about their experiences at the institute in order to document the impact of DMAC on their professional development and answer questions like, "What evidence is available that will allow us to examine the influence of DMAC's instructional experience and the significance of its related pedagogical, scholarly, and community outcomes to its attendees?" In this chapter, we report on part of this study as it relates to the professionalization of multimodal composition, showing how individual professionalization at workshops like DMAC can lead to broader institutional and disciplinary impacts.

BACKGROUND

In 2015, Cheryl E. Ball, Dánielle Nicole DeVoss, Scott Lloyd DeWitt, and Cynthia L. Selfe (Ball et al. 2015; DeVoss et al. 2015; DeWitt et al. 2015) edited a three-part collection of articles and web texts titled "CIWIC, DMAC, and Technology Professional Development in Rhetoric and Composition." This scholarship was featured in *Computers and Composition: An International Journal* (print), *Computers and Composition Online* (webtexts), and *Showcasing the Best of CIWIC/DMAC* (webtexts) and celebrated thirty years of combined CIWIC/DMAC workshops. The editors state in their introduction, "These special issues mark [the thirtieth] anniversary by exploring how rhetoric and composition scholars who attended CIWIC or DMAC have integrated that technological professional development experience into their academic lives. These special issues are a scholarly tribute and celebration of these internationally known workshops" (Ball 2015). Authors featured in these publications tell stories about how their personal experiences at DMAC allowed them to effect change at their home institutions with their colleagues and with their students. In other words, they were invited to explore and reflect on topics related to technology professional development that emerged from their CIWIC/DMAC experiences.

Nicky Adams, Margaret M. Strain, and Patrick W. Thomas (2015) describe how their motivation to produce multimodal scholarship, to teach multimodal composing, and to develop new administrative practices was strengthened by the range of professional-development experiences DMAC offers, writing, "What each of our stories has in common is that our interest in attending DMAC stemmed from our own perceived 'lacking.' Each of us had a felt sense that in order to advance in some aspect of our professional work, we needed to pay attention to multimodal composition and digital media." Laura McGrath and Letizia Guglielmo (2015) argue that attending DMAC allowed them to provide professional development to colleagues at their home institution in the form of technology and pedagogy workshops that emphasized DMAC's commitment to hands-on learning, collaborative problem solving, and community building (46–49). Harley Ferris (2015) reminds readers DeWitt and Selfe often referred to professional development as "professional activism," with an emphasis on "making the case," the ability to make persuasive arguments "at our home institutions—to our faculty, administration, students, and perhaps even ourselves—that these non-traditional modes of composition are valid, valuable, and indeed vital to today's writing program." In a cautionary tale, Rik Hunter, Alanna Frost, Moe Folk, and Les Loncharich (2015) remind us that despite the efforts of institutes like CIWIC/DMAC, the material conditions of home institutions (funding, career demands, resources) can limit the ability to sustain technology professional development.

Collectively, these reflections paint a picture of CIWIC/DMAC attendees pursuing individual professional development in order to further their own development and effect change at their home institutions with colleagues and with students. This evidence, however, is narrow, focused on the authors' personal experiences. Two writers in the CIWIC/DMAC collections take up the question of impact by looking at larger-scale evidence, the first by collecting publicly available documents and the second by surveying past DMAC attendees. Julia Voss (2015) utilizes systematic documentary analysis (Journet 2007) to analyze DMAC texts, both the institute's curriculum and documents produced by attendees—"social media posts made during the institute, publications developed at the institute, and online professional documents created by alumni after attending the institute" (Voss 2015, 18). Voss includes in those professional documents "CVs; university profile pages; professional websites; LinkedIn profiles, and academic networking sites like Academia.edu, Mendeley, and ResearchGate" (18). By collecting and analyzing these documents, Voss is able to show that "tracing how . . . teachers and scholars have returned to their home institutions to shape curriculum, champion new technologies and labs, and more is another method of analyzing the influences of the institute" (21). Voss concludes, "Further research is needed to study systematically whether and how institute ideas have been implemented at [attendees'] home institutions" (22).

In his webtext, "Keeping Track of DMAC," Trey Conatser (2015) studies the impact of DMAC's technology professional development by modeling data collected from registration materials and from a survey sent to all attendees from 2006 to 2014, along with video recordings of interviews with attendees of the 2014 institute that were part of a partner project. His survey asked attendees to identify or describe when they attended DMAC, their home institution, professional position, and motivations for attending DMAC, the kinds of support they received to attend, and the professional networking that resulted from attending DMAC. Conatser's analysis further illustrates a relationship between motives/goals for attending CWIC/DMAC and the results/effects of that attendance, where the divergence is most often categorized as "a shift from expectations involving the individual to results involving professional communities and collaborative work." Conatser also found a high frequency of attendees reporting they received partial financial support, as opposed to full support, to cover the institute fee and travel expenses, a finding that "[indicates] a need to refine how we make a case in our local contexts for institutional support of digital media and composition studies." He writes, "Professional development institutes like DMAC rely on a diverse ecosystem of individuals and institutions, each looking to use the institute not only as a resource for individual literacies but also as a model for technology-driven professional development and networking in participants' local contexts."

These studies point to a number of factors that can influence the professionalization of a field, such as building on personal professional development (Adams, Strain, and Thomas 2015), advocating for multimodal composition in one's institution (Ferris 2015), and finding institutional support. Like these studies, our survey documents DMAC's impacts on individual development, showing this professional development can lead to professionalization by creating infrastructural and institutional spaces for multimodal composition. This study expands on previous research of CIWIC/DMAC's impact on the field of multimodal composition by surveying DMAC attendees from 2006 to 2019 and analyzing submissions of research and pedagogical materials attendees produced after their DMAC experience.

RESEARCH-STUDY METHODS

Since the publication of the three-part collection in 2015, DMAC has undergone significant changes. After Selfe's retirement in 2016, DeWitt became the sole director of DMAC and expanded the number of faculty teaching at DMAC, emphasizing and expanding the institute's specialization in digital accessibility, access, writing program assessment, activism, and writing analytics. In 2018, John Jones became the codirector of DMAC and in 2019 the director, with DeWitt remaining as codirector. Due to the 2020 COVID-19 pandemic, DMAC 2020 was cancelled, and in 2021 the institute was moved entirely online.

In response to these changes, we designed an impact study that seeks to respond to Voss's (2015) call for further systematic research by tracing the impact of DMAC on attendees and the field of multimodal composition. We constructed a data-driven impact study to examine the influence of DMAC's instructional experience on attendees' professional development and analyze the significance of related pedagogical, scholarly, professional, and community outcomes. Impact studies are important tools for tracking these influences and the changes brought about by the institute (Global Libraries 2015). As the Global Libraries Initiative Impact Planning and Assessment Road Map[2] (Global Libraries 2008) argues, collecting impact evidence will show

1. whether projects are being conducted effectively, in order to learn from and improve project activities;

2. whether the program is making a difference to people, groups, organizations or communities; and

3. [how] to use that evidence of impact to advocate for continued support and/or funding from relevant stakeholders.

The data used in this study is self-reported, "collected directly from people who interact with the enterprise" (Global Libraries 2008). We invited all past DMAC attendees to provide us with data, relying on them to not only choose to engage with our surveys but also to share evidence that illustrates impact as they define it.

Between 2006 and 2019, 446 professionals attended DMAC. A research team of the two study PIs and seven undergraduate assistants spent significant effort locating current contact information for our past attendees. Beyond identifying current contact information, we did not collect any publicly available professional information about attendees. Of 446 past attendees, we were unable to locate current contact information for twenty-seven people. We learned that four were deceased.

120   DEWITT AND JONES

Therefore, our recruitment size was 415. Our IRB research protocol allowed us to recruit study participants using email.

We invited attendees to submit two types of evidence of DMAC's influence on their work. The first was a deidentified, aggregable survey. This survey was organized in three sections, with the first and third sections nearly identical. The first section asked participants questions about *when they attended DMAC*: year, type of institution, professional position, kind of academic or professional unit or setting, and professional expertise. The third section asked nearly identical questions about *their current professional status* with an additional question: Have you moved to a new institution or employer since attending DMAC? The second section asked attendees to apply their DMAC experience to work they had completed at their home institutions, workplaces, and/or communities, that is, to document how DMAC impacted their professional development by considering direct and indirect connections from DMAC to their work.

The second data set consisted of material examples of class assignments, courses, academic programs, professional-development opportunities, awards, and community engagement and outreach. This included assignment prompts, syllabi, workplace documents, or participants' CVs with highlighted information. Participants could also copy and paste text, including URLs, to online materials and documents. In addition to document uploads, participants were provided with a comment box to provide us with context for these materials, if necessary. Participants were able to submit to one or both datasets.

FINDINGS

Of the 415 DMAC attendees contacted, 163 respondents completed the survey (39.3% response rate) and 86 respondents (20.7% response rate) submitted 188 items to the examples dataset. For many questions on the survey, respondents could select more than one option, and not every respondent answered every question, so the total responses for individual questions can be higher or lower than the total number of respondents. In cases where percentages are reported, they are based on the total number of survey responses to make comparisons across questions easier. For example, when asked about their current professional position, respondents were able to choose multiple categories. As some respondents held positions in multiple categories, there were 172 total responses to the question, but the percentages for individual categories are based on the total number of respondents to the survey.

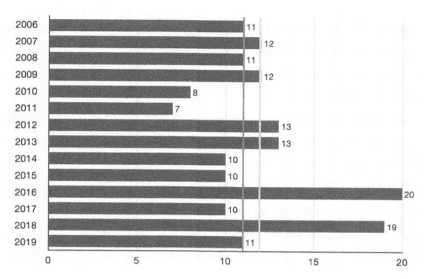

Figure 6.1. Years respondents attended DMAC. The darker vertical line is the median (11) and the lighter vertical line the mean (11.9).

PARTICIPANT INFORMATION

There was generally consistent representation from the start of DMAC in 2006 to the most recent incarnation in 2019 (see fig. 6.1). After DMAC 2020 was cancelled, the DMAC curriculum was offered as a class for OSU students in May 2020, but these participants were not included in this study. The years with the most responses were 2016 (twenty) and 2018 (nineteen); the years with the least were 2011 (seven) and 2010 (eight). The median response was 11 and the mean was 11.9.

Respondents' institutions and professional positions are recorded in table 6.1. Most respondents, 97.5 percent, were affiliated with an institution of higher education at the time they attended, with most of those (65.6%) hailing from four-year colleges with graduate programs (see fig. 6.2 and 6.3). Of the remaining respondents, two (1.2%) were located in K–12 education and one (0.6%) was nonacademic.

These numbers shift only slightly when looking at respondents' current positions: 88.3 percent were affiliated with higher education, with the largest movement being the number taking nonacademic positions, which grew from less than 1 percent (one) to nearly 5 percent (eight). The number of respondents currently at two-year colleges and private four-year colleges grew slightly, while those at public four-year colleges decreased slightly.

122 DEWITT AND JONES

Table 6.1. Respondents' institutions and positions when attending DMAC and at present. Percentages are calculated from total responses to the survey.

	When attending DMAC		Current	
Question	Total responses	% of respondents	Total responses	% of respondents
Institution				
K-12	2	1.2%	1	0.6%
Two-year college	8	4.9%	11	6.7%
Four-year college, private	13	8.0%	17	10.4%
Four-year college, public	30	18.4%	21	12.9%
Four-year college with graduate program, private	10	6.1%	17	10.4%
Four-year college with graduate program, public	97	59.5%	75	46.0%
HBCU	1	0.6%	3	1.8%
Nonacademic	1	0.6%	8	4.9%
Total	162		153	
Professional position				
Graduate student	78	47.9%	18	11.0%
Faculty, non-tenure track	30	18.4%	40	24.5%
Faculty, tenure track, not tenured	14	8.6%	29	17.8%
Faculty, tenured with promotion to higher rank possible	21	12.9%	29	17.8%
Faculty, tenured with highest rank achieved	11	6.7%	21	12.9%
Staff, nonfaculty	3	1.8%	6	3.7%
Administrator	2	1.2%	16	9.8%
Professional, nonacademic	1	0.6%	8	4.9%
Retired	0	0.0%	5	3.1%
Total	160		172	

The largest group of respondents were graduate students (47.9%) when they attended DMAC (see fig. 6.4). The next largest group, 18.4 percent, were non-tenure-track faculty. Not surprisingly, most graduate students moved on to other positions in the years following their DMAC attendance, and, in aggregate, 48.5 percent of attendees currently hold tenure-track and tenured faculty positions, up from 28.2 percent at time of attendance. The single largest category for current positions was non-tenure-track faculty, at 24.5 percent. Attendees

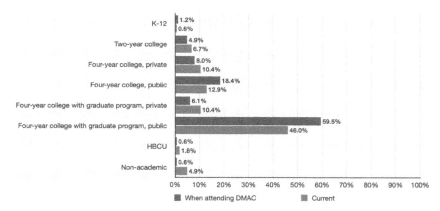

Figure 6.2. Respondents' institutional affiliation. Percentages are calculated from total responses to the survey.

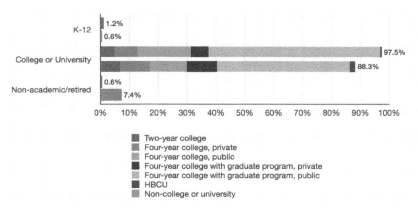

Figure 6.3. Respondents' institutional affiliation with colleges and universities aggregated (higher education institution types are identified in the legend). For each category, the top bar represents respondents' affiliation when attending DMAC and the bottom bar their current affiliation. Percentages are calculated from total responses to the survey.

also reported an increase in administrative (9.8%) and nonacademic positions (4.9%).

Table 6.2 contains respondents' self-reported departmental affiliations and subject-matter expertise. The majority of attendees were affiliated with English departments (71.8%) or composition and rhetoric programs (12.9%) when they participated in DMAC (see fig. 6.5). In their current positions, respondents' English affiliations dropped to 53.4 percent and composition and rhetoric rose to 16.6 percent.

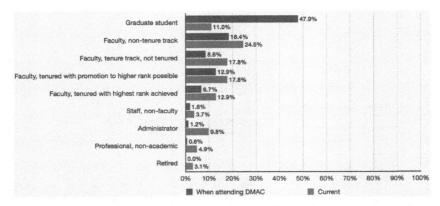

Figure 6.4. Respondents' rank, at time of attendance and currently. Percentages are calculated from total responses to the survey.

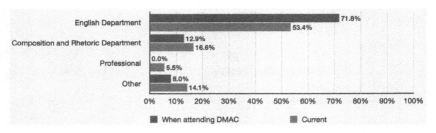

Figure 6.5. Respondents' departmental or professional affiliation. Percentages are calculated from total responses to the survey.

Respondents were asked to self-report their areas of subject-matter expertise, and the largest areas at the time of attendance were composition and rhetoric (70.6%) and computers and writing/digital media studies (19.0%) (fig. 6.6). The current numbers dropped for composition and rhetoric (63.8%), but computers and writing/digital media studies grew (28.8%), as did disability studies (3.1% to 6.1%), critical race studies (3.7% to 9.8%), education (3.7% to 13.5%), professional and technical communication (9.8% to 17.8%), and rhetorical theory (7.4% to 12.9%).

DMAC IMPACTS

The responses in table 6.3 address how DMAC impacted respondents' academic output. The questions were grouped into five categories—teaching, research, service, community engagement, professional development, and production.

Table 6.2. Respondents' department affiliations and areas of professional expertise when attending DMAC and at present. Percentages are calculated from total responses to the survey.

	When attending DMAC		Current	
	Total responses	% of respondents	Total responses	% of respondents
Department or division				
English Department	117	71.8%	87	53.4%
Composition and Rhetoric Department	21	12.9%	27	16.6%
Professional	0	0.0%	9	5.5%
Other	13	8.0%	23	14.1%
Total	151		146	
Areas of professional expertise				
African American studies	3	1.8%	3	1.8%
Asian American studies	1	0.6%	1	0.6%
Book history	1	0.6%	1	0.6%
Business management	0	0.0%	4	2.5%
Composition and rhetoric	115	70.6%	104	63.8%
Computers and writing/digital media studies	31	19.0%	47	28.8%
Creative writing	10	6.1%	6	3.7%
Critical race studies	6	3.7%	16	9.8%
Cultural studies	3	1.8%	1	0.6%
Design	0	0.0%	5	3.1%
Digital humanities	1	0.6%	4	2.5%
Disability studies	5	3.1%	10	6.1%
Education	6	3.7%	22	13.5%
Film, media, and popular culture	14	8.6%	19	11.7%
Folklore	3	1.8%	3	1.8%
Gender and sexuality	19	11.7%	22	13.5%
Journalism	1	0.6%	1	0.6%
Literacy studies	10	6.1%	15	9.2%
Literature	25	15.3%	19	11.7%
Narrative theory	3	1.8%	3	1.8%
Policy studies	1	0.6%	1	0.6%
Professional and technical communication	16	9.8%	29	17.8%

continued on next page

126 DEWITT AND JONES

Table 6.2—*continued*

| | When attending DMAC | | Current | |
	Total responses	% of respondents	Total responses	% of respondents
Religious studies	0	0.0%	3	1.8%
Rhetorical theory	12	7.4%	21	12.9%
Writing across the curriculum	2	1.2%	6	3.7%
Writing center practice and theory	5	3.1%	5	3.1%
Writing program administration	15	9.2%	14	8.6%
Total	308		385	

Some highlights from these professional-development impacts are that 77.9 percent of respondents reported developing a new assignment and 42.3 percent a new course (see fig. 6.7); 49.1 percent presented at a conference; 30.7 percent published an article or chapter; 24.5 percent published a webtext; 41.1 percent served on a committee within their department or unit; 20.2 percent created a digital project used by their community; 17.8 percent collaborated with a group in the community; and 30.0 percent attributed a new position, either with their current employer or a new employer, to attending DMAC. After attending DMAC, most attendees reported being better able to teach digital-media production, produce their own digital-media texts for teaching and their workplace, and design accessible texts.

Respondents were asked whether DMAC had enabled them to better advocate for multimodal work (74.2% yes), hiring (23.3% yes), producing multimodal works in their professional setting (75.5% yes), or move to a new institution (44.8% yes) (see fig. 6.8).

The material-examples dataset includes a range of resources produced in response to or influenced by respondents' time at DMAC. We categorized these materials into fifteen types (table 6.4). The largest category was research articles (fifty-one), followed by teaching assignments (forty), course syllabi (twenty-five), teaching handouts (thirteen), and documentation of service activities (twelve).

THE IMPACT OF DMAC ON PROFESSIONALIZING MULTIMODAL COMPOSITION

We suggest DMAC has impacted the professionalization of multimodal composition in two ways: providing for individual professional

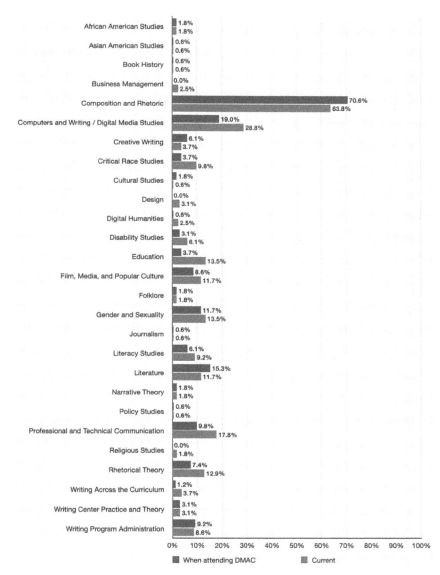

Figure 6.6. Respondents' areas of expertise. Percentages are calculated from total responses to the survey.

development and creating infrastructure and institutional support for multimodal composition. We further argue that the individual professionalization provided by DMAC can seed broader impacts for a discipline.

Table 6.3. Respondents' professional-development and academic impacts. Percentages are calculated from total responses to the survey.

	Total responses	% of respondents
Teaching		
Developed a new assignment or assignment sequence	127	77.9%
Developed a new course	69	42.3%
Developed a new academic program	17	10.4%
Created a student award	3	1.8%
Created a teaching award	1	0.6%
Created an administrative/staff award	0	0.0%
Total	217	
Research		
Presented at a conference	80	49.1%
Published an article or chapter (print or digital)	50	30.7%
Published a webtext	40	24.5%
Published a monograph (print or digital)	5	3.1%
Received a grant	20	12.3%
Total	195	
Service		
Served on a committee within your academic or professional unit	67	41.1%
Served on a committee outside your academic or professional unit	29	17.8%
Served on a state-wide or national committee	9	5.5%
Total	105	
Community engagement		
Collaborated with a group in my local community	29	17.8%
Conducted a workshop in my local community	24	14.7%
Developed a program in my local community	4	2.5%
Created a digital project used in my local community	33	20.2%
Total	90	
Professional Development		
Acquired a new position within my institution/employer	24	14.7%
Acquired a new position at a new institution/employer	25	15.3%

continued on next page

DMAC at Fifteen 129

Table 6.3—*continued*

	Total responses	% of respondents
Teaching		
Promoted to a new rank	18	11.0%
Received certification or licensure	7	4.3%
Received an award or recognition	23	14.1%
Total	97	
Production		
I am better able to teach digital-media production to students	119	73.0%
. . . produce digital-media texts for teaching	123	75.5%
. . . produce digital-media texts for research	68	41.7%
. . . produce digital-media texts for my workplace	83	50.9%
. . . design accessible texts, instructional materials, and/or learning experiences	111	68.1%
. . . produce materials and/or learning experiences that integrate social justice and access in digital contexts	77	47.2%
Total	581	

Conatser's (2015) evaluation of the impacts of DMAC concludes with four takeaways: individual aspiration becomes institutional action, professional development succeeds when it seeds itself elsewhere, professional development is professional destabilization, and professional development remains a professional luxury. Our results support these observations. While we are limited to the demographic data in the survey and the types of materials we collected, several results from our study suggest attendees have implemented the skills they acquired at DMAC in new institutions and they have driven institutional action to advance the field of multimodal composition. In the first case, attendees have facilitated change by their movement between institutions; attendees have moved to two-year colleges, private colleges and universities, and nonacademic positions—categories that show growth—and away from public colleges and universities, where there are declines. Additionally, out of the 44.8 percent who moved jobs (fig. 6.8), 15.3 percent of attendees reported they changed institutions or employers because of their DMAC attendance (fig. 6.7). Taken together, these results suggest multiple opportunities for individuals trained at DMAC to apply their expertise in multiple institutional settings and therefore

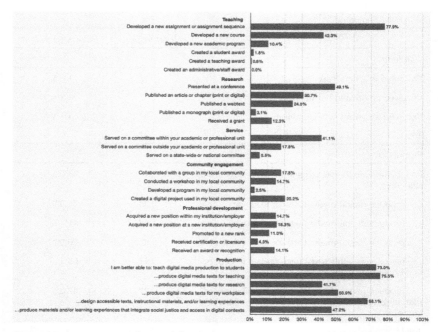

Figure 6.7. Impacts on professional development. Percentages are calculated from total responses to the survey.

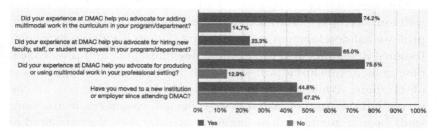

Figure 6.8. Impacts on advocacy. Percentages are calculated from total responses to the survey.

make possible the seeding effect of individual professional development (Conatser 2015).

In the second case, attendees self-reported a range of institutional actions that resulted from their DMAC experiences and that would support professionalization of the field. Attendees reported developing new courses (42.3%), new academic programs (10.4%), and serving on departmental (41.1%), college or university (17.8%), and outside committees (5.5%) (fig. 6.7). While some of these percentages are small,

Table 6.4. Material submissions by document type. Percentages are calculated based on the number of submissions.

Type	Count	%
Assignment	40	21.7%
Award	4	2.2%
Community engagement	9	4.9%
Conference presentation	8	4.3%
Course design	3	1.6%
Dissertation	2	1.1%
Grant	1	0.5%
Handout	13	7.1%
Professional development	4	2.2%
Program document	6	3.3%
Research article	51	27.7%
Research monograph	2	1.1%
Service documentation	12	6.5%
Syllabus	25	13.6%
Website	4	2.2%
Total	184	

as a group they show how the individual professional development provided by DMAC has enabled institutional changes necessary for professionalization. The individual impacts of professional development documented in the study support the professionalization of multimodal composition, as individual professional development is a necessary stepping stone to professionalizing a field. The individual training provided by DMAC not only leads to the production of research and pedagogical materials but also helps create the infrastructural and institutional conditions necessary for a field to achieve institutional status. These results suggest DMAC has met a need, noted by Alison Witte, Stacy Kastner, and Kerri Hauman in this volume, to facilitate the implementation of individual professional development at attendees' home institutions when they return from DMAC.

Professionalizing an academic subject requires the production of scholarship and teaching materials that serve as a literature for the field and training materials for new scholars. Of course, research on, and the teaching of, multimodal composition predates the existence of DMAC and the fifteen-year period covered by this study. There is

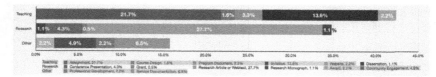

Figure 6.9. Aggregated example-document submissions. All values are percentages of the total documents submitted.

evidence, however, that DMAC has promoted both the development of pedagogical materials for teaching multimodal composition and multimodal scholarship, key features in the continuing professionalization of multimodal composition.

TEACHING MULTIMODAL COMPOSITION

Pedagogy plays a significant role in professionalization, both in articulating the professional identity of a field and training new scholars (cf. Rosner, Boehm, and Journet 1999). The most widely reported impact of DMAC on respondents was in their teaching. Over three-quarters of respondents (77.9%) developed a new assignment or assignment sequence because of their time at DMAC, and 42.3 percent developed a new course (fig. 6.7), results supported by the example-materials data. When all teaching materials from the dataset are aggregated, they constitute the largest category of submissions (fig. 6.9).

Attendees also reported their DMAC attendance made them better able to teach digital media to students (73.0%), improved their ability to produce digital-media texts for their classes (75.5%), and made them better able to produce accessible texts for learning (68.1%) (fig. 6.7). These results suggest DMAC has had a notable impact on the teaching of digital production, providing support for the professionalization of early-career digital-media scholars.

SCHOLARSHIP IN MULTIMODAL COMPOSITION

A key development in the professionalization of multimodal composition was the foundation of research venues like conferences (Gerrard 1995), journals (Moran 2003), and monograph series (Hawisher and Selfe 1997, 115). As noted above, respondents to our survey reported that DMAC impacted and contributed to their scholarship in these venues. Nearly half the respondents (49.1%) noted that because of their DMAC attendance, they had presented at a conference, and 55.2 percent generated a research publication. The survey data note these publications consisted of both traditional academic essays (30.7%) and webtexts (24.5%). Overall, 41.7 percent reported they were better able to produce digital-media texts for research (fig. 6.7), a finding that suggests the institute's impact on the shift to institutional recognition of digital scholarship (Voss 2015, 27). Respondents also reported DMAC led to their publication of a print or digital monograph (3.1%) or receiving a grant (12.3%).

The research impact of DMAC was further documented in the materials supplied by attendees. The largest single category of submissions in the dataset was research articles (fifty-one) and, taken together, presentations, dissertations, grants, articles, monographs, and web projects account for 36.2 percent of the total submissions, representing the significance respondents gave these projects (fig. 6.9). These reported impacts paint a compelling picture of DMAC's influence on the research trajectories of participants; it not only impacted the materials they produced but also provided professional development with technology that enabled attendees to incorporate digital media in their work.

INDIVIDUAL PROFESSIONALIZATION AND DISCIPLINARY PROFESSIONALIZATION

Research and teaching are important factors in the professionalization of a field not only because they are instrumental in training new scholars and advancing knowledge, but also because they provide the grounds for institutional recognition. DMAC attendees have produced a range of scholarship, pedagogical materials, and programmatic changes that have created institutional spaces for recognizing multimodal composition. As noted in table 6.3, a small, but not insignificant, number of respondents (10.4%) reported their experience at DMAC helped them create a new academic program at their institution. DMAC attendees created new courses and awards and served on departmental, college or university, and national committees. As we note, attendees acquired new positions, were promoted and licensed, and received awards or recognition for their work.

Self-reported comments about hiring and service work suggest DMAC has contributed to the advancement of multimodal composition within the university. The cumulative weight of these examples of personal professional development suggest the impacts of DMAC on the professionalization of the field—attendees who were able to create new programs provided greater access to multimodal composition

134   DEWITT AND JONES

instruction. Creating new classes and new assignments—together with program development—normalizes and professionalizes multimodal composition practices and helps establish them within the academy. Awards allow for greater visibility of multimodal and other digital work, and committee service, at all levels, allows attendees to advocate for multimodal composition as a field. Attendees were positioned to become advocates for multimodal teaching and scholarship, as Li, Michael Strickland, and Paula Rosinski do in this volume, as well as for hiring new multimodal scholars within their institutions.

Perhaps the clearest sign of DMAC's impact on the professionalization of multimodal composition is the increase in attendees' reporting scholarly specializations in computers and writing or digital media. DMAC has primarily appealed to attendees from higher education, particularly four-year colleges and universities (fig. 6.3). The largest category of respondents in the study were graduate students when they attended DMAC, with the next largest group being non-tenure-track faculty (fig. 6.4). Although the data do not show direct movements between respondents' positions after attending DMAC, they generally continued at institutions of higher education. All rank categories except graduate students saw increases (fig. 6.4), as respondents were hired, promoted, or moved to staff or administrative positions, began careers outside academia, or retired. No doubt some of this movement represents the natural progression of academic careers—students graduate and take jobs, junior scholars are promoted and/or move into other positions—and this progression is conspicuous in the data because of the high level of graduate participation at DMAC.

DMAC draws largely from programs historically associated with English and composition and rhetoric, which together accounted for 84.7 percent of attendees' departmental affiliations at the time of attendance (table 6.2). For this study, the most notable change in participants' careers is the increase in the number of respondents who currently identify computers and writing/digital media studies as an academic specialty (fig. 6.6). Only 19.0 percent of respondents identified digital studies as a specialty when they attended DMAC, but this share jumped to 28.8 percent after their attendance. This 9.8 percent change is the highest in the data set, tied with education, which was a specialty for 3.7 percent of respondents at the time of their attendance and is 13.5 percent currently. The number of attendees currently affiliated with English or composition and rhetoric departments dropped to 70.0 percent. English affiliations dropped from 71.8 percent to 53.4 percent, while composition and rhetoric affiliations increased from 12.9 percent to 16.6 percent of attendees.

Some of this movement can be accounted for by attendees entering the nonacademic workforce, moving into administrative positions, or retiring. Yet the rest suggests the diversity of academic approaches Conatser (2015) identifies as "destabilization." The engagement with a range of methodological approaches, Conatser argues, provides openings for new areas of research and inquiry, destabilizing the commonplaces and practices of a field. We add that this professional development can further promote the professionalization of the field. As researchers move to new disciplines and adopt new methodologies, they can bring multimodal methods and pedagogy to these fields. Even if they do not blend these methods, they can be advocates for them elsewhere in the university, helping to reinforce the presence of the field in the academy.

MOVING FORWARD

The professionalization of a field requires infrastructure. Not only must there be scholarship and teaching to establish a field, this work must be accepted and advocated for within an institution to maintain it. This analysis of survey and materials data indicates DMAC has been a means of training and providing professional development for scholars in multimodal composition. The training provided by DMAC has led some participants to make digital studies part of their professional specializations. Further, it has directly impacted the use of multimodal projects in participants' classrooms, providing for the "institutional action" Conatser argues helps support and maintain multimodal composition practices at the level of the institution. DMAC also led to research opportunities for respondents, including the publication of multimodal research, supporting "knowledge-making" that is disseminated through the field (Voss 27). This suggests institutes like DMAC are a means of increasing the number of multimodal scholars in rhetoric and writing, as well as other fields, and DMAC can be a model for furthering professionalization of multimodal composition. It is important to document how individual professional development is connected to professionalization, and DMAC suggests avenues by which other organizations can drive this professionalization.

As DMAC has evolved, areas for future study include understanding the impact of DMAC's focus on digital accessibility and access, writing program administration, activism, and analytics. In this survey, 68.1 percent of respondents reported DMAC enabled them to make digital materials and learning experiences more accessible, and 47.2 percent said they were better able to integrate social justice and access in their teaching (fig. 6.7). Future studies of the impact of DMAC could focus more granularly on issues of access and accessibility, as well as on topics like writing analytics. Additionally, the content of the example documents will benefit from a closer analysis for trends and commonalities.

As mentioned earlier, this impact study coincides with a period of change for DMAC, including a distinct shift in how we deliver the institute and, thus, the kinds of data we can collect in the future. In 2021, DMAC became a fully online, rather than residential, institute. While the eight-day duration of the institute remained the same, sessions and workshops were offered both synchronously and asynchronously using course-management and video-conferencing platforms (synchronous meetings were recorded and shared with those who could not participate). This move presented challenges—such as attendees needing to secure their own technology rather than having it supplied by the institute and to work independently (with virtual staff support)—but it also made possible greater access. Costs associated with attending the institute were reduced significantly—tuition was cut nearly by half, and attendees' personal expenses related to travel, housing, food, and house sitting were eliminated, as potentially were extra expenses related to pet sitting and childcare, thus reducing the amount of funding necessary to support DMAC participation. Lifting the burden of luxury, as Conatser (2015) and Witte, Kastner, and Hauman in this volume remind us, allows DMAC to reach teachers who otherwise would not be able to attend the institute. These populations may include two-year college instructors, high-school instructors, adjunct faculty, or those who simply cannot be away from work or home for eight days. Future research can explore how online delivery might alter how attendees respond to questions about curriculum and outcomes. Both DMAC and the field, by necessity, must think more critically about multimodal composing, access, and accessibility in distanced learning environments. Also in 2021, DMAC hosted an inaugural cohort of fellows, embedded teacher/scholars creating cross-disciplinary instructional modules on the broad topics of equity, diversity, and inclusion in digital contexts. Supported by the Global Arts and Humanities Discovery Theme at Ohio State, these teams created assignments, syllabi, curricula, workshops, classroom activities, bibliographies, and community-engaged project ideas to share with attendees. The interruption caused by the COVID-19 pandemic has offered DMAC a powerful moment to reflect on our past achievements while imagining new directions related to the format of the institute, its curriculum, and the types of instructional materials and modes of delivery that best meet participants' needs.

NOTES

1. Scott Lloyd DeWitt and John Jones wish to thank Nalijah Daniels, Lill Edwards, Carmen Greiner, Natalie Keener, Hana Le, Cynthia Lynn Schneider, Jade Werner, and their supervisor, Katie Stanutz, all of the Department of English at The Ohio State University. Their early efforts at locating current contact information for all past DMAC attendees made this impact study possible. They would also like to thank former DMAC attendees who completed our survey and who provided us with examples of their work for this study. Your generosity is greatly appreciated.
2. The Global Libraries Initiative is funded by the Bill and Melinda Gates Foundation and the Impact Planning and Assessment Road Map, and it outlines "the process Global Libraries (GL) grantees use to plan, measure, and report on the impact their programs have on the lives of people in the communities they serve" (Global Libraries 2015).

REFERENCES

Adams, Nicky, Margaret M. Strain, and Patrick Thomas. 2015. "'There and Back Again': How DMAC Shaped the Professional Growth of Three Departmental Colleagues." http://www.dmacinstitute.com/showcase/issues/n01/adams-strain-thomas-there-back.

Ball, Cheryl E. 2015. "CIWIC, DMAC, and Technology Professional Development in Rhet/Comp." Special issue, *Computers and Composition* 36. http://ceball.com/tag/open-access/.

Ball, Cheryl E., Dànielle Nicole DeVoss, Cynthia Selfe, and Scott Lloyd DeWitt, eds. 2015. "CIWIC, DMAC, and Technology Professional Development in Rhetoric and Composition." Special issue, *Computers and Composition Online* 36. http://cconlinejournal.org/ciwic_dmac/CC_ONLINE_INTRO/.

Conatser, Trey. 2015. "Keeping Track of DMAC: Visualizing Influence Across Space and Time." *Computers and Composition Online* 36. http://cconlinejournal.org/ciwic_dmac/conatser/.

DeVoss, Dànielle Nicole, Cheryl E. Ball, Cynthia Selfe, and Scott Lloyd DeWitt, eds. 2015. In "CIWIC, DMAC, and Technology Professional Development in Rhetoric and Composition." Special issue, *Computers and Composition* 36:1–66.

DeWitt, Scott Lloyd, Cynthia Selfe, Cheryl E. Ball, and Dànielle Nicole DeVoss, eds. 2015. "Showcasing the Best of CIWIC/DMAC." http://www.dmacinstitute.com/showcase/.

Ferris, Harley. 2015. "Making the Case DMAC as Professional Activism." *Computers and Composition Online* 36. http://cconlinejournal.org/ciwic_dmac/ferris/.

Gerrard, Lisa. 1995. "The Evolution of the Computers and Writing Conference." *Computers and Composition* 12 (3): 279–92.

Global Libraries. 2008. IPA Road Map. Seattle, WA: Bill & Melinda Gates Foundation.

Global Libraries. 2015. *Global Libraries Impact Planning and Assessment Guide.* Seattle, WA: Bill & Melinda Gates Foundation.

Hawisher, Gail E., and Cynthia L. Selfe. 1997. "The Edited Collection: A Scholarly Contribution and More." In *Publishing in Rhetoric and Composition*, edited by Gary A. Olson and Todd W. Taylor, 105–18. Albany: SUNY Press.

Hunter, Rik, Alanna Frost, Moe Folk, and Les Loncharich. 2015. "Like Coming in from the Cold: Sponsors, Identities, and Technological Professional Development." *Computers and Composition Online* 36. http://cconlinejournal.org/ciwic_dmac/hunter-et-al/.

Journet, Debra. 2007. "Inventing Myself in Multimodality; Encouraging Senior Faculty to Use Digital Media." *Computers and Composition* 24 (2): 107–20.

McGrath, Laura, and Letizia Guglielmo. 2015. "Communities of Practice and Makerspaces: DMAC's Influence on Technological Professional Development and Teaching Multimodal Composing." *Computers and Composition* 36: 44–53.

Moran, Charles. 2003. "*Computers and Composition* 1983–2002: What We Have Hoped For." *Computers and Composition* 20 (4): 343–58.

Rosner, Mary, Beth Boehm, and Debra Journet. 1999. *History, Reflection, and Narrative: The Professionalization of Composition, 1963–1983*. Westport, CT: Greenwood.

Voss, Julia. 2015. "To Teach, Critique, and Compose: Representing Computers and Composition through the CIWIC/DMAC Institute." *Computers and Composition* 36: 16–31.

7

LOOKING BEYOND THE WRITING PROGRAM
Institutional Allies to Support Professional Development in the Teaching of Digital Writing

Alison Witte, Stacy Kastner, and Kerri Hauman

Undoubtedly, the field of writing studies is concerned about how technology affects teaching writing (e.g., Banks 2006; DeVoss 2018; Graupner, Nikoson-Massey, and Blair 2009; Halbritter and Lindquist 2018; Hawisher et al. 1996; Kynard 2010; Palmeri 2012; Yancey 2004). As early as NCTE's 1972 Resolution on Preparing Students with Skill for Evaluating Media, educators recognized the importance of technology in the teaching and learning of writing. Since then, major professional organizations (e.g., CEE, MLA, NCTE, TYCA, WPA) have issued dozens of documents stating best practices for designing, teaching, and assessing writing courses responsive to technological shifts in literacy. Common across these documents is the positioning of teachers as learners in a technological landscape that is and always will be in flux.

In positioning teachers as learners and thinking about the digital as something we will always be learning, we must consider technological professional development (TPD). And indeed, governing entities in our field have done just this. The "CCCC Statement on Teaching, Learning, and Assessing Writing in Digital Environments," for example, states, "Administrators with responsibilities for writing programs will . . . assure that faculty have ready access to diverse forms of technical and pedagogical professional development before and while they teach in digital environments. Such support should include regular and just-in-time workshops, courses, individual consultations, and Web resources" (Yancey et al. 2004). Writing program administrators (WPAs), then, are responsible not only for leading the design and facilitation of first-year writing (FYW) curricula but also for developing wide-ranging TPD to support the ongoing learning of educators in their programs, in-field or

https://doi.org/10.7330/9781646424184.c007

not, with a variety of institutional statuses, including MA, MFA, or PhD students; contingent or part-time faculty; or tenure-track or tenured faculty. Despite this essential but heavy charge, Michael Faris's (2019) bibliographic essay attending to forty years of WPA scholarship argues, "Little scholarship has addressed both technology and the work of WPAs" (106).

Given major governing bodies' iterative calls for WPAs to develop robust TPD for writing teachers, Faris's work reveals an important shortcoming in our research. In scanning *Computers and Composition Online*'s professional-development section's archive (spring 2003–2018), we find narratives describing individuals' experiences at external TPD such as the Computers in Writing-Intensive Classrooms Summer Institute (CIWIC) or the Digital Media and Composition Summer Institute (DMAC),[1] but we don't find many narratives about how individuals are leveraging and networking TPD experiences at their home institutions.

While our field has long recognized writing teachers must attend to technological influences and consistently emphasized the importance of TPD for writing teachers, it has not as consistently attended to the institution-specific ecological and material realities of deploying effective TPD in support of digital multimodal writing curricula. The 2003 CCCC statement serves as evidence of this, as its focus on WPAs as the singular party responsible for TPD makes invisible TPD's material and institutional realities, which involve various individuals who are not WPAs and various institutional spaces that are not writing programs.

On one hand, TPD's wide-ranging involvement is pragmatic: WPAs do not have the time nor the resources to provide TPD on their own. On the other hand, TPD decisions are not always in the WPA's purview. For example, a participant in Kerry Hauman, Stacy Kastner, and Alison Witte's (2015) survey of technopedagogy preparation for English studies PhD students notes their department was prevented from developing formal or informal technology pedagogy graduate curricula because "the [Faculty Development Institute] is *the* unit on campus that delivers instruction on the use of pedagogical technology" (52). WPAs, then, are not, and do not have to be, the only ones responsible for developing wide-ranging curricula to support the ongoing learning of educators who teach in FYW programs with digital components. In their conclusion, the authors of chapter one in this collection encourage WPAs to seek out cross-campus partnerships, citing positive experiences working with the CTL at MSU "to leverage their experiences in providing all-university support and utilizing their broad networks and resources." For WPAs and writing teachers interested in developing relationships across campus to support the professionalization of digital multimodal composition, our chapter offers case studies investigating how six different writing programs collaborated with colleagues across campus and leveraged institutional resources to initiate and sustain the teaching of digital writing within FYW curricula.

Before bristling at the idea of people beyond the writing program exercising disciplinary expertise, consider that, in some cases, there are people and spaces within institutions who are better positioned (e.g., have dedicated staff, budgets) to take on the responsibility for educators' pedagogical development and technological literacy acquisition. And, before bristling at the idea of people beyond the program having resources to exercise disciplinary experience, consider Isis Artze-Vega, Melody Bowdon, Kimberly Emmons, Michele Eodice, Susan K. Hess, Clarie Coleman Lamonica, and Gerald Nelms's (2013) research showing that "a growing number of faculty members with composition and rhetoric (comp/rhet) backgrounds and affiliations have assumed interdisciplinary faculty development leadership positions at their institutions" (162).

As a field, we must learn more about how writing teachers interface with institutional entities in order to support the digital multimodal dimensions of our work. Mary Jo Reiff, Anis Bawarshi, Michelle Ballif, and Christian Weiser (2015) provide a methodological invitation for researchers to study and profile writing programs "as complex ecological networks" (4). To do so, the authors advise "shift[ing] the emphasis away from the individual unit, node, or entity, focusing instead on the network itself as the locus of meaning" (6). Taking up this call, this chapter presents data collected at six institutions with writing programs that require digital writing assignments: Marquette University, The Ohio State University (OSU), Purdue University, Salt Lake Community College (SLCC), the University of Texas at El Paso (UTEP), and the University of North Carolina at Charlotte (UNCC). Three research questions from our larger project guide the findings discussed here:

1. Why do teachers of digital writing seek out TPD, where on campus do they access that support, and what do they identify as characteristics of meaningful TPD?

2. From developing and facilitating such opportunities, what insight about successful TPD and support do individuals beyond the writing program, maybe even beyond our field, have to offer?

3. What campus-wide technoecologies and commitments support the teaching and learning of digital writing?

142   WITTE, KASTNER, AND HAUMAN

In this chapter, after discussing methods of program selection and data collection, we provide snapshots of the institutions we visited and their FYW curricula. We then discuss what we learned from FYW educators and various TPD stakeholders across campus about what makes TPD experiences meaningful. Across all six institutions, we found the following elements characterized and/or facilitated meaningful TPD: (1) personalized and just-in-time TPD for specific curricular and pedagogical needs; (2) PD and technology-rich programmatic cultures that include colleague-collaborators and compensation; and (3) institutional infrastructures in which physical proximity of the writing program to university resources and relational proximity to staff within technology-focused divisions were equally important. Finally, in our discussion section, we encourage WPAs to consider ways to interface with their campus technoecologies to elevate the institutional status and influence of the writing program, including emphasizing the pedagogical and technological expertise of the program's teaching staff.

PARTICIPANT SELECTION AND DATA COLLECTION

We selected programs that hold a CCCC Writing Program Certificate of Excellence (WPCE) and that, at the time of our data collection (fall 2018–spring 2019), assigned a digital writing project in at least one required writing course. Our first criterion ensured programs we researched offered "exemplary ongoing professional development for faculty of all ranks, including adjunct/contingent faculty" (Conference on College n.d.). While we recognize many exemplary writing programs with digital writing assignments and innovative TPD models do not hold a WPCE, using the WPCE as a selection criterion gave us a valid and reliable way to identify a manageable group of programs to work with that we could be assured positioned teachers as learners.

The programs profiled here (see fig. 7.1) are located in five regions of the United States and represent three Carnegie classifications. Additionally, these institutions include one community college (SLCC), one private university (Marquette), three public universities (OSU, Purdue, UNCC), and one public Hispanic-serving institution (UTEP). The writing program at one participating institution was independent (UNCC), while the rest were housed within English departments.

In contrast to other studies of writing programs' TPD—including our 2015 study—that rely on WPAs as the primary (and often only) on-campus informants, this chapter draws on interviews with WPAs and educators within the writing program, as well as staff members from

Looking beyond the Writing Program 143

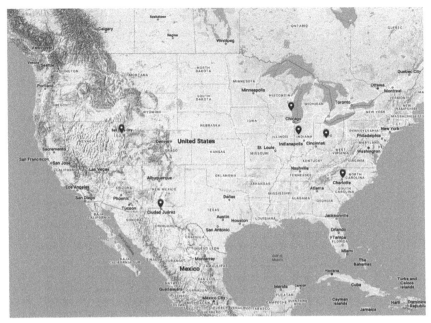

Figure 7.1. Map of participating institutions. The map identifies participating institutions, from left to right: Salt Lake Community College (Salt Lake City, Utah), University of Texas at El Paso, Marquette University (Milwaukee, Wisconsin), Purdue University (West Lafayette, Indiana), The Ohio State University (Columbus, Ohio), the University of North Carolina at Charlotte.

institutional sites like academic technologies, centers for teaching and learning, and libraries who work in service of and in collaboration with writing programs. Table 7.1 helps contextualize whom we spoke with and what we asked.

PROGRAM SNAPSHOTS

While no two institutions have identical programmatic or institutional structures, and although local context is crucial, we grouped program snapshots into three categories based on the writing program's location within a larger techecology: (1) programs whose WPA articulated an uncertain digital future based on shifts in campus culture and priorities, (2) programs positioned within institutions with technology-centered priorities and initiatives, and (3) programs whose implementation of digital writing curricula and whose networking across campus to support that implementation influenced the digital culture on campus.

144 WITTE, KASTNER, AND HAUMAN

Table 7.1. Overview of interview and focus group protocols

Interview Type	Interview questions consulted for this chapter
Interviews with writing program administrators	- What PD opportunities are available to you/educators on campus beyond the program? - Do you advertise these opportunities to your educators or provide incentives (or does the university provide incentives)?
Mapping focus groups with educators in the writing program	- What do you think it means to teach digital writing? - Do you teach digital writing in your classroom? If so, how did you learn to do so? - How do you leverage/use current campus resources to support your (a) PD in terms of learning to teach digital writing and/or (b) implementation of digital writing projects in your classes? - Mapping activity: (1) First, please list the experiences you feel have best prepared you to teach digital writing. (2) Then, number them in order of influence—1 being the most influential; ties are okay :). (3) Create a map of your university's technology infrastructure. Be sure to think broadly and expansively about the components you include. - What digital technologies are available to students, staff, faculty, or visitors? - Who are the individuals on campus who support and facilitate technology use on campus? - Who/what are the campus centers, groups, departments, or labs supporting and facilitating technology use on campus? - In what spaces is technology used, housed, or made available? - Now that you've created a linear list of PD you access and ranked it and also mapped the technology infrastructure on your campus based on your experience, talk to us about how your PD list correlates (or not) to the map you created.
Interviews with nonprogrammatic campus partners: (1) academic technologies, (2) centers for teaching and learning, (3) libraries, (4) other tech units specific to institution	- What is your unit's role in digital writing instruction support? In what capacities do you work with the writing program (educators, the WPA)? - What instructional services do you provide for educators, staff, and students? - What PD opportunities do you offer for educators? What is attendance like? What kinds of support do people seem to be seeking? - What (if any) kinds of digital writing projects have you consulted with educators to implement in their classrooms? - What kinds of support do people seem to be seeking? - What kinds of successes and barriers have educators faced in designing or implementing digital projects?

Programs in which the Digital Future Is Uncertain

> **Purdue University, Introductory Composition at Purdue (ICaP)**
>
> **UNDERGRADUATE ENROLLMENT:** 31,006
>
> **WPA/PRIMARY CONTACT:** Bradley Dilger (associate professor of English and director of ICaP)
>
> **COURSE SEQUENCE:** ENGL 106: First-Year Composition
>
> **DIGITAL WRITING PROJECT:** Remediation project; students choose from many forms of digital remediation including video and podcasts
>
> **TEACHING STAFF:** Primarily graduate students—MA, MFA, or PhD students in the Department of English—and a small number of full-time lecturers and adjuncts in the Department of English

> **Marquette University, First-Year English**
>
> **UNDERGRADUATE ENROLLMENT:** 8,335
>
> **WPA/PRIMARY CONTACT:** Jenn Fishman (associate professor of English)
>
> **COURSE SEQUENCE:** ENGL 1001: Rhetoric and Composition I and ENGL 1002: Rhetoric and Composition II
>
> **DIGITAL WRITING PROJECT:** Remix project stemming from students' production of a white paper; project was not required to be digital, but many were, and those that were not often used digital tools to produce a multimodal project
>
> **TEACHING STAFF:** Mix of graduate students—PhD students in the Department of English—lecturers and tenure-track/tenured faculty in the Department of English

At the time of our site visits, the writing programs housed within English departments at both Marquette and Purdue Universities were encountering unprecedented institutional revisions of their core curricula that condensed and restructured FYW in ways that took responsibility for designing curricula, teaching writing, and facilitating TPD away from specialists in writing studies. At Marquette, that meant eliminating the FYW program and WPA position, as well as trading the second course in the FYW sequence, the course in which students completed a digital writing project, for a writing-intensive upper-division course offered by any department. Similarly, at Purdue, the revision meant no longer requiring students to take the FYW program's course in which students would be exposed to digital writing and instead giving them the option to satisfy their writing requirement with a humanities-based course called Transformative Texts. At both institutions, broad pragmatic issues influenced the decisions impacting these programs: cuts in funding for graduate students and non-tenure-track faculty and prioritizing student contact with tenure-track and tenured faculty, who were increasingly seeing lower enrollments in their nonrequired, primarily humanities-based courses. Likewise, curriculum committees on both campuses did not recognize the value and transferability of FYW courses that taught digital writing nor did they recognize the importance of a writing studies specialist steering decisions about writing curricula. Our study does not include the outcomes of these changes.

146   WITTE, KASTNER, AND HAUMAN

Programs Influenced and Supported by Broader
Campus Commitments and Initiatives

The Ohio State University, First-Year Writing Program

UNDERGRADUATE ENROLLMENT: 45,946

WPA/PRIMARY CONTACT: Edgar Singleton (director of first-year writing)

COURSE SEQUENCE: ENG 1110: First-Year English Composition and a second course taught as a WAC course and offered by departments across campus

DIGITAL WRITING PROJECT: Research symposium Adobe Spark presentation that moves through multiple images and includes an audio element; evolved from a remix project and the Commonplace project, which was an op-ed type of project

TEACHING STAFF: Primarily graduate students—MA, MFA, or PhD students in the Department of English—and also by full-time lecturers and adjuncts in the Department of English

---

Salt Lake Community College, Composition

UNDERGRADUATE ENROLLMENT: 60,000 across 10 campuses

WPA/PRIMARY CONTACT: Jennifer Courtney (professor of English); Stephen Ruffus (associate dean of English)

COURSE SEQUENCE: ENGL 1010: Intro to Writing and ENGL 2010: Intermediate Writing or ENGL 2100: Technical Writing

DIGITAL WRITING PROJECT: Faculty chose the type of digital assignments they felt were best for their classes; often students could complete a project in whatever modality they felt was most rhetorically effective; SLCC also had a campus-wide ePortfolio requirement, which ENGL 1010, 2010, and 2100 faculty have incorporated into their course.

TEACHING STAFF: Mix of full-time and adjunct faculty in the Department of English, Linguistics, and Writing Studies

---

When visiting OSU and SLCC, we witnessed campus-wide initiatives bolstering TPD opportunities for FYW educators. While it was not the explicit intention of these initiatives to support FYW, educators benefited from increased attention to digital texts and tools and the recognition that educators needed preparation and/or support to meet the goals of institutional initiatives. OSU was in the first year of their Digital Flagship program, which was the result of a partnership with Apple that provided every incoming first-year student with an iPad, keyboard, and stylus. The Office of Distance Education and eLearning (ODEE) facilitated the Digital Flagship program and required any faculty who wanted to teach

Digital Flagship courses to complete a five-week cohort-style training. SLCC required all students to complete an ePortfolio, and as part of their efforts to reduce student costs; they had been developing open educational resources (OER) for several years. OER funds allowed English-department faculty to create new internal TPD opportunities like workshops. At both OSU and SLCC, unlike at Purdue and Marquette, digital writing within FYW gained security from broader college/university initiatives that also recognized the value/necessity of students' digital literacy. In addition to experiencing less pushback against digital curricula, the FYW programs at both institutions enjoyed affordances from these broader campus initiatives as well (e.g. access to TPD and material technologies beyond the writing program's own capacity and budget).

Programs Influencing Broader Campus Commitments and Initiatives

---

The University of North Carolina at Charlotte, University Writing Program[2]

UNDERGRADUATE ENROLLMENT: 23,914

WPA/PRIMARY CONTACT: Joan Mullin (professor of English and executive director)

COURSE SEQUENCE: UWRT-1104, a four-credit-hour course with three seated hours and one hour of online studios facilitated through the LMS

DIGITAL WRITING PROJECT: A digital portfolio focused on a semester-long inquiry project, and the required studios may also involve the production of digital or multimodal projects

TEACHING STAFF: Primarily full-time, non-tenure-track faculty from the university writing program, and a small number of sections were taught by adjuncts and tenure-track faculty in the Department of English

---

The University of Texas, El Paso, First-Year Composition Program

UNDERGRADUATE ENROLLMENT: 21,341

WPA/PRIMARY CONTACT: Judith Fourzan (director FYC)

COURSE SEQUENCE: RWS 1301: Rhetoric and Composition I and RWS 1302: Rhetoric and Composition II

DIGITAL WRITING PROJECT: Visual rhetoric project for which they had the option of creating a documentary or an OER

TEACHING STAFF: Primarily graduate students—MA or PhD students in the Department of English—and a small number of core full-time lecturers in the rhetoric and writing studies program within the Department of English

During our UNCC and UTEP site visits, as we met with staff members beyond the writing program, three things were consistent: (1) staff members in techpedagogy units had experience teaching FYW, often within the program we were visiting, and/or were collaborating with FYW educators to develop and facilitate their unit's TPD offerings; (2) institutional visions, missions, and fiscal priorities included focuses on TPD (e.g., at UTEP there was a push for OER to encourage faculty to create digital course materials, and at UNCC, funding for PD is included in the College of Arts and Sciences' mission statement); and (3) staff members clearly articulated that FYW's curricular shift to digital writing influenced their unit's abilities to grow and thrive, whether structurally (at UTEP they were able to secure and grow campus labs, equipment, and staff in their academic technologies unit) or pedagogically (at UNCC writing program faculty were leading the way in supporting their university's Quality Matters [QM] certificates and training).

FINDINGS: MEANINGFUL TECHNOLOGICAL PROFESSIONAL DEVELOPMENT

In our data, we found exigencies for accessing TPD that we expected: people reported accessing TPD because of personal interest in teaching with technology; because it was required by the program or institution; and because it came with financial, material, or professional incentives.

Not surprisingly, at all the institutions we visited, TPD was required to teach within the writing program or to teach particular classes (e.g., online courses). For example, all the writing programs we visited had some kind of required new-instructor orientation (e.g., ODEE's five-week training for OSU faculty wanting to be part of Digital Flagship). Programs staffed with graduate students had practicum courses or pre-semester workshops (Marquette, OSU, Purdue, UTEP).

TPD accessed for financial incentive took many forms, including participation in off-campus training, in new on-campus programs/initiatives, and in ongoing campus TPD. As examples, UTEP has an annual Teach Tech research group with a stipend of up to $2,000 for faculty to study teaching or researching with a particular technology, and SLCC provides ongoing TPD throughout each semester, with hourly compensation for adjunct faculty who attend. TPD was also accessed for material incentives. For example, instructors who participated in the OSU Digital Flagship training received an iPad, keyboard, stylus, and case. Other times, the incentive was professional, such as a CV-line, status as an on-campus expert, or the opportunity to shape new campus initiatives as an early adopter. For instance, at Marquette, the WPA (Jenn Fishman) was directly involved in the development of the Digital Scholarship Lab and in linking the composition courses to that facility.

However, our discussions with WPAs and educators revealed that some of the most influential reasons people chose to participate in TPD and/or find TPD meaningful were anchored to personalized support, programmatic culture, and institutional infrastructure; thus, the remainder of our chapter focuses on these motivators, as well as key challenges.

Personalized Support

In interviews with educators, we learned people are less inclined to value abstract TPD. A graduate student and TA at OSU noted, "I feel like the most helpful things for me are very personalized." Likewise, educators within Marquette's writing program noted they did not attend their CTL's programming because it was too "big picture," focused on teaching theory and concepts in general rather than providing programming that could be directly applied to individual classes, sections, and instructors.

Interview participants across all six site visits also overwhelmingly indicated immediate teaching needs motivated their participation in TPD. In short, we found both educators and faculty developers were tired of the "brownbag" model of TPD and were innovating and experimenting with models of TPD that were more impactful because they were more tailored to direct needs of specific educators and classrooms. At Marquette, Elizabeth Gibes, digital scholarship librarian, explained they now provide a list of on-demand workshops groups of three or more can request; otherwise, they offer an individual consultation. UNCC's CTL addressed this desire for personalization and specificity in a similar manner, offering "customized" workshops and partnering with FYW educators to coteach workshops. Jaesoon An, a senior instructional designer within UNCC's CTL, explained, "We always try to cultivate faculty champions in academic programs we work with. . . . It is crucial to have faculty champions because they can enhance PD experience tremendously by providing more systematic and personalized PD to their section instructors."

We observed this same trend in designing personalized TPD within UTEP's Academic Technologies unit. Steve Varela, associate director of Creative Studios, described their Blackboard Institute as showing educators "how to use Blackboard from a teaching and learning point of view, not a point and click kind of thing." Further, Varela explained the institute is designed "with the idea that we'll build you something so you can use it for the next class you teach." Similarly, Tara Koger, educator programs manager for Digital Flagship at OSU, explained that ODEE's redesign of TPD intentionally increased personalized content by shifting from an all-day boot-camp model to a five-week cohort model. Koger explained, "We do the two hours in class where we try and make it as active as possible. We ask them all by their second week to identify a course project, meaning a project for a course they teach that they want to build, improve, revise, whatever, and it's really incredibly open. We just want them to leave the five weeks having something tangible for their teaching."

Programmatic Culture

Programmatic culture also influenced educators' choice and ability to participate in TPD. In some cases, that culture involved building TPD into other structures to reduce time commitments for participants and make it easier for people to engage with TPD opportunities. For example, UTEP's Blackboard Institute occurs during the break between semesters to reduce conflicts between TPD and teaching responsibilities. Additionally, at Purdue, graduate students serving as tech mentors visit the practicum course weekly, providing TPD during a time when TAs are already in class. Likewise, at UNCC, the administrative team integrated TPD into regularly scheduled faculty meetings, combining program business and TPD.

A programmatic culture that provided necessary resources, like time and money, also encouraged participation in external TPD. For example, at UNCC, WPA Joan Mullin procured funds for travel, lodging, and registration to allow FYW educators to attend DMAC. As Jan Rieman, a senior lecturer at UNCC with administrative responsibilities, explained, "We funded people to go to DMAC because we wanted people to get digital composing experience. And then, the idea was that whoever went came back and taught people who didn't want to go or who couldn't go." Important, this model demonstrates how WPAs can create an infrastructure in which a program's investment in individual TPD can be intentionally scaled to support both the program and, as Scott DeWitt and John Jones's research in chapter 6 of this collection shows, the professionalization of the field of multimodal composition itself.

SLCC has both an institutional and programmatic ethic concerning faculty compensation for PD. Jason Pickavance, director for faculty development, described part of his position as being able to secure funding for PD by articulating its necessity for accomplishing institutional priorities. For instance, he tells upper-level administrators that issues they care about, like student completion, cannot be achieved without offering compensated PD opportunities to faculty, including adjuncts, at strategic points in their careers. Pickavance also advocates for institutional culture in which PD is the default rather than an opt-in for full-time and adjunct faculty. One of the standing faculty within the writing program at SLCC noted that thinking ethically about adjunct faculty and PD ultimately served as a retention tool: "We have longevity with [part-time] faculty members because they want to stick around; there's professional-development opportunities there for them."

Programmatic culture extends beyond integrating and supporting formalized TPD opportunities to also involve more personal relationships and informal interactions. One interesting finding that emerged from our map-making focus groups with teaching staff was how meaningful talking with colleagues—informal and serendipitous, as well as pointed and help-seeking, dialogues—was. At each of the institutions we visited, focus-group participants noted these informal conversations were some of their most meaningful TPD experiences. For example, Sherita Roundtree, a doctoral candidate and graduate assistant for WAC at OSU indicated, "I rank asking colleagues and talking to colleagues as pretty high on my list as far as informing my work with technology and teaching digital writing." Likewise, Debarati Dutta, a senior lecturer at UNCC, articulated that "even outside the circles of official faculty development, faculty have a culture of supporting each other. Impromptu office as well as hallway conversations allow faculty to interact with each other, share knowledge about teaching, and problem solve together."

Institutional Infrastructure

Physical proximity (where the writing program was located on campus in relation to external units), relational proximity (former and/or concurrent teachers of FYW positioned in various roles outside writing programs), and interdependency between the writing program and external units had considerable influence on individuals' participation in external TPD.

Physical proximity of the writing program to other units was one factor that made TPD visible and accessible. For example, the academic technology unit at UNCC is located within the same building as the writing program. When we asked Rich Preville, director of Audiovisual Integration and Support for Learning Environments at UNCC, how his unit interfaced with the writing program, his response was simple: "A lot, mostly because they're our neighbors, so just being proximal to us, and because they have a bunch of cool ideas." At OSU, an instructional technologist located within the same building as the writing program was listed by many focus-group participants as a key part of their TPD. Additionally, FYW educators have easy access to digital tools and training because one of ODEE's Digital Unions is located in the same building as the English department. Similarly, at SLCC, participants attributed the strong connection between their FYW Online Plus program and the library to having historically shared the same physical space.

In addition to physical proximity, relational proximity—particularly relationships with people who had been part of the writing program or English department and moved into university-wide roles—facilitated engagement with TPD outside the writing program. Jason Pickavance at SLCC summarized this well, positing it was not uncommon to find "a preponderance of English people in teaching and learning centers. . . . We like to write and talk, and just talk about teaching. I think there's something to the idea that writing is a kind of teaching subject." Though Pickavance's comment focused on CTLs, our research confirms this extends to other faculty-development sites across campus as well.

At OSU, educational technologist Mike Bierschenk started as a program coordinator working closely with the FYW online program in the English department. Doing this work, he was identified and recruited by the College of Arts and Sciences' Technology Services unit to occupy his current position as the educational technologist for the English department. Though he's no longer in the English department, in his current role, Bierschenk provides tech-support services to English-department faculty, including regularly visiting the GTA summer workshop and practicum class. Similarly, a librarian at UNCC who had taught FYW explained she was hired for her position heading the makerspace and other innovation spaces "because of my instructional background and my creativity." In our interviews, this librarian's former colleagues noted that having her in that role made FYW educators more aware of the opportunities available to them.

At UTEP, Varela is currently working in Learning Environments, but he holds a BA in English from UTEP and previously served as a senior lecturer in the English department. In talking with us, Varela noted he was recruited to support faculty teaching with technology at the university level because of his faculty background. He believes his classroom experience gives him "street cred," helping to build his ethos with other faculty, especially because he can draw directly on his teaching to provide examples of successes and failures and can talk to faculty as a fellow practitioner.

Finally, a culture of intentional interdependency between the writing program and other units on campus sometimes led to more robust pedagogical resources. For example, according to Mike Pitcher, director of Academic Technologies and Learning Environments and codirector of UTEP's Center for Research in Engineering and Technology Education (CREaTE), his unit evolved and grew in response to the FYW program's digital writing curriculum: "Originally, we were instructional support services, and before that we were kind of more traditional IT. We've really evolved based in part on the [rhetoric and writing studies] program. . . . We evolved partly because of [their redesign that integrated digital assignments], partly just because of student need and kind of our take on technology."

We found interdependency at UNCC also: writing program faculty who first participated in CTL workshops now facilitate CTL-sponsored workshops for the campus community and have leadership roles in supporting the university's QM initiative. At SLCC, Emily Dibble, the ePortfolio coordinator for the college, noted she partnered with Tiffany Rousculp, director of Writing Across the College, to develop and facilitate ePortfolio workshops for faculty because faculty, like students, are evaluated by assembling digital portfolios: "We do a workshop for faculty called Creating your Professional Portfolio. She does the narrative, content part, and then I focus more on the technology part. So it's been a good partnership," and she added that many faculty have attended.

Key Challenges and Mitigations

A question we repeatedly heard from participants within writing programs was, *How do I know if this TPD is worth my time?* And a question we repeatedly heard from people providing TPD was, *How do I get people to show up?* Two concerns are central to these questions: salience and accessibility. As GTA and assistant WPA Alisha Karabinus from Purdue cogently put it, "There are resources, but are they actually resources if they don't really help anybody? . . . If they're not, if you can't find them, if you don't know they exist, if they're not offered to everybody, if everybody doesn't have equal access? When does a resource stop being a resource and just start being a place where we put money?"

One difficulty educators on many US college campuses face is the challenge of identifying and accessing PD opportunities beyond one's own program/department. We heard this repeatedly in our interviews, both from educators and from people in faculty-development roles. Speaking about the environment at Purdue from an educator's standpoint, Karabinus aptly put it this way: "It's difficult to navigate a campus with so many departments that are not paying attention to what the other departments are doing and not working together. . . . But it's a whole campus culture. I think it's a university culture, honestly." Speaking about the culture at OSU from a faculty developer's perspective, Koger likewise talked with us about the challenge of reaching diverse stakeholders. Koger noted specifically that GTAs and adjunct instructors felt excluded from PD, that people in "funky roles" are sometimes explicitly told they cannot participate in PD, and emphasized that communication barriers, like the absence of a listserv of all GTAs, can complicate advertising TPD opportunities broadly.

Speaking from a faculty developer's perspective at UTEP, Varela explained that the challenge of sustainable cross-campus connections was the exigence for designing their Blackboard Institute as a cohort-based learning experience that includes short-term and longer-term follow-up. The week-long class draws twenty-five people with varying levels of technology expertise from across campus. Postinstitute, members are invited to an informal monthly Lunch and Learn about new tools or approaches, and then a year and a half after the initial class, institute facilitators reach out to participants to offer support tailored to the participants' teaching, learning, or research. Using this model, within a year and a half, Varela and his colleagues were working with 130 to 140 faculty across campus—faculty who were then connected with one another and with Academic Technologies (AT). He noted the reciprocally beneficial relationship between AT and faculty, explaining that if they're trying out a new workshop, he "can send an email to [his] list and say, 'Hey y'all, you want to come have lunch, we want to try out this new thing.' I got twenty, thirty people just coming to hang out."

Committed to encouraging cross-campus collaborations at UNCC, Preville and his team approached the same problem Varela and his colleagues faced by creating a website that streamlined the project-management process. Doing so made identifying and connecting with potential collaborators possible and ultimately bolstered cross-campus collaborations.

On campuses we identified as having writing programs that influence broader campus commitments and initiatives, we spoke with heads of AT units who were purposefully creating infrastructures—whether in-person institute or web platform—to instigate and support cross-campus connections: the design of faculty-development programs at UTEP, communications technology at UNCC.

DISCUSSION: THE BENEFITS OF TECHNO-ECOLOGICAL THINKING FOR TPD STAKEHOLDERS

Our research shows that drawing on external units for support significantly expands writing programs' opportunities to communicate their value, particularly in supporting students' and educators' acquisition of technological literacies. Likewise, when writing programs sought opportunities to collaborate with TPD entities across campus, meaningful TPD experiences emerged. In some cases, this included funding for educators to participate in TPD, and in other cases, this included invitations to collaborate and be compensated for designing and facilitating TPD. Thus, writing programs can be well served by intentionally and proactively pursuing opportunities to collaborate across campus, leveraging existing relationships, as well as forging new ones as broader college or university initiatives emerge.

Aligned with Artze-Vega et al.'s (2013) research, an additional notable trend from our research is that writing studies educators, like Varela and several other staff members we spoke with in libraries, CTLs, and AT units, are being recruited to hold positions that position them as bridges between writing programs and extraprogrammatic TPD sites. On the campuses we visited, having writing studies educators in bridge roles resulted in writing programs being connected with external resources, staff members, expertise, and tools for designing and facilitating high impact TPD.

Certainly, ineffective TPD exists. As Rik Hunter, Alanna Frost, Moe Folk, and Les Loncharich (2015) note, "It has been our experience that we remain mired in local training of the 'brown bag' variety—quick, non-disciplinary training experiences on the most recently, institutionally supported software" (under "Conclusions"). Likewise, Jeffrey Arellano Cabusao, Cathy Fleischer, and Bilal Polson's (2019) NCTE position statement, Shifting from Professional Development to Professional Learning: Centering Teacher Empowerment, asserts many educators loathe/resist PD because rather than being "a true learning experience," much of it is "a top-down, one-size-fits-all, one-shot model, directed at teachers rather than inclusive of teachers and their diverse classroom experience" (under "Issue Defined"). Yet, we agree with the National Council of Teachers of English's statement's conclusion that "professional development doesn't have to be this way" because, as our research reveals, meaningful TPD that supports FYW educators teaching digital writing exists (under "Issue Defined").

Rather than concluding our discussion of this research, we instead invite readers to the "Teaching Resources" page on the WAC Clearinghouse website (https://wac.colostate.edu/resources/teaching/), where they can find a database of the artifacts collected for this research, including faculty-development materials and the writing assignments that make technopedagogy on these particular campuses exigent. While creating and sustaining meaningful TPD is undoubtedly difficult, time-consuming work, we hope these institutional snapshots and recommendations encourage engaging TPD to proliferate.

NOTES

> **Acknowledgments.** *This project was made possible by an Emergent Researcher Award from the Conference on College Composition and Communication (2017–2018). We are grateful to Shirley Rose for her mentorship; to Dànielle Nicole DeVoss, Bump Halbritter, and Julie Lindquist, who arranged a pilot site visit with us that was invaluable in shaping the design of this study and data collection; and to Lee Nickoson and Kristine Blair, who have supported this project's origins since our graduate studies at Bowling Green State University. Likewise, we are indebted to the WPAs and administrative support staff at each of the six institutions we visited, who were beyond generous with their time in helping us arrange site visits, and to each of the individuals on campus who shared their experiences, insight, and reflections.*

1. See DeWitt and Jones in this collection for more information regarding CIWIC and DMAC.
2. Since our site visit, the independent writing program at UNCC has become an independent academic department titled Writing, Rhetoric, and Digital Studies, with Joan Mullin transitioning from executive director to chair.

REFERENCES

Arellano Cabusao, Jeffrey, Cathy Fleischer, and Bilal Polson. 2019. "Shifting from Professional Development to Professional Learning: Centering Teacher Empowerment." National Council of Teachers of English, Position Statements. https://ncte.org/statement/proflearning/.

Artze-Vega, Isis, Melody Bowdon, Kimberly Emmons, Michele Eodice, Susan K. Hess, Clarie Coleman Lamonica, and Gerald Nelms. 2013. "Privileging Pedagogy: Composition, Rhetoric, and Faculty Development." *College Composition and Communication* 65 (1): 162–84.

Banks, Adam. 2006. *Race, Rhetoric, and Technology: Searching for Higher Ground.* Mahwah, NJ: Lawrence Erlbaum.

Conference on College Composition and Communication. n.d. "CCCC Writing Program Certificate of Excellence." https://cccc.ncte.org/cccc/awards/writingprogramcert.

DeVoss, Dánielle Nicole. 2018. "Digital Writing Matters." In *The Routledge Handbook of Digital Writing and Rhetoric,* edited by Jonathan Alexander and Jacqueline Rhodes, 9–17. Abingdon: Routledge.

Faris, Michael. 2019. "Writing and Technology in WPA: Toward the WPA as an Advocate for Technological Writing." *WPA: Writing Program Administration* 42 (3): 106–12.

Graupner, Meredith, Lee Nickoson-Massey, and Kristine Blair. 2009. "Remediating Knowledge-Making Spaces in the Graduate Curriculum: Developing and Sustaining Multimodal Teaching and Research." *Computers and Composition* 26 (1): 13–23.

Halbritter, Bump, and Julie Lindquist. 2018. "It's Never About What It's About: Audio-Visual Writing, Experiential-Learning Documentary, and the Forensic Art of Assessment." In *The Routledge Handbook of Digital Writing and Rhetoric*, edited by Jonathan Alexander and Jacqueline Rhodes, 317–27. Abingdon: Routledge.

Hauman, Kerri, Stacy Kastner, and Alison Witte. 2015. "Writing Teachers for Twenty-first Century Writers: A Gap in Graduate Education." *Pedagogy* 15 (1): 45–57.

Hawisher, Gail E., Paul LeBlanc, Charles Moran, and Cynthia Selfe. 1996. *Computers and the Teaching of Writing in American Higher Education, 1979–1994: A History.* Norwood, NJ: Ablex.

Hunter, Rik, Alanna Frost, Moe Folk, and Les Loncharich. 2015. "Like Coming in from the Cold: Sponsors, Identities, and Technological Professional Development." In *CIWIC, DMAC, and Technology Professional Development in Rhetoric and Composition*, edited by Cheryl Ball, Dánielle Nicole DeVoss, Cynthia L. Selfe, and Scott Lloyd DeWitt. Special issue, *Computers and Composition Online.* http://cconlinejournal.org/ciwic_dmac/hunter-et-al/index.html.

Kynard, Carmen. 2010. "From Candy Girls to Cyber Sista-Cipher: Narrating Black Females' Color-Consciousness and Counterstories In and Out of School." *Harvard Educational Review* 80 (1): 30–53.

National Council of Teachers of English. 1972. "Resolution on Preparing Students with Skill for Evaluating Media." https://ncte.org/statement/skillforevalmedia/.

Palmeri, Jason. 2012. *Remixing Composition: A History of Multimodal Writing Pedagogy.* Carbondale: Southern Illinois University Press.

Reiff, Mary Jo, Anis Bawarshi, Michelle Ballif, and Christian Weiser, eds. 2015. *Ecologies of Writing Programs: Program Profiles in Context.* Anderson, SC: Parlor.

Yancey, Kathleen Blake. 2004. "Made Not Only in Words: Composition in a New Key." *College Composition and Communication* 56 (2): 297–328.

Yancey, Kathleen, Andrea Lunsford, James McDonald, Charles Moran, Michael Neal, Chet Pryor, Duane Roen, and Cindy Selfe. 2004. "CCCC Position Statement on Teaching, Learning, and Assessing Writing in Digital Environments." *College Composition and Communication* 55 (4): 785–90.

8

A FRESH CATALYST
Invigorating the University with Integrated Modalities

Daniel Schafer and Josh Ambrose

INTRODUCTION

"What *exactly* is the value of the liberal arts? What is the financial return on investment?" As much as faculty may instinctively recoil from evaluative questions, they are what students and their families are asking our colleges and departments.

Because we are relatively young English instructors from working-class backgrounds, these questions are familiar and personal. McDaniel College—where Daniel and Josh both taught for the better part of a decade—has led the way in diversifying its student population over the past decade, continuing to serve a student body well over 45 percent first generation. So in our own practice, we create the classes we wish we had as undergrads, looking to bridge the practical with the theoretical, the abstract with the experiential. We contend that we can empower students by placing them in multimodal moments of development, believing that the academy is relevant to developing one's agency and that the development of professional skills is not opposed to the idealized educational values often seen in liberal arts colleges and higher education more broadly.

A liberal arts education equips students with crucial skills that allow them to succeed as professionals and live a balanced life outside the workplace (Logan and Curry 2014). We are teachers at a liberal arts college, so much of what we discuss in this chapter focuses on our experience working at a small college. But what we suggest can work anywhere—from the smallest community college to the largest university. We argue that as part of providing a well-rounded education, the liberal arts community should embrace professionalization, leveraging the value of internship-based courses that privilege multimodal composition.

https://doi.org/10.7330/9781646424184.c008

Our own experience with the ongoing debate around the professionalization of the liberal arts reflects conversations throughout the field, on listservs, at conferences, and in articles. We do not advocate for the suspension of any literature or creative-writing class or work to diminish the absolute value of rhetoric; on the contrary, we advocate for classes that complement and translate skill sets for students eager to figure out how to apply their love of Shakespeare to an off-campus experience, harnessing the writing and communication skills employers say they privilege.

Take Lauren—an English major at McDaniel College who wasn't sure what to do with her degree yet possessed a clear sense that she wanted to make a difference in the world. She got solid marks in her literature classes and was an accomplished tutor in the college's writing center. But when it came to her senior year, she was unsure how to translate her skills to the world outside academia. So, she signed up for the Writing for Nonprofits course, where she was paired with a partner organization in town and put to work creating press releases, social media initiatives, and new website content.

Together with her classmates, Lauren learned about the national nonprofit landscape through talks from people like entrepreneur Dan Pallotta (2016) and books such as *Forces for Good* by Heather McLeod and Leslie R. Crutchfield. Students were also guided through long-form grant applications and discussions around media depictions of poverty through Zoom conversations with global nonprofit executives. Equipped with this broader context for the challenges faced and the work done by nonprofits, Lauren experienced and learned about messaging across different platforms as she worked for her partner. Each assignment was unique, most were composed in multiple modes, and all were conducted under the guidance of the course instructor.

After graduating, Lauren signed up for a year with AmeriCorps, which led to a full-time job with a literacy nonprofit, and, in time, a director job with a citywide organization pulling together over three hundred nonprofit partners dedicated to education. The knowledge she gained about the nonprofit landscape, as well as the opportunities in her internship, served as catalysts for Lauren's career.

Another student, Lucy, a history and Spanish major, interned with a local running store as part of Writing for Main Street, a course that teaches students about small businesses in the community around McDaniel College. Lucy had this to say about the class:

> Without the internship, I would never have started work in the digital marketing field. This course taught me how to write for a professional

> business through hands-on-learning: the work I created in class was actually used in advertising. . . . The knowledge I gained from the "Writing for Main Street" class is used in my life on a daily basis.

Doing this kind of work was a new experience for Lucy—and she was good at it. So good at it, in fact, that when her supervisor traveled from Maryland to Florida for a national conference, several people surprised him by knowing his store purely from the social media content Lucy generated. He was so impressed that he retained Lucy as a part-time freelancer after she graduated, even as she went on to another full-time job at a web firm.

Lucy's and Lauren's stories are just two of dozens of similar stories from students who have taken Writing for Main Street or Writing for Nonprofits at McDaniel College. And these courses are just two of many courses at McDaniel College that blend the academic with the practical, the theoretical with apprenticeship. These courses have directly led to the implementation of the McDaniel Commitment, a new programmatic academic-value proposition. The McDaniel Commitment is a team-led, campus-wide initiative increasing student engagement, breaking down town-gown barriers, and ultimately improving retention and graduation rates (Association of American Colleges and Universities 2012). Moreover, it is leading to success after success for students like Lucy and Lauren. Its emphasis on experiential learning was met with the largest incoming class in school history in both 2020 and 2021 and is already earning national recognition for its articulation of what a liberal arts degree guarantees. Moreover, this campus-wide model—in which multimodal composition is vitally important—is one that can be implemented at any college or university.

It's clear: multimodal composition is integral not just to creating a healthy sense of vocation but also to articulating a liberal arts education in the twenty-first century. Our experience continually affirms our conviction that one of the most powerful ways to effect connection and catalytic action is to infuse the curriculum with local engagement. In continuing to scale up that engagement holistically, liberal arts at universities are not only demonstrating their relevance but are also ensuring their very survival. Fully engaged, multimodal composition courses are well poised to demonstrate this at a higher frequency and volume than ever before. With the right mindset, English departments should take up the mantle and lead the way forward in engagement in the midst of open questioning of the liberal arts value proposition.

MULTIMODAL RESEARCH OVERVIEW

> *For compositionists, of this time and of this place, this moment—this moment right now—is like none other. Never before has the proliferation of writings outside the academy so counterpointed the compositionists inside. Never before have the technologies of writing contributed so quickly to the creation of new genres.*
>
> — Kathleen Blake Yancey

Daniel remembers working as an editor at an educational publisher in 2010 after a graduate education steeped in the early work of digital rhetoric scholars such as Kristin Arola and Cheryl Ball. The landscape of rhetoric and composition across the country, though, was not generally accepting multimodal composition. In creating textbooks for undergraduates studying composition, educational publishers had to navigate a profession in which some thought traditional, monomodal writing was still highly preferred.

Much has changed in the last decade. Today multimodal composition is widely accepted within our field. Still, this acceptance was almost a quarter century in the making.

In 1996, the New London Group published what may be scholars' first attempt to bring visual design into the field of rhetoric and composition. The New London Group describes the ways composing texts in multiple modes—using different tools in various permutations—allows writer-designers "to treat any semiotic activity, including using language to produce or consume texts as a matter of Design . . . emphasiz[ing] the fact that meaning making is an active and dynamic process, and not something governed by static rules" (194). By appealing to multiple senses, texts can create meaning more effectively than the linguistic alone.

Rhetoric and composition embraced multimodal composition slowly. In 2002, Diana George famously advocated for multimodal composition, but her use of these types of assignments in her own classes wase not greeted with enthusiasm. George recounts conversations with colleagues in the year 2000 this way:

> When I told other faculty teaching sections of the same course that I would be asking my students to construct a visual argument, many were more than skeptical. They wanted to know if such a genre existed and, if it does, how can it be taught, and for what reason might I use it—except, perhaps, to keep students doing "interesting projects." Primarily, faculty asked how I could evaluate visual arguments since some students, according to these faculty, are "just more visual/more visually talented than others." (225)

In her 2004, CCCC chair's address, Kathleen Blake Yancey underscored the importance of multimodal composition, observing that text creation outside academia was both increasingly multimodal and ever changing. Yancey, in this instance, correctly foresaw composition would grow to include the many digital spaces we use today—many of which also require design literacy in addition to wordcraft. Riding the wave of Yancey's address, in 2005, NCTE published its "Position Statement on Multimodal Literacies" (Yancey 2014), equipping instructors with the institutional might many needed to justify incorporating multiple modes in our composition classrooms. Since that time, some of the most influential scholars in composition studies publish in multiple modes and teach digital literacies at all levels, from first-year composition to graduate seminars. Since the turn of the century, our field has generated highly respected journals, publishing high-quality scholarship, that are fully online. Indeed, today many graduate students in rhetoric and composition are learning about multimodal literacies as they prepare for careers teaching in the field using texts such as Victor Villanueva and Kristin Arola's (2011) *Cross-Talk* reader, which contains a section dedicated to digital work.

We—Daniel and Josh—learned to write, design, and teach amid this transition toward multimodal. We have participated in and observed changes in scholarship and pedagogy over the last twenty-five years. It has taken work and time—from all of us in the field—to reach the level of acceptance for multimodal composition we see today. This acceptance is reflected in our courses and the vision of multimodal composition. Josh remembers that as both an undergrad and graduate student, he was part of the first wave of students to take new media courses that set out to explore blogging, social media, and more—classes other professors openly disdained and questioned.

Today, multimodal composition requires both students and instructors to be flexible, as well as rhetorically and digitally savvy. Daniel Schafer and Paul Muhlhauser (2018) describe the way multimodal composition allows students to be builders and sharers of knowledge, which we view as a powerful use of rhetorical awareness, offering new opportunities for effective communication (62). We strive to create opportunities for students to compose multimodally often and for multiple audiences and purposes in order to build their skills. This sentiment is echoed by Marisa Sandoval Lamb, Jenna Sheffield, and Kristin Winet (2016), who—in talking about infographics—urge composition instructors this way:

We encourage our students to move beyond being analyzers of visuals to composers; we teach visual design concepts as being grounded in rhetoric; we encourage low-stakes experimentation and play with new technologies; and we suggest that this type of "play," when geared toward a particular audience, can help students inductively learn formal design principles in a way that transfers to the creation of a variety of professional and technical communications documents.

We also see the courses offered at McDaniel College reflected in Paula Rosinski's work, whose research, in 2016, suggests that

> to encourage the potential transfer of rhetorical strategies between students' digital self-sponsored and academic writing, instructors could ask students to:
>
> > • Examine their rhetorical knowledge/strategies in non-academic writing domains;
> > • Consider the rhetorical knowledge/strategies they use in their own self-sponsored digital writing; and
> > • Reflect on these strategies, examine their value and effectiveness, and consider applying them in academic writing.
>
> These suggestions are meant to invite students to bring the entirety of their writing lives and their writing experiences into the classroom for discussion and reflection; they encourage students to value, and imply that faculty also value, the writing that they do in internships, on-the-job, for themselves, and for their friends and family. (267)

We think that's what we've done in the courses we've designed. We've taken what is best about multimodal composition and built on it, with the understanding that it leads to a more relevant and engaged experience.

DISCONNECT BETWEEN EMPLOYERS AND STUDENTS

> *NACE's Job Outlook 2020 survey found that beyond a relevant major for the position and a strong GPA, problem-solving skills and the ability to work as part of a team are the attributes employers most want to see on resumes. Ninety-one percent of employer respondents are seeking signs of a candidate's problem-solving skills, and 86 percent want proof of a candidate's ability to work as part of a team*
>
> — National Association of Colleges and Employers' "The Top Attributes Employers Want to See on Resumes"

Employers consistently report that they privilege and desire the skills liberal arts students bring to the table. And yet students increasingly question the relevance of a college degree. Why?

Jessica McCaughey and Brian Fitzpatrick (2017) of George Washington University, in working with those who compose for a living, identified "gaps between perception (at all stages—student, new employee, established workplace writer), expectation, and experience" as well as "gaps between the modes and authenticity of writing in-classroom and in the workplace." Their study, in particular, identified gaps between workplace expectations and reality among recent graduates, in part by providing a database of workplace writing students could access. McCaughey and Fitzpatrick observe, and we agree, that "as students hear the voices of those creating real workplace writing, they are exposed to these authentic writing situations, and they begin to see the extremely complex and diverse audiences, purposes, and modes that will be expected of them." They further observe that each document in their database "offers teachers an opportunity to help students develop a flexibility in their thinking, as they work to inhabit various writing roles, each with its own complexities and constraints, and adapt to modes and genres across contexts."

Internship-based courses at McDaniel College seek to address common misconceptions students and graduates have about the working world by providing guidance amid experiences of composing in professional contexts. Much like McCaughey and Fitzpatrick, we seek to offer students opportunities to "try on" different writing identities by providing connections to local businesses and organizations that may be otherwise unattainable. As a result, in these courses, multimodal composition is taught with a tangible audience and purpose, with real consequences associated with writing and design decisions, resulting in exceptional learning opportunities and outcomes.

In the early days of multimodal composing, emphasis was placed on first learning to analyze texts others created. Then, students would move on to creating their own works, often mirroring existing scholarship enhanced by visuals (see Anderson 2014 for examples). In these early days, instructors often provided assignments with "real-world" contexts. Instructors also incorporated multimodal composition into research and reflection, particularly in first-year composition classrooms. Debra Journet, Tabetha Adkins, Chris Alexander, Patrick Corbett, and Ryan Trauman (2008) saw the value of multimodal composition as a means of reflection, observing that

> multi-modal reflection encourages experimentation and "play" which can encourage students to confront and conquer anxieties relating to voice, technological ability, or presentation of self. In turn, teachers can also benefit from reflecting upon a new learning experience in order to better understand apprehensive freshman entering college classrooms.

Scholars in our field have published on these practices. But as valuable as these resources are, they remain somewhat limiting because they isolate single projects. Following their experience in college, students are expected to take on communication practice that is continuous, ever changing, and within a particular institutional and historical context. We offer an alternate approach, one that extends the simulation from one single project to a semester-long, fully immersive learning opportunity.

One of the most important tasks in these classes is create an integrated portfolio-building experience that clearly signals relevance to employers. While it is true that output from many composition courses can provide writing samples for a prospective employer, there also is no denying that a successful grant application, or a robust social media account, clearly communicates value to those entrenched in business. These kinds of classes help students translate what they are learning while helping employers wrap their minds around the relevance of the liberal arts skills. Some might decry this approach as cheapening the public discourse and "professionalizing" the academy; we affirm it as enriching and empowering and politely suggest the naysayers may be reflecting a perspective that belies their privilege.

Immersive partnerships with local stakeholders forge connections between students and community otherwise difficult to engineer. In addition to serving as an example of the value of the liberal arts and multimodal composition, these courses ensure a sense of belonging and place for students and instructors alike.

In his work at the Othering & Belonging Institute at the University of California, Berkeley, john a. powell stresses the importance of belonging—that it is perhaps the crucial component to humans' well-being. In powell's (2016) view, the path to a truly antiracist society is through the recognition of connection and the rejection of practices, such as color blindness, that ultimately divide. Powell's work speaks to us because part of what we seek at our institution is community connection—breaking the barriers between the town and the college, finding ways to shape our shared space together for the better. In a 2016 talk, powell asks, "How do we organize structures to support and celebrate and facilitate our connectivity? Our belongingness?" He begins to answer his own question by continuing, "And in doing so that means those structures have to be open to being revised." In our own experience, this openness is all the more vital as student demographics continue to evolve (at McDaniel, we've moved from a majority white institution to a majority BIPOC student population).

166   SCHAFER AND AMBROSE

Returning to Yancey's 2004 CCCC address, "This moment—this moment *right* now—is like none other" (Yancey 2014). The moment we're in now—almost twenty years later—offers different opportunities, different challenges. But what remains the same is the importance of rhetorical awareness and the necessity—for all of us composing texts—to use all the tools at our disposal to create the most effective text for our audience.

The twin strategies of forging local connection through internship-based courses and teaching students skills associated with multimodal composition offer opportunities to work toward belonging. powell stresses the importance of structures being flexible, just as Yancey celebrates multimodal composition's ability to—by its very nature—adapt to fit the current moment. At the heart of these efforts is the necessity for students to compose and communicate in multiple modes. These are skills we must teach, but they must be taught in context—in such a way that their influence can be fully realized, and utilized, for the betterment of our communities and the lives of our students.

CLASSES

The small liberal arts institution of McDaniel College is about a thirty-minute drive northwest of Baltimore. The campus is situated atop a hill (indeed, people refer to the college as "The Hill") that gently slopes downward toward a quaint, but economically checkered, downtown. Household income is significantly lower in the city than it is in the surrounding suburbs, there is an acknowledged challenge with absentee landlords, and local shops struggled to survive after the 2008 recession and during the COVID-19 lockdown. Despite its relative proximity to major urban centers, the area borders rural areas and otherwise is marked by many of the challenges endemic to "rust-belt cities." In the midst of all of this, the college's proximity to Main Street would seem to afford logical engagement, yet in the first decade of the 2000s, the disconnect between the two communities was pronounced. Outright hostility was expressed toward the "elites on the hill" and suspicions reciprocated back regarding local crime, "hick" mindsets, and more.

In 2011, English Professor Dr. Julia Jasken partnered with a group of local nonprofit leaders to launch Writing for Nonprofits, designed to provide substantive writing and design opportunities to students and aid local partners in their efforts. After a decade of intentional work, the relationship between the college and the community has evolved into a productive, close-working one, reaping significant rewards and serving as a changemaker force, both on campus and in the community. In recent years, Dr. Jasken became the college's president and empowered Josh to spearhead efforts to transform the college's connection with the local community.

From membership in the Chamber of Commerce, to revamping student orientation to include time downtown for the entire incoming class, to continual presence at downtown meetings, to intentional patronage of local restaurants, these efforts have reaped significant dividends:

- increase in local opportunities listed in careers database (jobs, internships, volunteer engagement);
- remarkable change in goodwill and awareness between McDaniel and the local community;
- dramatic differences in first-year students' sense of the surrounding community (ascertained via surveys).

Instructors may ask, "How do I make the kinds of connections described here?" Creating these connections does take time and effort. Josh spent the last seven years attending community events, meeting with nonprofit and business leaders, and otherwise looking for ways for the college to serve the town. As part of this effort, Josh founded the first town/gown council with faculty, staff, and local stakeholders, held interest meetings for faculty looking to make connections along main street, and brokered many conversations.

Meanwhile, Daniel has worked to form substantive relationships with local nonprofits in order to provide rich partnership opportunities for students. Together, in spring 2016, Josh and Daniel walked the streets of our town, Westminster, Maryland, to visit as many local shops as possible. The purpose of these excursions was to ask local small-business owners if they would participate in the course Writing for Main Street, either by taking on a student intern or participating as a guest speaker. Not all business owners were enthusiastic, but some of the people we spoke to in 2016 have become valuable, consistent partners in our courses and with the college more broadly.

At present there are two dedicated internship-based courses at McDaniel College in which multimodal composition is a central component of the student experience. Other multimodal courses outside the English department incorporate work with partners to a lesser extent, while two new internship-based courses are in the development process. We describe these courses briefly below.

Dedicated Internship-Based Courses

- Writing for Nonprofits: The class evolves with the nonprofit landscape in Carroll County. Writing for Nonprofits played a leading role in transforming McDaniel College's connections with the local community. Each spring, for instance, the class is prominently featured at a yearly community-engagement breakfast, where students present on the work they've done with nonprofit partners.
- Writing for Main Street: This course, designed by the authors of this chapter, partners students with internships at local small businesses. The class is eligible to fulfill requirements for English, marketing, business, and entrepreneurship.

Additional Courses

- English 1101: Discovering Westminster: This first-year composition course serves as an introduction to the town of Westminster, which is new to many students just arriving at the college. As part of the course, the class created a tourism website, which eventually led to the creation of an official town tourism website.
- The Forest Online: In this year-long interdisciplinary course (English and environmental studies), students spend the three-week January term working with a conservation NGO in Peru. Fall term is spent preparing for the experience, while the spring term is spent publishing and sharing stories about the NGO's work.
- Professional Communication: This course takes on four nonprofit clients each semester for which students assess needs and create texts. Students learn how to create and implement a communications plan and use various design tools.
- Digital Publishing: Josh taught this course while serving as a visiting faculty member at McDaniel College's campus in Budapest, Hungary. Students launched an online arts and literature magazine.

Of course, experiential learning and internships are nothing new to college courses. What *is* new is how these experiences are privileged and woven into the class structure. We are seeing moves for more holistic, multimodal integration across campus in this direction, including classes in kinesiology, social work, and education. The community-engagement and internship experiences embedded into these courses go beyond simply short-term fieldwork and into varied assignments to help privilege real-world application of the liberal arts skills learned in the classroom.

All these courses provide opportunities for students to create multimodal texts of their own while serving local businesses and organizations. The model employed at McDaniel College addresses shortcomings observed at other institutions. For instance, in a 2016 a study conducted by Jenna Pack Sheffield at the University of New Haven, "Respondents indicated that practice in critically reading and analyzing electronic texts is more important than creating them. However, this was generally not because they did not value composing but because of time constraints and/or faculty expertise." In Sheffield's study, students learned by analyzing multimodal texts—as do students at McDaniel College. However, to succeed as multimodal composers, students must understand how to compose an effective text both in theory and in practice. The model we employ in these courses accomplishes both.

ASSIGNMENTS AND RECOMMENDATIONS

For the courses described in the previous section—and particularly those courses housed in the college's English Department—a combination of long-form and short writing assignments is required. Students read case studies, full-length books, and magazine articles, watch TED talks, and more.

The internship-based course, Writing for Nonprofits, requires

- a grant research report, for which students seek out and present funding opportunities for their partner organization;
- a collaborative project proposal, for which small groups design and pitch a service project. Students submit their project to be evaluated for funding;
- a fundraising event proposal designed to help partner organizations find new funding sources;
- a messaging pitch for which students assess their partner organization's outward-facing communications, make recommendations, and design several sample texts such as video, social media graphics, and print;
- a community luncheon at which students present their work at the end of the semester.

The internship-based course, Writing for Main Street, offers

- a memo-writing assignment;
- a ten-second branding video in which students synthesize the story of their business;
- an "idea pitch" to business partners, building a case for a new product or process;
- a community-wide social media experiment;
- a "create-your-own-business" assignment.

Special Guests

Each internship-based course at McDaniel College includes guest speakers. These guests are important components of the course for several reasons, which vary as widely as the speakers themselves.

Josh and Daniel leverage their connections to bring—either face to face or via video chat—nonprofit and business leaders into the classroom. For example, executives from numerous international nonprofits have joined Writing for the Nonprofits to discuss fundraising and storytelling. Students are often excited by the scale of the work conducted by these guests, and the perspective these guest speakers provide is also invaluable. When discussing fundraising, for example, one speaker—a child-sponsorship nonprofit executive—shared strategies that worked for them throughout a career raising over one hundred million dollars.

If an instructor doesn't have personal connections with the kind of guests they'd like to invite to class, there are other options such as drawing on a school's alumni network. In 2020, Josh invited the president of the San Diego Foundation to speak with students. This guest—a McDaniel College alumnus and member of the college's board of trustees—was in town for the college's annual board meeting and was willing to speak with students during the visit.

Interns also have the opportunity to interact with community leaders in ways not always available to college students. The year 2016 was the first-time offering Writing for Main Street—the course in which students intern with small businesses in the community. In addition to working with a small-business partner, students also participated in a research study that sought to understand the social media habits of people who lived in the area.

The social media experiment featured an incentivized shop-local campaign, tracking engagement across platforms. Conducted in partnership with a local technology nonprofit, the results of the experiment were shared with business leaders, the local Chamber of Commerce, and a town-council member. Local leaders were generous with their time and also visited class for a question-and-answer session. The local business leaders that attended the event shared their knowledge and perspective and, most important, listened to students. The most tangible result of this course was the eventual creation of a tourism website for the town ("Discover Westminster" 2020).

Guest speakers are essential to an internship-based course. Guests who work on a national or global scale give students a glimpse of what is possible in their careers, and students are often excited by the scale of the work conducted by these guests. The perspective these guest speakers provide is invaluable. Meanwhile, meetings with local leaders offer a tangible vision of what is happening around them, what is possible, and what it takes to create a positive change.

THE MCDANIEL COMMITMENT

These types of classes and their proven successes have directly helped lead to the implementation of the McDaniel Commitment, a new comprehensive, programmatic academic-value proposition set in motion by the provost and president, voted on by the faculty, used as a central part of the messaging of the school, and recognized by national trade publications. The McDaniel Commitment, of which Josh was a chief architect, is completed by all students at the college and is made up of four distinct components:

1. **My Place** (zero credits but required to graduate): As part of a summer-to-January term series of orientation experiences, students develop a sense of belonging, cultivate a growth mindset, and make connections with the community. Because My Place occurs over the course of several months, it is designed to grow with students over the course of their first-year experience. During the summer, students participate in a service-learning project, either planting trees on a college-owned farm property or facilitating activities with children at the local Boys & Girls Club (McDaniel College 2020). Early in the My Place process, students also visit local businesses, where they're given a free meal and have the opportunity to meet many of the people who serve as partners in the college's internship-based courses.

2. **My Design** (two-credit January term course): First-year students live on campus during this January term. In the two-credit course, students look for patterns in their experiences and interests in order to chart possible college and career paths, identify their strengths, and articulate the liberal arts. In addition to the academic side of the course, the college's career center coordinates numerous field trips and alumni engagement opportunities for students.

3. **My Experience** (required to graduate): Each student at McDaniel College must complete at least one hands-on experience that helps them reflect on and articulate the relationship between theory and practice, exhibit fluency in professional standards and practices, and make meaningful professional connections outside the college.

4. **My Career** (one-credit class): In their junior year, students make a concerted effort to plan for life after college. In this course, students learn how to articulate their unique value to employers; research careers, scholarships, and fellowships; network with alumni and other professionals; and polish job-search materials.

The McDaniel Commitment was informed by years of student surveys, research, faculty discussion, and pilots. In most cases, a small cohort of students participates in an experience during year one, a larger group participates in year two, and all students complete the commitment by year four.

The commitment's emphasis on experiential learning has been met with two successive years of the largest incoming classes in school history and is earning national recognition for its articulation of what a liberal arts degree guarantees. For instance, among other accolades, McDaniel College was listed as a top college by the Princeton Review in 2019 and 2020 for the first time ("Best 386 Colleges"; Edelman 2019).

"WHERE DO I START?"

This chapter describes many of the programs faculty and administrators can adopt if they wish to undertake an effort similar to the one currently in effect at McDaniel College. In addition, we recommend the following practical action items:

- Network with your career services office and faculty. Forge connections between those in your institution with expertise in communications, English, business, entrepreneurship, and more.

- Connect with your local Chamber of Commerce (or downtown partnership group) and ask what local businesses and organizations need. In doing this, your institution can seek to meet a need in the business and/or nonprofit community.

- Create syllabi and design courses with an emphasis on multimodal assignments. Instead of launching an entire program right away, consider starting with just one course that involves an integrated internship.

BELONGING AND A BALANCED EDUCATION

> *Structures are never neutral. They're always doing some work.*
> *So how do we organize structures to support and celebrate and*
> *facilitate our connectivity? Our belongingness?*
>
> — john a. powell

The opportunities described in this chapter offer much more than a résumé line—they serve as dynamic think tanks, designed to transform both the community and our students. Local engagement demonstrates relevance of multimodal composition, encourages design thinking, and fosters community participation. Relevant, local multimodal composition experience also equips students to consider how their skills, experiences, and interests can inform professional and personal decisions, encouraging students to engage in the kind of design thinking that can help them lead happier and more productive lives (Brooks 2010; Burnett and Evans 2016). Furthermore, in a world that is increasingly segmented, internship-based courses help students develop a sense of place, belonging, and identity (powell 2015; Turkle 2011).

The integrated internship model requires effort, cooperation, and support at the institution and departmental levels. The results, however, are worth the investment of time and energy required to develop such a program. There are many ways institutions and departments can build in similar real-world writing experiences that promote community engagement and leverage multimodal composition as a powerful skill for students and local stakeholders.

Internship-based courses that privilege multimodal composition at McDaniel College provide a template we firmly believe can work in a variety of contexts. When institutions amplify what is exciting about their city or town, find ways to connect students with existing local initiatives, and commit to providing substantive opportunities to create texts for a variety of audiences and purposes, students develop a suite of new skills and apply them to the world in innovative ways. It also adds great value for all stakeholders in creating the kind of communicative, empowered community that attracts growth, partnership, and investment.

Partnership with our neighbors is entering into a dynamic, collaborative laboratory that positions the academy as a genuine catalyst for economic and social change. While the model is relevant to all majors, we are proud to champion the ways English departments can lead the charge in this necessary work. Whether it is a first-year composition course or an upper-level new-media course (and everything in between), as we iterate and learn from each other, the relevance of reciprocal relationships—and the perspective and skills taught—are proven every step of the way.

REFERENCES

Anderson, Daniel. 2014. "The Low Bridge to High Benefits: Entry-Level Multimedia, Literacies, and Motivation." In *Multimodal Composition: A Critical Sourcebook*, by Claire Lutkewitte, 360–80. New York: Bedford/St. Martin's.

"Best 386 Colleges: 2021 Edition." 2020. *Princeton Review*. www.princetonreview.com/college-rankings/best-colleges.

Brooks, Katharine. 2010. *You Majored in What? Mapping Your Path from Chaos to Career*. New York: Viking.

Burnett, William, and David J. Evans. 2020. *Designing Your Life: How to Build a Well-Lived, Joyful Life*. New York: Alfred A. Knopf.

"Discover Westminster." 2020. Discover Westminster Maryland. discoverwestminstermd .com/.

Edelman, Gilad. 2019. "2019 College Guide and Rankings." *Washington Monthly*, August 25. washingtonmonthly.com/2019college-guide.

George, Diana. 2014. "From Analysis to Design: Visual Communication in the Teaching of Writing." *Multimodal Composition: a Critical Sourcebook*, by Claire Lutkewitte, pp. 211–232. New York: Bedford/St. Martin's.

Journet, Debra, Tabetha Adkins, Chris Alexander, Patrick Corbett, and Ryan Trauman. 2008. "Digital Mirrors: Multimodal Reflection in the Composition Classroom." *Computers and Composition Online*. Cconlinejournal.org/Digital_Mirrors/tabetha_adkins_home_01.htm.

Logan, Jerry, and Janel Curry. 2014. "A Liberal Arts Education: Global Trends and Challenges." *Christian Higher Education* 14: 1–2.

McCaughey, Jessica, and Brian Fitzpatrick. 2017. "Didn't Get the Memo: Refining Professional Writing Transfer Strategies through the Study of Authentic Writing Spaces." Paper presented at the Conference on College Composition and Communication, Portland, OR, March 16, 2017. https://s3.amazonaws.com/workplace-writing/archive/CCCC2017.pdf.

McDaniel College. 2020. *Become a Force of Nature*. April 16, 2020. https://www.youtube .com/watch?v=E70EImqxj2g.

New London Group. 2014. "From a Pedagogy of Multiliteracies: Designing Social Futures." *Multimodal Composition: a Critical Sourcebook*, by Claire Lutkewitte, pp. 193–210. New York: Bedford/St. Martin's.

Pallotta, Dan. 9 Mar. 2013. "The Way We Think about Charity Is Dead Wrong." TED video, 18: 08. www.ted.com/talks/dan_pallotta_the_way_we_think_about_charity_is_dead _wrong?language=en.

powell, john a. 2015. *Racing to Justice Transforming Our Conceptions of Self and Other to Build an Inclusive Society*. Bloomington: Indiana University Press.

powell, john a. 2016. "Putting Racism on the Table: John a. Powell on Structural Racism." Washington Regional Association of Grantmakers, May 31. Video, 1:08:39. www .washingtongrantmakers.org/resources/putting-racism-table-john-powell-structural -racism-video.

Rosinski, Paula. 2016. "Students' Perceptions of the Transfer of Rhetorical Knowledge between Digital Self-Sponsored Writing and Academic Writing: The Importance of Authentic Contexts and Reflection." In *Critical Transitions: Writing and the Question of Transfer*, edited by Chris M. Anson and Jessie L. Moore, 247–71. Fort Collins, CO: WAC Clearinghouse.

Sandoval Lamb, Marisa, Jenna Sheffield, and Kristin Winet. 2016. "Three Ways In: Teaching Visual Rhetoric through Web-Based Infographic Programs." *Kairos: A Journal of Rhetoric, Technology, and Pedagogy* 21 (1). https://praxis.technorhetoric.net/tiki-index .php?page=PraxisWiki%3A_%3AThree+Ways+In.

Schafer, Daniel, and Paul Muhlhauser. 2018. "The Ps of a POOC: Participatory, Professional Points of Presence in a Personal Open Online Course." In *Designing and Implementing Multimodal Curricula and Programs*, edited by J. C. Lee and Santosh Khadka, 55–70. New York: Routledge.

Sheffield, Jenna Pack. Fall 2015–Fall 2016. "Thinking Beyond Tools: Writing Program Administration and Digital Literacy." *Computers and Composition Online*. www .cconlinejournal.org/sheffield/index.html.

Turkle, Sherry. 2011. *Alone Together Why We Expect More from Technology and Less from Each Other*. New York: Basic Books.

Villanueva, Victor, and Kristin L. Arola. 2011. *Cross-Talk in Comp Theory: A Reader*. Urbana, IL: NCTE.

Yancey, Kathleen Blake. 2014. "Made Not Only in Words: Composition in a New Key." *Multimodal Composition: A Critical Sourcebook*, by Claire Lutkewitte, pp. 62–88. New York: Bedford/St. Martin's.

9

EMBEDDING MULTIMODAL WRITING ACROSS A UNIVERSITY AT THE INSTITUTIONAL, ADMINISTRATIVE, AND CURRICULAR LEVEL
The Undergraduate Professional Writing and Rhetoric Major as Agent of Change

Li Li, Michael Strickland, and Paula Rosinski

INTRODUCTION

The significance of multimodal writing has been increasingly studied and acknowledged in the field of rhetoric and composition (Alexander and Rhodes 2014; Lutkewitte 2014; Palmeri 2012; etc.). While the *what* (nature) and *why* (value) of multimodal compositions have been deeply explored, the *how* (practice) question can still appear daunting to writing program administrators and instructors because of the lack of institutional support, resources, and instructor expertise with multimodal writing and instruction (Khadka and Lee 2019). Even less scholarship has studied the synergy between institutional support and program development of multimodality. Situated in the context of our midsized liberal arts primarily undergraduate institution, this chapter offers a case study on *how* multimodal writing has been advocated for at the institutional and administrative levels, integrated across the university at a curricular level, practiced at the course level with innovative multimodal projects and interdisciplinary perspectives, and anchored in and nurtured across the campus by a small but dynamic Professional Writing and Rhetoric (PWR) major operating as an agent of change. We argue institutional initiatives bring a culture change on campus and prompt document revisions of goals and outcomes at the program level, which finally leads to effective course-level implementation of multimodal composition. As proposed by chapter 4 in this collection, we also believe rhetoric programs and instructors have the advantage and can be the initiators to professionalize multimodal composition across curricula.

https://doi.org/10.7330/9781646424184.c009

LITERATURE REVIEW

The call for multimodal pedagogy started with the New London Group's (1996) seminal work "A Pedagogy of Multiliteracy" in the 1990s and continued with the National Council of Teachers of English (NCTE)'s position statement on multimodal literacies in 2005. As defined by NCTE, multimodality is "the interplay of meaning-making systems (alphabetic, oral, visual, etc.) that teachers and students should strive to produce" (NCTE Executive Committee 2005, para. 1). In the past two decades, multimodal writing has been increasingly studied in the field of rhetoric and composition (Alexander and Rhodes 2014; Lutkewitte 2014; Palmeri 2012; etc.). Multiple studies of students' writing practices have found our students are writing in a great variety of composing technologies and platforms (Gold, Day, and Raw 2020; McClure 2011; Moore et al. 2015; Purcell, Buchanan, and Friedrich 2013; Wolff 2013; Yancey 2009; etc.). For example, Jessie L. Moore, Paula Rosinski, Tim Peeples, Stacey Pigg, Martine Courant Rife, Beth Brunk-Chavez, and Dundee Lackey (2015) found students are using a range of writing technologies and platforms for self-sponsored purposes and to participate in public life. Students have been pushing boundaries of traditional technologies and using them in flexible ways faculty haven't expected. Randall McClure (2011) explored the advancement of the Semantic Web. He argued that the Semantic Web would alter the research-writing relationship of our students and, in turn, our ways of teaching writing. In her study for the National Council of Teachers of English, Kathleen Blake Yancey (2009) claims that "we can and should respond to these new composings and new sites of composing with new energy and a new composing agenda" (7). Erin Frost (2011) also argues that student innovations in using technology should drive pedagogical practice.

However, studies also found discrepancies between our writing pedagogies and students' writing practices. Moore et al. (2015) reported that "students have much more fluid ways of using composing technologies than we typically acknowledge in our writing pedagogies" (2). Therefore, "we need new models of composing and new pedagogies for teaching writing." Daniel Anderson, Anthony Atkins, Cheryl Ball, Krista Homicz Millar, Cynthia Selfe, and Richard Selfe (2006) surveyed college composition instructors across US universities on how individual teachers and their program integrate multimodality into college writing classes. They found instructors were in great need of effective professional-development opportunities offered by their institutions. Yancey (2009) reported that we are facing three challenges and opportunities today: "developing new models of writing; designing a new curriculum supporting those models; and creating models for teaching that curriculum" (1).

Developing a new writing model and applying it to our curriculum is clearly a challenging and complex process. In their book *Bridging the Multimodal Gap: from Theory to Practice*, Santosh Khadka and J. C. Lee (2019) point out that although the value of multimodal writing has been persuasively argued, "the implementation of multimodal instruction has remained nominal in many writing programs" (4). Scholarship on the implementation of multimodality is still far from adequate. Nevertheless, a few scholars have illustrated the successes and difficulties in their attempts to develop and/or implement a multimodal initiative at their institution. Dànielle Nicole DeVoss, Ellen Cushman, and Jeffrey T. Grabill (2005) delineate the process of developing a multimedia writing course at Michigan State University. The authors articulate that the new curriculum's difficulties were related to the changes in the university's technology infrastructure. Patricia Ericsson, Leeann Downing Hunter, Tialitha Michelle Macklin, and Elizabeth Sue Edwards (2016) illustrate how multimodality was built into the first-year writing program of Washington State University. They suggest a multivocal and multi-theoretical approach to develop a multimodal composition program. Chanon Adsanatham, Phill Alexander, Kerrie Carsey, Abby Dubisar, Wioleta Fedeczko, Denise Landrum, and Cynthia Lewiecki-Wilson (2013) provide an account for the process of institutional changes initiated at Miami University to promote multimodal writing in the classroom. They emphasize the importance of building alliances across campus and teacher training in the development of multimodal writing in the first-year composition curriculum. Traci Fordham and Hillory Oakes (2013) also discuss how they introduced multimodal pedagogies into their curriculum at St. Lawrence University. They started with a Rhetoric and Communication Initiative in the university, with a focus on the promotion of rhetorical concepts in multimodal pedagogies.

All these studies show institutional support is essential for developing multimodal initiatives, programming, and curriculum on college campuses. However, few studies have looked at how the institution, programs, and course instructors have worked *together* to further multimedia writing on their campuses. In this chapter, we describe how we took a university-wide Quality Enhancement Plan as an opportunity to develop multimodal writing on our campus broadly and in our PWR major specifically, moving from changes in the major's internal and public-facing documents, to changes in the major's curriculum, and onto professionalizing faculty across the curriculum by offering development

EMBEDDING MULTIMODAL WRITING ACROSS A UNIVERSITY AT THE INSTITUTIONAL AND ADMINISTRATIVE LEVELS

Elon University, a medium-sized, liberal arts, primarily undergraduate institution prides itself on engaged teaching and learning. When it came time to select a topic for our Southern Association of Colleges and Schools (SACS) accreditation requirement for a Quality Enhancement Plan (QEP), our community overwhelmingly decided on writing after a year-long process of vetting several excellent ideas. We named our proposal the Writing Excellence Initiative (WEI), and a team of faculty, staff, and administrators across the university wrote a five-year plan designed to develop a culture of writing on our campus that would help improve the teaching and learning of writing for faculty, staff, and students in academic, disciplinary/professional, and personal contexts, while also committing the resources necessary to build and sustain such a culture. It was an ambitious proposal, designed to build ongoing processes, physical spaces, and budgets that would exist beyond the limited five-year focus of the required WEI. While we conducted a great deal of ongoing assessment of the WEI every year, as well as at its official conclusion two years ago, this section focuses on how, at the institutional and administrative levels, Elon laid the groundwork for growing multimodal writing instruction on our campus by building it into our institution's five-year WEI.

The overall goal of Elon's WEI, which was launched in fall 2013, was to create a robust and sustainable culture of writing on our campus that would enhance the teaching and learning of writing in academic and cocurricular spaces. To achieve this overall goal, the WEI guided Elon to (1) develop, and help students achieve, student learning outcomes defined by, for, and within specific writing contexts, including all academic departments, general education, and Student Life, and (2) build an infrastructure that would contribute to a sustained culture of writing on our campus by supporting students, faculty, and staff as they work towards achievement of the student learning outcomes. Four of the major ways the WEI encouraged multimodal writing at the institutional and administrative level were:

1. Integrating best practices in writing pedagogy into the initial WEI plan, thereby recognizing and encouraging multimodal writing

2. Tying the initiative to our university's mission, thereby securing adequate funding

3. Modeling a bottom-up process supplemented with multiple faculty-development opportunities, thereby inviting and encouraging faculty across the curriculum to research writing, including multimodal writing, in their disciplines

4. Raising the profile of and celebrated multimodal writing

Each of the above strategies provided us with opportunities, to different extents, to speak about, encourage, develop, and support multimodal writing at the institutional and administrative level.

A WEI That Integrated Best Practices in Writing Pedagogy into the Initial Plan, Thereby Recognizing and Encouraging Multimodal Writing

It was essential that several writing and rhetoric faculty members were on the committee that wrote the five-year plan; they ensured best practices in writing instruction were woven throughout each part of the plan and that writing was broadly conceived to include digital documents, visuals, movement, video, and sound. While the writing and rhetoric experts on the committee already understood all writing is already multimodal (Ball and Charlton 2016), they explicitly referred to writing in this way to expand discussions across campus about multimodal writing and to encourage faculty to research and identify multimodal writing that was timely and appropriate for their own disciplines. The WEI stated, "An additional best practice related to the definition of good writing is to expand the definition to encompass writing done in multimedia genres as well as in print or digital files that resemble print (Council, Council et al., Grabill et al., Porter, Porter, Sheridan, WPA, Yancey, *Miami, Minnesota, and Stanford*). Many university graduates will need to be able to communicate in twenty-first century modes" (Elon University, "Quality Enhancement Plan: Writing Excellence Initiative," n.d., 25). So the WEI took a multimodal view of writing, referencing the American Association of Colleges and University's "Written Communication VALUE Rubric" that acknowledges and allows for written, oral, and visual texts. Additionally, faculty-development workshops offered by the Writing Across the University program included at least one workshop every term focusing on integrating best practices in multimodal writing instruction into classes across the disciplines.

To encourage consistency across multisection courses in the general education program (which included a first-year composition and a core first-year seminar course), faculty teaching these classes worked on achieving the common writing outcome of "foster(ing) instruction that helps students communicate effectively using 21st century digital media and genres" (Elon University, "Quality Enhancement Plan: Writing Excellence Initiative," n.d. 36). Faculty and staff were asked to consider what students in their major/minor/cocurricular organizations should be able to *write*, *do* with writing, or *understand* about writing at the point of graduation so they could be successful writers in their personal, professional/disciplinary, and civic lives. This part of the process encouraged faculty and staff to survey their graduates about the genres they were writing in their postacademic lives, to reconsider whether they were teaching important newer or emerging multimodal genres in their professions and disciplines, and to deepen the already existing multimodal writing instruction in their existing curriculum. Indeed, several majors/minors/cocurricular groups developed multimodal writing outcomes. A full list of writing outcomes for majors, minors, and cocurricular experiences can be found at Elon's Center for Writing Excellence website (Elon University, "Aspirational Writing Outcomes," n.d., para. 5). The document-level changes of goals and outcomes resulted in real changes at curriculum and class level. End-of-year WEI reports also indicated students were now being asked to write more and a greater variety of multimodal texts, including video journalism articles; visual stories; a wide variety of video projects such as public-service announcements, explainer or instructional videos, or video advertisements; blogs; websites; infographics; multimedia reports; and podcasts.

A WEI Tied to Our University's Mission, Thereby Securing Adequate Funding

Because the WEI aligned with Elon's mission and strategic goals, the university committed to providing the extensive resources necessary for its success. A majority of these resources were dedicated to promoting work at the grassroots level, supporting the efforts of faculty and staff in departments and programs across campus to develop new writing outcomes and their corresponding learning experiences.

Early on, Elon created a Center for Writing Excellence by combining and expanding the existing Writing Center and the Writing Across the Curriculum program (which, with its expanded role, was reenvisioned as Writing Across the University). The Writing Center's existing small space on the first floor of our library was renovated and expanded into a much larger, visible, and technologically enhanced space designed to encourage and to make visible all kinds of writing—including multimodal writing—as well as the collaborative nature of writing. Large, heavy furniture was replaced with flexible seating and tables, ones that encouraged movement and collaboration. The floor plan of the physical space was altered to add two multimodal rooms, with new Apple computers and full Adobe Suite software, along with a third presentation practice room. The university contributed substantial resources to redesigning the CWE, which acts as the symbolic and physical representation of the WEI; its architecture, design, furniture, and resources make visible all kinds of collaborative, multimodal writing.

The university also contributed significant funding to the budgets of the Writing Center (WC) and Writing Across the University (WAU) for extended and enhanced programming. The Writing Center increased consultant training (including training in multimodal writing and consulting) and extended consulting sessions up to forty-five minutes. The WAU program began offering writing pedagogy grants and research into writing grants; expanded faculty-development workshops throughout the year (which provided lunch); and a new three-and-a-half-day Summer Writing Institute. An expanded Disciplinary Writing Consultant program was a joint venture between the WC and WAU. Each of these offerings also provided participating faculty and staff with stipends and WC consultants with a higher hourly wage. Much of this programming, to different extents, encourages discussions about multimodal writing on our campus and provides faculty with professional-development opportunities to learn about teaching multimodal writing.

A Bottom-Up WEI Process Supplemented with Multiple Faculty-Development Opportunities, Thereby Encouraging Faculty across the Curriculum to Integrate Writing, Including Multimodal Writing, into Their Disciplines

The WEI provided faculty with a model for developing writing outcomes important to their discipline/major, examining past curriculum and student writing strengths and weaknesses in regard to these outcomes, and then designing at least three "interventions" to help students more effectively achieve those writing outcomes. Every major and minor was required to engage in this process, and all faculty and teaching staff were expected to contribute to the teaching of writing across the curriculum and in cocurricular spaces. This process was bottom-up, encouraging faculty/staff to draw upon their own strengths and disciplinary/professional expertise to define their major's/minor's writing outcomes, while WAU offered professional-development opportunities and compensated participants for their time and efforts.

As mentioned above, many of these faculty-development opportunities were opportunities to teach and encourage faculty/staff to teach multimodal writing. For example, the Summer Writing Institute walks faculty through the entire process of designing effective writing assignments, including a component on multimodal writing. Faculty are encouraged and indeed have applied for both pedagogy and scholarship grants to develop/study the teaching of multimodal writing. Faculty-development workshops every year include some multimodal-writing teaching workshops, such as Evaluating Visuals and Multimedia; Teaching 2-Column Script Writing; Teaching Information Design and Data Visualization in Writing Assignments; Strategies for Designing Multimodal Writing Assignments; and Simple Videos that Encourage Students to use Feedback to Improve their Writing.

Raised the Profile of and Celebrated Multimodal Writing

In an effort to further raise the profile of and celebrate multimodal writing across the disciplines, the WC and WAU directors created a new Multimodal Writing Competition.

Up to a total of nine awards are given (for individual or group projects), based on the context in which the multimodal project was created so the contest would recognize multimodal writing happening *across* the disciplines and in cocurricular contexts such as on-campus employment and internships. The nine contexts include projects created in a class from the Schools of Arts/Sciences, Communications, Business, Education, Health Sciences, Law, and General Education; in Student Life/Campus Employment; and in an internship.

Example multimodal projects submitted to the competition include research posters, essays with graphs or images, websites, animations, podcasts, videos, infographics, or graphic novels. Students also submit a rhetorical reflection on their projects, and entries are judged based on how well they integrate the multiple modes to effectively reach a target audience in order to achieve a specific purpose (as articulated by the writers). For each of the nine categories, there's a first-place winner, a runner up, and one grand-prize winner. Now in its fourth year, the competition has grown and become more competitive; winners are invited to a celebration along with their faculty member/ work supervisor for whom they created the project; awards are presented and pictures are taken for our university's newspaper and social media accounts.

While the required five-year plan of the WEI was completed two years ago, the infrastructure and processes we created to build a culture of writing are still in place, as are the efforts to raise the profile of multimodal writing on our campus. In our final WEI report to SACS, we explicitly referenced the range of multimodal projects our students are now writing: "Reports from units across campus indicate that students across Elon have been engaged in writing a wide variety of context-specific forms and genres, include the following: advocacy projects, analysis papers, annotated bibliographies, executive briefs, grants, multimodal projects, videos, blogs, podcasts, op-eds, poems, proposals, reflective essays, reports, research papers, and teaching unit plans. The WEI sought to give students experience writing a range of texts for different audiences, and as this select list shows, this goal was achieved" (Elon University, "Writing Excellence Initiative: Final Report," n.d., 5–6). One of the ways some students gained more experience with multimodal writing was by taking classes in or majoring/minoring in PWR, a program that also took advantage of the opportunities provided by our institution's WEI to further embed multimodal ways of writing into its curriculum.

EMBEDDING MULTIMODAL WRITING ACROSS A UNIVERSITY AT THE CURRICULUM LEVEL

Overview of the PWR Program and History

The Professional Writing and Rhetoric (PWR) major is housed in the English Department in the College of Arts and Sciences of Elon University. Initially one of four concentrations (PWR, literature, creative writing, and teacher licensure) in the English Department, in 2018, PWR became a stand-alone bachelor of arts major in the English Department. In addition to a BA in PWR, students can also double major with any concentration in English or with other majors across the university. Surrounded by well-respected professional communications and business schools, the PWR program has developed its unique program identity, described as follows:

> The BA major in Professional Writing and Rhetoric (PWR) reflects a national trend in higher education, as well as a long tradition within the discipline of rhetoric, to more clearly connect the liberal arts to worlds beyond the walls of academia. . . . Though distinctly not a pre-professional program, PWR prepares students to be successful communicators in their daily lives and, primarily, workplace and or civic contexts. (Elon University, "Professional Writing & Rhetoric" n.d., para. 1 and 2)

In other words, the PWR program bridges the liberal arts and professional programs to benefit students in their professional, civic, and individual lives. With that purpose in mind, PWR's programmatic goals are:

184   LI, STRICKLAND, AND ROSINSKI

1. Students will learn, often through working hands-on with actual clients, how to analyze, reflect on, assess, and effectively act within complex contexts and rhetorical situations.

2. Students will learn to approach a wide variety of communication practices (e.g., visuals, multimedia, collaboration, and research) from the perspective of writing and rhetoric.

3. Students will study a wide variety of rhetorical techne (i.e., strategies) and, by working within and reflecting on actual rhetorical contexts, learn to adapt and develop rhetorical strategies and heuristics appropriate to specific situations.

4. Students will show an ability to integrate theoretical knowledge and professional practice.

5. Students will adopt a disciplinary identity as a writer and see themselves as experts (i.e., professional writers/rhetors) who bring rhetorical ways of seeing and acting in and on the world around them.

6. Students will understand that writing participates in socially constructing the worlds within which we live, work, play, etc. (Elon University, "Programmatic Assumptions" n.d., para. 2)

Historically, the PWR program was an early adopter of new writing technologies in our classrooms. In 2002, the PWR program created a dedicated computer writing lab, the Center for Undergraduate Publishing and Information Design (CUPID), to cater to the pedagogical needs of writing and publishing with new technologies. CUPID is "a physical computer lab and collaboration space dedicated to involving students in the design and production of Professional Writing and Rhetoric projects in desktop publishing and multimedia design" (Elon University, "CUPID," n.d., para. 1). Equipped with updated design software, CUPID allows for integration of images, audio, and video into the teaching of writing. With all PWR courses taught in this space, CUPID is more than a lab. It is "a community hub that affords students the opportunity to collaborate with other writers, to interact with internal and external clients, to improve computer-mediated writing skills, and to acquire experience completing complex writing tasks" (Elon University, "CUPID," n.d., para. 2). The affordance provided by CUPID enabled PWR faculty members to be among the first groups at the university to apply for WEI funding to embed multimodal writing further across its curriculum.

Integrating Multimodality at the Curriculum Level

Answering the call of the WEI's multimodal initiative, the PWR program applied for and received a Writing Pedagogy Grant meant to encourage best practices in writing pedagogy. We used this grant to study and then integrate more multimodal writing across the PWR curriculum. We made multiple curriculum-level "interventions," including revising the program outcomes, redesigning several courses and a major project in the methods course, and adopting a multifaceted program assessment, leading to the integration of multimedia writing and rhetorics across the entire curriculum.

Revising Program Outcomes to Include Multimedia Specific Outcomes

Revising our major's goals and outcomes was the essential first step before we could make changes in the curriculum. As a writing major, the PWR program already addressed multimodal writing in our program goals; but, to enable a systematic application of multimodality across the curriculum, we added the following multimodal student learning goals to the existing goals.

- Graduates should be able to demonstrate they can create/compose/ design multimedia projects that respond appropriately to specific rhetorical situations (audience, purpose, context, delivery).

- Graduates should be able to demonstrate they can rationalize and justify the choice of media for texts.

- Graduates should be able to demonstrate they can apply their understanding of PWR to lead effectively in personal, social, civic, and professional contexts when appropriate (examined through the lens of multimedia).

The added multimedia outcomes emphasize the programmatic focus of rhetorics (e.g., audience, purpose, context, and medium) rather than technical skills. As advocated by Fordham and Oaks (2013), approaching multimodal writing from a rhetorical perspective allows us to "move beyond the 'transmission' and 'acquisition' of skills or literacies and toward the fostering of a critical and rhetorical approach to multimodal pedagogies" (316). Tiffany Bourelle also argues in chapter 4 of this collection that rhetoric is essential to multimodal composition and rhetorical training should be woven into the teaching of multimodal composition. Further, this approach reinforces the program's liberal arts identity and differentiates it from other professional-school programs that offer multimedia communication courses; the central role of multimodal skill sets in the PWR major is to professionalize such practices not as discrete elements of specific courses but as fully integrated skills within the entire program, building towards a professional ePortfolio.

186   LI, STRICKLAND, AND ROSINSKI

Redesigning the Curriculum with Multimedia-Focused Courses

Revising the program goals and outcomes prompted the redesign of specific courses to achieve the multimedia objectives. In order to provide students with the technical skills needed to practice multimodal writing, we created a new required course in the major titled Professional Writing and Technology Studio. In this course, students learn about how professionals use various types of software in real-world contexts, and they work with different writing technologies, especially learning new technologies, critiquing the affordances and limitations of those technologies, and practicing those technologies by designing multiple multimodal projects. The professional writing and designing skills acquired in this course provide a foundation for students to produce multimodal projects in other PWR courses.

In addition to adding the new course, we redesigned two existing multimodal-focused courses already in the curriculum (Multimedia and Visual Rhetorics I and Multimedia and Visual Rhetorics II), recognizing that multimodal and visual rhetoric are closely related and that more scaffolding on these topics could be helpful. The first class now provides an introduction to the theories and practices of multimodal and visual rhetorics, while the second class builds on the knowledge students gain in the previous class while also giving students the opportunity to create a large-scale multimodal project for real audiences. Taken as a whole, these three multimodal-focused courses—created or redesigned as part of the PWR faculty members' work for our institution's WEI—provide students with scaffolded opportunities to gain both depth and breadth in multimodal writing.

Assessing Student Progress Using Multifaceted Program Assessment

Our revisions of program goals and outcomes also guided our program assessment. Besides the course-based direct assessment, we use three other assessment strategies to measure students' learning and systematic practices of multimedia writing pedagogy in the program: an external assessment of senior ePortfolios, a capstone project showcase, and a collaborative and evaluative exit dinner.

Instead of individual student-exit interviews typically conducted in our department, we adopted **exit dinners** as part of a senior assessment strategy. At the exit dinner, PWR faculty and students share a meal together while students collaboratively discuss topics that address their understanding of rhetoric and their professional identities. Students prepare ahead of time (with example questions) to ensure they speak to issues otherwise asked in the interviews. These collaborative discussions are much preferred by faculty and students over the individual exit interviews, as they are collaborative, supportive environments in which students can showcase their knowledge. Given our addition of multimodal learning outcomes to the PWR curriculum, the exit dinners now always include discussions about multimodal writing.

The ePortfolio serves as a graduate requirement for PWR majors, as well as an external program assessment tool and an essential facet of professionalizing specific practices and skill sets, such as multimodal writing. PWR-major students submit an ePortfolio to an external reviewer in the fall semester of their senior year. The ePortfolio includes an introductory letter; a résumé; an organizational plan with sections that represent the student's identity as a professional writer; eight to fifteen artifacts; and a contextual reflection for each artifact. Students are encouraged to develop and revise professional documents in several of our courses and in PWR faculty-mentored internships and undergraduate research projects. In their senior year, the PWR program coordinator works closely with seniors to review their drafts and provide feedback before they are submitted to an external reviewer.

As part of their WEI work, the PWR faculty refined the ePortfolio process to remind students to highlight and reflect on the multimodal writing knowledge they gained from PWR courses. After adjusting this process, almost all PWR seniors now choose to include some multimodal writing artifacts in their ePortfolios and also reflect critically on their multimodal rhetorical choices, especially the ways these artifacts serve to professionalize their identities as seniors about to enter the job market. Several years after revising the ePortfolio process, a majority of PWR seniors also identify and articulate multimodality as part of their professional identity.

Since the ePortfolios collect student work from various PWR courses, internships, and client projects, their assessment allows us to examine multimodal learning outcomes across the curriculum. The external reviewer (a reputable scholar in the field who works at another university) examines students' ePortfolios according to how well their artifacts and rhetorical reflections show they achieved the PWR program learning outcomes. The PWR faculty select established scholars in the field who are working or have worked in institutions similar to our program as our potential external reviewers, and they are compensated based on the number of student ePortfolios in that given year. The external reviewer provides us with an outside perspective that helps us assess our program's strengths and weaknesses and guides us to revise our curriculum accordingly. Passages from our recent external reviewer's reports show we successfully met our program learning goals, especially the multimedia learning outcomes:

> Your program is particularly strong at teaching a theoretical core in rhetoric studies while encouraging students to embrace multimedia and multimodal genres.

> All portfolios demonstrated reflective practice across a range of media including both "old" and "new" media, reflecting the program's commitment to diverse semiotic modes. I was impressed at the diversity of genres represented, including short videos, infographics, blog posts, social media, brochures, logos, mailers, and many others.

> The high production-quality of most student projects was also impressive; students are clearly learning a range of digital, design, and production tools, but their reflections demonstrate how they approach those technical tools with a foundation in rhetorical theory.

One critical goal of the ePortfolio is to prepare the students for job interviews. Students post their portfolios online, and in applications point their potential employers to these portfolios and refer to specific artifacts in their application letters, inviting employers to look them over, read the contextual narratives, and ask questions about the projects.

We credit the opportunity provided to us by our university's WEI to focus on enhancing the teaching and learning of multimodal writing across our curriculum with our most recent external evaluators' recognition of our students' strengths in this kind of writing.

The Capstone Showcase is another senior assessment the PWR program uses to examine student learning outcomes. Students develop a research-based project in the senior seminar course in the spring semester of their senior year and present it in a poster-presentation style senior showcase at a university-wide student research conference held in late April. The deliverables of the Capstone Showcase include a handout for the showcase audience that summarizes the project; an in-depth personal statement declaring the student's definition and understanding of professional writing and rhetoric; a poster highlighting the research and rhetorical strategies the student used; and project deliverables that range from more traditional alphabetic texts such as reports and surveys to multimodal genres such as webpages, visual designs, social media campaigns, podcasts, and video productions.

As a multimodal project, the senior Capstone Showcase prompts students to integrate, synthesize, and reflect on their learning of multimodal writing. Completing this comprehensive multimedia project, students showcase creativity, their multimedia skills and rhetorical knowledge, and their awareness of audiences and writing's power to shape and represent identities. According to our alumni survey, both the ePortfolio and the Capstone Showcase are significant for student's professional development, as they identify these projects as having lasting impact on their multimodal writing abilities and their successes on the job market. In the following section, we share the redesign of a successful large-scale multimedia project in one of our courses, a revision guided again by the WEI initiative and prompted by our outcome revisions.

INTEGRATING MULTIMODAL WRITING AT THE CLASS LEVEL

In the hierarchical design of the PWR major, the methods course (Writing as Inquiry) was originally intended to be primarily a preparation for the research required for the culminating senior seminar project, always taught in the spring of the senior year. Typically, students took Writing as Inquiry in the preceding fall term. The final project for the course was an in-depth proposal for a potential senior seminar project and focused on timeline management, stakeholder relations, and applicable research methodologies.

In recent years however, we moved more towards using the course as an earlier introduction to research, encouraging students to take on independent, guided research projects earlier in their academic career and to apply appropriate research methods in other course work before the senior year. To facilitate this, we changed the course number to a lower level and via advising tried to move the course demographic from mostly first-semester seniors to juniors. All aspects of the course and its place within the PWR curriculum are now designed to fit closely with both the goals of the PWR major and the WEI emphasis on multimodal practices and a scaffolded approach to preparing students. Spurred on by our institution's WEI, we strengthened the multimodal writing component of the Highway 64 project in this methods course. The project specifically addresses the multimedia goal to "create/compose/design multimedia projects that respond appropriately to specific rhetorical situations (audience, purpose, context, delivery)."

The Highway 64 project itself, the centerpiece of the course, is defined as "travel and food writing through a rhetorical lens." In the syllabus for the course we describe it thus:

> The framework of the course will be built around the theme of travel and food writing, and we will analyze travel writing as a rhetorical field and put this into practice with both personal projects and a large semester-long group multimodal project of publishable quality. The focal subject of this fieldwork will be North Carolina's historic Highway 64, which runs

the entire width of the state from the mountains of the TN border to the Atlantic Ocean.

As this description shows, the Highway 64 project was always multimodal. Students practiced researching food and travel through interviews, surveys, and case studies. They wrote microethnographies and composed image-driven restaurant reviews, traditional travelogues, and cultural profiles. Much of this content included visual elements, from basic charts, figures, and maps to photos and videos.

The new multimodal component added to this course, as a result of faculty members' work on our institution's WEI, is a collaboration with students in the Environmental Studies Senior Seminar. The goal of this collaboration is for the Highway 64 project to transition into a long-term collaboration between students in the two majors: Environmental Studies and Professional Writing and Rhetoric. As this collaboration develops, we intend for the project to become a large-scale multimodal project and digital repository; we expect it to become institutionalized, with students from both PWR and environmental classes becoming editors of website content, earning internship credit and eventually stipends.

The Highway 64 website will then become more of a destination, rather than serving as only an archival site for collective work, as it currently does. A primary goal is be for the PWR students to run the website from within another course, CUPID Studio, a year-round PWR workshop on multimedia projects, working with the Writing as Inquiry class for ongoing cultural content and the environmental students for updated information on climate-resilience data and activities in North Carolina. This more generative, ongoing, and collaborative version of the Highway 64 project will provide PWR students experience with much more complex, ongoing, and collaborative multimodal writing, as well as more experience working within the community, both of which are now specific goals of the PWR major.

Conclusion

Adsanatham et al. (2013) state that the essential components to sustain a program-wide focus on multimodal pedagogy include "preparing and supporting instructors, developing curriculum, securing and maintaining materials and administrative resources, and conducting program-wide assessment" (302). Our multilevel approach to multimodal pedagogy has created a successful balance of these elements. Our institution's QEP for SACS accreditation was a major motivating force for advocating for multimodal writing at the institutional and administrative levels. The WEI raised discussions about multimodal writing across campus, helping us integrate it across the university and disciplines at a curricular level; it encouraged us to revise our program goals, which led to curriculum change and an innovative multimodal project in the PWR program; and as a whole, multimodal writing is now anchored in, nurtured, and professionalized across the campus by a small but dynamic PWR major.

In addition, the key to the PWR program's growth and development has been our successful alignment with the WEI and the institutional resources and support that come with such a university-wide, dynamic enterprise. By building on existing strengths and alliances, and embedding strategic facets of the WEI within our curriculum, PWR has been able to successfully navigate the often stormy waters of today's academic reformations. Using the momentum of the WEI helped us recalibrate significant redesign of our curricular plans, and the clear alignment of our major with WEI institutional initiatives across all schools of the university helped move our profile from a small specialized major to a recognized agent of change across the university landscape.

Our future plans to strengthen the multimodal program include but are not limited to hiring faculty members with multimodal writing expertise, maintaining and expanding the Highway 64 project, developing the CUPID Studio course so it connects with the Highway 64 project, and launching an online publication that highlights the best student multimodal work. We will use our successes in PWR to continue to work for an even richer university-wide practice of professionalizing and supporting multimodal pedagogy.

REFERENCES

Adsanatham, Chanon, Phill Alexander, Kerrie Carsey, Abby Dubisar, Wioleta Fedeczko, Denise Landrum, and Cynthia Lewiecki-Wilson. 2013. "Going Multimodal: Programmatic, Curricular and Classroom Change." In *Multimodal Literacies and Emerging Genres*, edited by Tracey Bowen and Carl Whithaus, 282–312. Pittsburgh: University of Pittsburgh Press.

Alexander, Jonathan, and Jacqueline Rhodes. 2014. *On Multimodality: New Media in Composition Studies*. Studies in Writing and Rhetoric. Urbana, IL: NCTE.

The American Association of Colleges and Universities. n.d. "Written Communication VALUE Rubric." Accessed January 8, 2023. https://www.aacu.org/initiatives/value-initiative/value-rubrics/value-rubrics-written-communication.

Anderson, Daniel, Anthony Atkins, Cheryl Ball, Krista Homicz Millar, Cynthia Selfe, and Richard Selfe. 2006. "Integrating Multimodality into Composition Curricula: Survey Methodology and Results from a CCCC Research Grant." *Composition Studies* 34 (2): 59–84.

Ball, Cheryl, and Colin Charlton. 2016. "All Writing Is Multimodal." In *Naming What We Know: Threshold Concepts of Writing Studies*, edited by Linda Adler-Kassner and Elizabeth Wardle, 42. Logan: Utah State University Press.

DeVoss, Dànielle Nicole, Ellen Cushman, and Jeffrey T. Grabill. 2005. "Infrastructure and Composing: The When of New-Media Writing." *College Composition and Communication* 57 (1): 14–44.

Elon University. n.d. "Aspirational Writing Outcomes, by Major and Department." Accessed January 7, 2021. https://www.elon.edu/u/academics/writing-excellence/writing-excellence-initiative/accomplishments/.

Elon University. n.d. "CUPID." Professional Writing and Rhetoric. Accessed January 4, 2021. https://www.elon.edu/u/academics/arts-and-sciences/english/professional-writing-rhetoric/experiences/cupid/.

Elon University. n.d. "Professional Writing and Rhetoric." Accessed January 4, 2021. http://www.elon.edu/e-web/academics/elon_college/english/pwr/.

Elon University. n.d. "Programmatic Assumptions." Accessed January 4, 2021. https://www.elon.edu/u/academics/arts-and-sciences/english/professional-writing-rhetoric/about/programmatic-assumptions-goals/.

Elon University. n.d. "Quality Enhancement Plan: Writing Excellence Initiative." Accessed January 4, 2021. https://www.elon.edu/u/academics/writing-excellence/writing-excellence-initiative/quality-enhancement-plan/.

Elon University. n.d. "Writing Excellence Initiative: Final Report." Accessed January 4, 2021. https://eloncdn.blob.core.windows.net/eu3/sites/921/2019/10/QEP-Final-Report_Writing-Excellence-Initiative_Elon-U_v2.pdf.

Ericsson, Patricia, Leeann Downing Hunter, Tialitha Michelle Macklin, and Elizabeth Sue Edwards. 2016. "Composition at Washington State University: Building a Multimodal Bricolage." *Composition Forum* 33. https://compositionforum.com/issue/33/wsu.php.

Fordham, Traci, and Hillory Oakes. 2013. "Rhetoric across Modes, Rhetoric across Campus: Faculty and Students Building a Multimodal Curriculum." In *Multimodal Literacies and Emerging Genres*, edited by Tracey Bowen, and Carl Whithaus, 313–36. Pittsburgh: University of Pittsburgh Press.

Frost, Erin A. 2011. "Why Teachers Must Learn: Student Innovation As a Driving Factor in the Future of the Web." *Computers and Composition* 28 (4): 269–75. https://doi.org/10.1016/j.compcom.2011.10.002.

Gold, David, Jathon Day, and Adrienne E. Raw. 2020. "Who's Afraid of Facebook? A Survey of Students' Online Writing Practices." *College Composition and Communication* 72 (1): 4–30.

Khadka, Santosh, and J. C. Lee, eds. 2019. *Bridging the Multimodal Gap: From Theory to Practice*. Logan: Utah State University Press.

Lutkewitte, Claire. 2014. *Multimodal Composition: A Critical Sourcebook*. Series in Rhetoric and Composition. Boston: Bedford/St Martin's.

McClure, Randall. 2011. "Writing Research Writing: The Semantic Web and the Future of the Research Project." *Computers and Composition* 28 (4): 313–26.

Moore, Jessie L., Paula Rosinski, Tim Peeples, Stacey Pigg, Martine Courant Rife, Beth Brunk-Chavez, Dundee Lackey, Suzanne Kesler Rumsey, Robyn Tasaka, Paul Curran, Jeffrey and T. Grabill. 2016. "Revisualizing Composition: How First-Year Writers Use Composing Technologies." *Computers and Composition* 39: 1–13. https://doi.org/10.1016/j.compcom.2015.11.001.

New London Group. 1996. "A Pedagogy of Multiliteracies: Designing Social Futures." *Harvard Educational Review* 66 (1): 60–93. www.pwrfaculty.net/summer-seminar/files/2011/12/new-london-multiliteracies.pdf.

NCTE Executive Committee, Multimodal Literacies Issue Management Team. 2005. "Position Statements." Accessed January 8, 2023. https://ncte.org/statement/multimodalliteracies/.

Palmeri, Jason. 2012. *Remixing Composition: A History of Multimodal Writing Pedagogy.* Studies in Writing and Rhetoric. Carbondale: Southern Illinois University Press.

Purcell, Kristen, Judy Buchanan, and Linda Friedrich. 2013. "The Impact of Digital Tools on Student Writing and How Writing Is Taught in Schools." Pew Research Center. http://www.pewinternet.org/2013/07/16/the-impact.

Wolff, William I. 2013. "Interactivity and the Invisible: What Counts as Writing in the Age of Web 2.0." *Computers and Composition* 30 (3): 211–25. https://doi.org/10.1016/j.compcom.2013.06.001.

Yancey, Kathleen Blake. 2009. "Writing in the 21st Century: A Report from the National Council of Teachers of English." Urbana, IL: NCTE. https://cdn.ncte.org/nctefiles/press/yancey_final.pdf.

PART III

Academic Leadership

This section strives to respond to the unusual gap between theoretical sophistication and implementation paucity of multimodal composing in the field of writing studies by bringing together academic leaders, scholars and instructors from diverse institutions who have, either institutionally or individually, designed and launched successful academic programs around multimodal composition. These leaders discuss the theoretical and logistical questions considered while designing and implementing those initiatives. Taken together, chapters in this section explore these questions: What departmental and institutional challenges to and opportunities for studying and teaching multimodal composition exist in today's higher education settings? How can those challenges be turned into opportunities? What challenges, struggles, and successes have been identified to integrate multimodality in first-year composition and other upper-division writing or writing-intensive courses across the curriculum or disciplines? How can writing faculty better integrate multimodality in their curricula?

In short, chapters in this section explore strategies for successful responsiveness to the multifaceted needs of developing a program that focuses on multimodal writing; discuss the theoretical, practical, and personal aspects of developing a digital-literacy curriculum; highlight how program culture informs multimodal practices in a doctoral-level course development on digital rhetoric; and stress the challenges to and rationale for the change while taking up multimodal writing and communication as the major focus in a program development.

https://doi.org/10.7330/9781646424184.p003

10

THE ART OF RESPONSIVENESS
The Ongoing Development of a Master of Arts in Composition, Rhetoric, and Digital Media (CRDM)

Claire Lutkewitte

INTRODUCTION: A PROGRAM IN CONTEXT

Using Nova Southeastern University's master of arts degree in composition, rhetoric, and digital media (CRDM) as an example, this chapter explores strategies for ensuring successful responsiveness to the multifaceted needs of developing a program that focuses on multimodal writing and preparing those who want to work in a variety of writing-related fields, including those who want to write or teach writing professionally. Time and again, this unique program, its faculty, and administrators have responded to the changing needs of (1) its students, (2) its faculty, (3) its institution, and (4) the workforce. In looking at these four needs, this chapter argues that ongoing reflection and the willingness of a program to adapt quickly by (1) offering experiential learning opportunities that extend beyond classrooms, (2) providing faculty development and support, and (3) facilitating collaboration across disciplines can aid in the success of a program. In what follows are examples of how one MA program built around multimodal composition reflected (and still reflects) and acted (and still acts) in order to ensure the success of the program and its stakeholders. Although the chapter uses CRDM as a specific example, one situated in a particular context, the strategies are applicable to other programs and do offer a means for reflecting on the discipline and what happens when we all (faculty, administrators, disciplinary leaders, and so forth) make multimodal composition the center of what we do.

In 2015, after months of researching, writing, and discussing, Nova Southeastern University's Department of Writing and Communication curriculum committee submitted a proposal to the dean of the College of Arts, Humanities, and Social Sciences outlining plans to revamp its

https://doi.org/10.7330/9781646424184.c010

master's program in writing to focus on multimodal composition, a move that responded to the needs of students, faculty members, the institution, and the workforce. The department described the new program in the following way:

> The Master of Arts in Composition, Rhetoric, and Digital Media provides students with a foundation for conducting and presenting research, applying rhetorical theories, teaching writing, and producing digital media. Through specialized coursework and experiential learning in the history and theory of composition, rhetoric, and production students develop expertise researching and practicing writing in a variety of professional genres. The CRDM program prepares students for careers in writing, publishing, and teaching, and doctoral study in Composition and Rhetoric and related disciplines. (Nova Southeastern University 2023)

After some negotiations with the dean and college curriculum committee, the plan was approved, and the MA in composition, rhetoric, and digital media was born. Excited, faculty immediately went to work developing coursework, recruiting new students, and creating workshops and initiatives with the goal of providing students with experiential learning opportunities that could help them develop their multimodal writing skills.

For the past five years, the program has grown. It has hired new faculty, added more classes, revised others, created assistantships, and collaborated with colleagues in other disciplines to provide students with diverse experiences relevant to their needs and interests. During this time, faculty learned important lessons, including the lesson of responsiveness: the ability to adapt to the changing needs and interests of stakeholders and to do so efficiently.

NSU is a diverse, private, not-for-profit research university. Designated a Hispanic-serving institution (HSI), students from all over the world attend classes online or in person on its many campuses. The main campus is located in South Florida and houses the CRDM program. The program is led by ten faculty members who all have PhDs in composition and rhetoric and who are involved in many other programs on campus, including NSU's COMP fellows program facilitated by NSU's Write from the Start Writing and Communication Center. In addition, classes are also taught by faculty who have PhDs in other fields, such as communication.

Initially, this program was housed in the Department of Writing and Communication. In the fall of 2019, NSU's College of Arts, Humanities, and Social Sciences combined several departments, including this department, into one School of Communication, Media, and the Arts.

The Art of Responsiveness   199

Faculty in this school taught in a variety other disciplines besides writing and communication, including dance, theater, music, and graphic design. With the institution of the new school came opportunities for faculty to share resources and expertise to make the CRDM program even more versatile, attracting, again, a diverse student population.

However, a year later, during the writing of this chapter, NSU was in the midst of yet another restructuring. During this restructuring, the College of Arts, Humanities, and Social Sciences merged with the College of Natural Sciences and Oceanography to create a new college, the Halmos College of Arts and Sciences and the Guy Harvey Oceanographic Research Center. The School of Communication, Media, and the Arts became the Department of Communication, Media, and the Arts. As with previous restructurings, CRDM responded to the changes in university structure in ways that took into consideration its many stakeholders. Indeed, it was through the multiple restructurings that faculty honed their responsive skills to ensure the program would continue to thrive.

Students who enroll in the CRDM program include, among others, local teachers, students who majored in communication and English at NSU as undergrads, writers, journalists, students who want to go on to PhD programs, and students who are interested in writing center studies. Throughout the program, students are mentored by faculty and can participate in graduate assistantship opportunities, from working in the writing center to working as a research assistant. They partake in workshops, attend and present at conferences, and serve as representatives in clubs and organizations on campus. During the program, students enroll in a variety of courses too, such as Teaching of Writing, Research Methods, Advanced Writing with Technologies, Theories of Composition, Social Media Writing and Strategy, and Transmedia Theory and Production. As of now, the degree culminates with a thesis project, but in the future, it will give students more options, including the choice of a thesis project, an internship and portfolio, or a culminating exam. Each of these three options will require that students work closely with a faculty committee to ensure their success.

A FOCUS ON MULTIMODAL COMPOSITION

Developing a program that highlights diverse meaning-making ways has made it clear to the CRDM faculty that being responsive is a necessity for the program's success. Being responsive, however, is not new to academia, which is not lost on the CRDM faculty. Nevertheless, the field of composition and rhetoric, more so than other disciplines, has proven well suited to responding to the needs and interests of others creatively, particularly because of the kinds of social practices we study and teach through multimodal composition. As Bruce Horner (2020) writes, "Modality is more appropriately, usefully understood as social practice" (21). Indeed, the "art" of responsiveness means having the wherewithal to recognize innovative ways of not just problem solving but also of making sure the needs and interests of stakeholders are addressed in creative and productive ways that benefit all. Hence, the program's, and thus faculty's, responsiveness takes into account the multifaceted, situated, and changing nature of writing. The art of responsiveness in the context of CRDM means being able to negotiate, listen, and adapt efficiently to the needs and interests of students, faculty, an institution, and the workforce. Each of these four needs requires specific kinds of reflection, questioning, and action.

In particular, CRDM's responsiveness mirrors the same kinds of responsiveness writers of multimodal composition engage in, ones nuanced, situated, and rhetorical. To be successful, multimodal composition must account for the needs of its audiences, as multimodal composition is about social action, about how humans interact with materials and people in a particular time, place, and space in order to communicate effectively. CRDM's courses show students multimodality is more about the practices of composing with multiple modes than it is about trying to identify specific, individual characteristics of modes. Modes themselves are multimodal; they are not static, as they evolve because of cultural, historical, economic, and social influences. The learning students do includes building a rhetorical awareness of the production practices valued or devalued by particular societies, thus empowering them to push back on inequalities and question the status quo through their own explorations of multimodal texts.

In CRDM, students take a core course called Studies in Multimodality and Digital Media. Even though this core course's title is the only one that includes the word *multimodal*, all courses in the program involve multimodal composition, from learning about theories to the practicing of multimodal composition. In fact, no matter whether they are working on smaller activities in the Teaching of Writing course or semester-long projects in the Research Methods course, students engage in discussions and practices of multimodal composition in each of the courses. Every text we create is multimodal and CRDM faculty have all been trained in various ways to facilitate courses that support and encourage an awareness of multimodal composing practices. By pointing this out, faculty do not mean to imply a dichotomy between multimodal composition and other compositions. Rather, the courses draw particular attention to the fact that when we write, we always use multiple modes. And they make clear that multimodal composition is not just relegated to composing using digital technologies, a point Shauna Chung, Stephen Quigley, and Tia Dumas also make in chapter 11 of this book. This focus helps students be more aware of the rhetorical, cultural, social, political, and material choices they make when using modes. In this way, students can see, for example, that multimodal composition is communication that uses "multiple modes that work purposely to create meaning" (Lutkewitte 2014, 2), as well as an assemblage; composers borrow from texts created in the past. In *Assembling Composition*, Kathleen Blake Yancey and Stephen J. McElroy (2017) explain, "Borrowing is multimodal in character as well: composers borrow words and passages; they borrow fonts, color palettes, images, and patterns. There are no texts that are absolutely original (though their assemblage may be), and naming texts as assemblages acknowledges that" (10). Throughout the program, students engage in such theories of multimodality and discuss their implications for borrowing from texts.

Moreover, the experiences of students help bridge the gap Santosh Khadka and J. C. Lee (2018) speak of in *Bridging the Multimodal Gap: From Theory to Practice.* This is most evident in the Teaching of Writing course, a course that helps merge "students' preferred literary practices and actual instruction in writing classrooms" (3). In this course, students see multimodal composing requires that "we interrogate and negotiate different tools, technologies, languages, and interfaces and that we also use them, experiment with them, make with them, and reimagine them" (Wysocki et al. 2018, 21). As students learn to teach their own composition classes, they must critically analyze pedagogical strategies, taking into consideration how we use materials to compose with modes. In their assignments and activities, they are asked to demonstrate their own strategies for teaching, and while doing so, they experiment with modes and technologies. They make with them, and they reimagine them.

Faculty are very aware of (and have contributed to) the scholarship on multimodal composition and its impact. A scan of the field's books, journals, and conference presentations shows this scholarship has grown substantially in the past two decades and includes a wide range of ideas for teaching and theorizing multimodal composition. To name a few, such directions include helping students develop "useful technological skills in the multimodal composition classroom" through gaming (Arduini 2018, 90), analyzing "emoji as a form of multimodal public writing" (Gray and Holmes 2020, 1), employing ethical actions with technologies by juxtaposing multimodal composition with user-centered design, rhetorical theory, and learner-centered design (Opel and Rhodes 2018, 74), and amplifying student agency through reflection and revision of multimodal work (Kitalong and Miner 2017, 41). Students in CRDM read a variety of resources and texts that give them a better understanding of the diverse ways people make meaning. They use these resources as inspiration for their own multimodal compositions. Often, students revise and rework these compositions over the course of several semesters and use them as a foundation for conference presentations, journal articles, or final thesis projects.

THE NEEDS OF STUDENTS

In studying faculty development and its relationship to graduate training in the field of composition and rhetoric, Isis Artze-Vega, Melody Bowdon, Kimberly Emmons, Michele Eodice, Susan K. Hess, Claire Coleman Lamonica, and Gerald Nelms (2013) write that "graduates need a wide range of skills to be prepared for varied career opportunities" (165). They add that "comp/rhet scholars are often flexible communicators; we are adept at making new ideas available and accessible to our colleagues" (167). This sentiment is most evident in multimodal scholarship that contends that since students write multimodally outside academia, academia should provide more opportunities for students to write multimodally in their classes. For instance, Jessica Kohout-Tailor and K. E. Sheaffer write that "today's students are already accustomed to interacting with information in a variety of ways" (11). Indeed, today's students are linguistically diverse, which is why we must teach multimodality. (For more on this, see Megan McIntyre and Jennifer Lanatti Shen's chapter 3 and Megan E. Heise and Matthew A. Vetter's chapter 12 in this book.) Ryan P. Shepherd (2018) likewise argues that we can take "the types of digital and multimodal composing students are engaging in outside of school" and put "these practices into conversation with practices in composition classes" so that "teachers may be able to foster learning transfer between students' various writing experiences" (103). He points to the writing students do on social media prior to entering college as examples of multimodal composition (104). He argues that students can have a hard time understanding a broader definition of writing, one that includes these kinds of examples. Shepherd is speaking of undergraduates, but CRDM faculty find even graduate students at first struggle to understand multimodal composition. Drawing on transfer scholarship, Shepherd claims that students "connecting writing contexts requires the more difficult high-road transfer and not the simpler low-road transfer" (110), that is, seeing the similarities in different writing contexts involves more conscious reflection on the part of students.

In their work on developing a dynamic feedback model for multimodal composition, Christa Teston, Brittany Previte, and Yanar Hashlamon (2019) focus on a specific professional-writing course, but their insights provide a means for seeing the contexts in which all writers write. They contend that "the spaces in which we work are in constant flux" and that "the material-discursive conditions in and through which we work are hardly stable" (204). So, it would be in our best interest to draw attention to the fluid nature of the contexts in which we write. When faculty provide feedback to students on their multimodal projects, this feedback "should sensitize its users to material-discursive conditions. These may include unexpected events, unreliable infrastructural supports, and, quite simply, change over time" (205). This attention to material-discursive conditions should be front and center in our pedagogy (207) because it highlights "ethical considerations about access, race, and linguistic diversity" (207). Additionally, students in the program often have discussions and participate in collaborative activities and assignments that help them see the diverse meaning-making ways multimodal composition demands and be responsive to those demands.

The CRDM program not only aids students in developing an awareness of the challenges they may face when writing multimodally but also helps them face these challenges head on. Scholarship in multimodal composition has a history of documenting such challenges. Using case studies on digital projects from undergraduate and graduate writing students, Michael-John DePalma and Kara Poe Alexander (2015) found that when "carrying out their multimodal composition projects, students encountered a range of challenges related to audience, ethics, composing processes, rhetorical constraints, technology, and collaboration" (191). To address challenges regarding audiences, the CRDM faculty spend time helping students identify and reflect on the real audiences they write for, whether on campus or beyond. For example, students participate in an exhibition of their work in one of the campus's galleries that is open to the public. In addition, students can participate in the Production & Preservation Project (P3), a digital archive and exhibition of students' artifacts, artifacts they create in the program's courses under the guidance of faculty. This project gives students another opportunity to build a web presence and portfolio and to rhetorically consider the many audiences they write for.

DePalma and Alexander (2015) recommend providing "students with rich examples of multimodal scholarship that they might model" (192) to further help understand audiences. The CRDM faculty certainly do so, choosing a wide range of examples for their courses, including both digital and nondigital ones. But, faculty also provide opportunities for students to collaborate and participate in scholarly activities alongside faculty, giving them the chance to contribute to the ongoing scholarly conversations in the field. This includes presenting at local and national conferences, participating in research projects, and writing scholarly articles with faculty.

To be responsive to the needs of students also means helping students see that multimodal composition tells a story about the people and materials that interact with one another before, during, and after a communication occurs in a specific context, a story that must consider the histories of people and their cultures, the histories of materials, and the histories of time, places, and spaces. Multimodal composition is, therefore, embodied—bodies shape multimodal composition but are also shaped by it—and embedded in contexts intertwined with other contexts (for more on this, see Christina V. Cedillo [2017]).

This awareness of embodiment is specifically evident in the work students do to create ePortfolios. Many of the CRDM classes help students compose a wide range of ePortfolios, ones that "suggest that our understanding of the form that ePortfolio artifacts can take is ever-evolving as the tools themselves move us from more alphabetic to visual, interactive modes and to forms of identity collection and representation that are assembled across multiple spaces and multiple genres" (Blair 2017, 136). As Kristine L. Blair (2017) points out,

> What makes assemblage an important term to add to the mix of nomenclatures is its presumption of pluralities and multiplicities of representation, identity, and making and circulating knowledge; ePortfolios themselves are genres aligned with these concepts. They are designed to be assemblages in the literal sense, rhetorically purposeful selections and deselections across genres and modalities and over time. (137)

In the Teaching Writing course, students compose a teaching ePortfolio, which helps them claim their voices in genres and modes that might have previously excluded them. Throughout this course, students discuss, analyze, and reflect on the many ways they learned literacy skills both in school and beyond and consider how they themselves will teach their own writing courses. These actions often highlight what Janine Butler (2017) writes about in her work on kinesthetic performance, that "our bodies are multimodal and our compositions are multimodal: We juxtapose, arrange, or disarrange modes to compose meaning" (74). Butler argues that "our bodies—and the differences between our bodies—shape how we interact with other modes and bodies in the spaces we share" (76). In the Teaching Writing course, students see this first hand in creating their own activities they then teach to the class. These activities are also included in their ePortfolios and serve to represent who the students are as composition instructors. During the teaching of their activities, students negotiate where their bodies are located in the class—sitting or standing in the front, in the back, or somewhere in between—in relationship with their students. Students are aware that "each one of us articulates meaning through different bodily qualities" (81). This awareness shows them how many bodies shape one text and how some bodies are privileged by particular modes. Such experiences in this class show students ways they "circulate meanings without disempowering certain bodies" (83). Providing students opportunities for empowerment makes for an inclusive program, one that celebrates each student's uniqueness.

Responsiveness to *students* means asking these questions:

- How can a program help students understand the diverse ways various communities communicate and how those ways are influenced by political, social, economic, and historical ideologies?
- What experiences can a program facilitate to help students effectively write in their communities by drawing attention to the materials they write with, the places and spaces they write in, and the people they write for?
- In what innovative ways can a program aid students in achieving their own professional and civic goals through multimodal writing?

THE NEEDS OF FACULTY

The CRDM program was created by dedicated faculty who are sensitive to the needs of each other, who complement and support the work of one another, who participate together in a wide range of scholarly activities, and who want to help the discipline grow in inclusive ways. The leadership of the program provides faculty with opportunities that help faculty thrive at NSU and beyond. They also help faculty collaborate with colleagues within the discipline and in other disciplines. Many of the faculty in the program, for example, have conducted grant-funded research studies, have written scholarly texts—books, articles, digital projects—and have presented at national conferences regarding a range of areas within the discipline, from comics to style to technology. Their scholarly pursuits, each in their unique ways, have given faculty the support they need to develop the courses in the program. In other words, by participating in multimodal composition themselves, they are better positioned to create and implement courses that attend to multimodal composition practices and theories. They put into practice what they discuss in their classrooms, thus modeling for students how multimodal composition is enacted.

One reason CRDM has found success has to do with faculty's beliefs that they too benefit from a program that focuses on multimodal theories and practice. While Butler (2017) draws attention to students' understandings of bodies, she writes that faculty have something to gain as well when they teach through the use of modes. As she contends, "By interacting through multiple modes of expression," instructors can create "a space for students *and* instructors to learn through multiple perspectives" (87–88). Interactions through modes is a hallmark of successful graduate education: students learn from faculty and faculty learn from students. They are a community of learners, working together to understand the diverse ways everyone composes. Butler is not the only scholar to make such an argument. Tina Arduini (2018) believes there is reciprocity that benefits instructors when a writing classroom focuses on multimodal composition. Using gaming as an example, she writes, "By designing courses that take students' at-home digital literacies into consideration, instructors can benefit from the digital expertise students bring to the classroom" (89). Pointing out that scholars "have noted one of the biggest literacy advantages afforded by gaming literacy is a fluency in multimodal composition," she contends instructors also learn rhetorical and technological skills from students when the students solve multimodal problems while gaming (90). The CRDM believes this too and has offered a special-topics course on gaming, which will be expanded into a permanent elective course.

In discussing multimodal composition as an assemblage, James Kalmbach (2017) writes that composers, especially digital composers, do not employ a "simple linear process"; rather they use a "coalition of *engagements* (technological engagements, architectural engagements, interface engagements, media engagements, etc.), as well as *negotiations* of the *embedded expertise* in those engagements" (60). Faculty are certainly included in these engagements and negotiations, working alongside their students. Every class, for example, encourages students to use various technologies to participate in scholarly discussions and to practice multimodal composition through a range of projects. In the program's Advanced Writing with Technologies course, students put together websites, videos, presentations, apps, blogs, and so forth, and they do so by thinking critically about the problems that occur along the way and with faculty by their side.

In addition to the problem solving that happens in their classrooms, the CRDM faculty have seen challenges along the way, from cuts to funding to changes in locations on campus to trying to highlight the value of the program to others beyond the field. Rick Wysocki, Jon Udelson, Caitlin E. Ray, Jessica S. B. Newman, Laura Sceniak Matravers, Ashanka Kumari, Layne M. P. Gordon, Khirsten L. Scott, Michelle Day, Michael Baumann, Sara P. Alvarez, and Dànielle Nicole DeVoss (2018) point out that "the multimodal work we do will not always be understood, supported, or valued by institutions or our students. We must anticipate this resistance and be prepared to articulate clearly why multimodality matters in the context of our classrooms, our curricula, and our programs" (22). Consistently, CRDM faculty have worked together and found creative ways to secure the materials, the spaces, and the resources needed to implement the courses they plan to teach each semester but to also help others, especially those outside the program, understand the work they do. These efforts are most evident in many of the marketing initiatives they have created over the years in order to show people the best the program has to offer.

Responsiveness to *faculty* means asking these questions:

- In what ways can a graduate program that focuses on multimodal theories and practices benefit the faculty who teach and oversee the program?
- What are the unique interests of faculty and how can a graduate program support faculty in pursuing these interests?
- What resources, materials, and spaces do faculty need in order to ensure their success in building, revising, and implementing a graduate program focused on multimodal theories and practices?

THE NEEDS OF AN INSTITUTION

Educating others about multimodal composing is and has been an ongoing endeavor for CRDM faculty but also more broadly for the field of composition and rhetoric. The history of composition and rhetoric certainly makes clear that such a diverse discipline has been challenged to make relevant the value of the theories and practices it supports time and again. CRDM faculty are well aware not all people know what multimodal composition means. This lack was most apparent when faculty first proposed the program to the dean. During that process, faculty had to think carefully and strategically about, among other things, the ways they worded or titled the proposed new program and its new courses. While they wanted to help teach those outside the field, such as administrators, that what they do in the field is much more than just words on a page, they had to be sensitive to the needs of the institution, including being conscious of the ways the institution marketed its programs. They needed to show CRDM could make money via enrollment and tuition dollars, and to do that they needed to choose their words carefully. Choosing to use the words *digital media*, for instance, instead of *multimodal* was a negotiated choice. People in the public, in other words potential students and the employers who would eventually hire them, knew what digital media is, but they were less likely to know what multimodal composition is. It has been well documented, most definitively by Claire Lauer (2009), that "though multimodal has become more commonly used in scholarly literature . . . , it is almost entirely absent from course titles, program names, and more public discussions outside of the academy where the term multimedia takes prevalence" (226). The faculty proposing the new CRDM program knew using a word like *media*, instead of *multimodal*, would require less explanation to those outside the field and ultimately decided upon "digital media" in its title with the intention of making sure multimodal composition was front and center in the program's course offerings, whether those course offerings used "multimodal" in their titles or not.

In addition, CRDM faculty are well aware, as are Wysocki et al. (2018), that "we must be attentive to the larger curricular, departmental, institutional, and professional contexts in which we work. Our courses do not exist in a vacuum, nor does multimodal composing. We should look toward committees, caucuses, community organizations, corporations, and others to help inform the ways in which we understand multimodal composing and how, where, when, and so on it enters the world" (22). To be responsive to NSU's needs, faculty often look beyond their institution, consulting and speaking with experts in the field at a number of different professional institutions. This happens regularly, as CRDM faculty are members of national organizations, participating in conference committees and special-interest groups that set forth best practices, ones they then use to negotiate with their own institution, making sure they continue to have a good, supportive relationship. For instance, faculty use best practices to develop classroom spaces that enable students to compose, whether that means capping the number of students in each of the courses or building classroom spaces that take into consideration the diverse bodies of students and faculty.

Therefore, responsiveness to *institutions* means asking these questions:

- How can a graduate program that focuses on multimodal theories and practices help an institution achieve its goals at the same time it recognizes the diverse ways we communicate?

- In what creative ways can a graduate program meet the challenges the institution faces and the challenges the institution poses on the program itself by working with all stakeholders?
- How can program faculty still achieve the work they wish to do, work integral to the field, while at the same time negotiating with institutional administrators to meet the needs of their college or university?

THE NEEDS OF THE WORKFORCE

Being responsive to an institution means being responsive to the workforce. It is no secret that higher education often relies on the promise of employment when recruiting students to its institutions. NSU is no different. NSU advertises it will help students launch their careers and achieve success while doing so. Calls to help students prepare for life beyond academia, likewise, are not novel in multimodal scholarship. Arduini (2018) argues that "by granting students experience in digital composing practices, multimodal composition instructors can ensure effective exposure to the twenty-first century literacies required to become successful professionals" (89). "According to the Bureau of Labor Statistics, demand for editors and writers will keep pace with other professions over the next several years, while demand for certain specialties, such as technical writing and public relations, will increase 7–10% faster than the average for all occupations from 2019–2029." (Nova Southeastern University 2023). In addition, the CRDM program contends that "the mandatory composition course requirement of most colleges and universities nationwide ensures the continued demand for qualified faculty in composition and rhetoric" (Nova Southeastern University 2023). With several courses focused on multimodal composition, the CRDM program offers a chance for students to understand the broad and diverse range of texts they produce and will produce in various writing-related jobs. In other words, they develop a more spacious understanding of writing. For a more detailed discussion on changing workplace literacies, see chapter 11 in this collection.

CRDM faculty scholarship has been attuned to the changing demands of the workforce. As an example, three of the faculty members in CRDM worked on a nationwide grant-funded study investigating the transitions composition and rhetoric students make from their PhD programs into the professoriate. Writing the subsequent book about their experiences—*Stories of Becoming: Demystifying the Professoriate for Graduate Students in Composition and Rhetoric* (Lutkewitte, Kitchens, and Scanlon 2022)—has led these faculty to reaffirm the important initiatives they provide to students in the CRDM program, as well as make significant changes that can better prepare students to succeed beyond the program, such as in PhD programs. Knowing new faculty in the nationwide study, for instance, valued the mentorships they had in their PhD program and on the job reinforced the existing mentorships between CRDM faculty and students and between the faculty too. It has also led to curricular changes, giving students opportunities to create portfolios that merge the diverse work they do in the program with the experiences they bring with them to the program. Such portfolios are then shared with potential employers.

Furthermore, CRDM provides students with several initiatives, including *Digressions*, the student-run literary and art journal. The journal is aptly named; digressions "are temporary departures or instances of divergence from a main theme," and this journal "invites students to move away from the rigidity of academia and scholarship" ("About Digressions" 2020). Students' experiences with this journal, from the writing of its contents to the creation of its publication, coupled with the other professional initiatives (like internships) students are involved with in the program, help prepare students for a number of writing careers beyond academia.

So, to end this section, responsiveness to the *workforce* means asking these questions:

- In what ways do graduate programs focused on multimodal composition prepare students for the careers they will pursue once they graduate?
- What experiences can such programs provide students to help them understand the diverse ways they may write in their careers?
- What roles do mentors play in helping students accomplish their career goals in a program focused on multimodal writing?

IMPLICATIONS

As a result of faculty and students' efforts over the past five years, the CRDM program has grown into a successful one. Such an approach can serve as a model for other master's programs in writing-related disciplines. The questions posed at the end of each section above can be used to generate conversations amongst program faculty and leadership, to guide decision-making practices, and to offer a chance for reflection. Beyond these, the art of responsiveness means to take into account what each program can do to be inclusive and to best serve all those involved. As a next step, programs are encouraged to research and understand their unique contexts and find a successful path forward for all stakeholders involved.

Moving on, the CRDM program will continue to innovate and revise its curriculum, its initiatives, and its activities along the way. Just recently, the program underwent an external review, a review that found the program to be strong, as it enhances the institution's mission and core goals at the same time it meets the needs of faculty and students. To continue, though, the review suggested, the program should look to the future and anticipate changes in teaching and technology. As a result, the faculty are already creatively and collaboratively working to respond to such changes to further strengthen the program. After all, the CRDM program has met the challenges it has faced over the years by being responsive to the needs of its stakeholders and will continue to do so as it evolves. With these goals in mind, the program hopes to expand its faculty resources, provide faculty and students with more funding opportunities, create a more comprehensive graduate school orientation, conduct more primary research alongside students, and incorporate newer technologies in the classrooms.

When so much of institutional leadership is driven by enrollment numbers, tuition dollars, and promises to students regarding job placements, humanities disciplines have struggled to convince students, administrators, and the public that what we do is of value in a time when STEM initiatives seem to have the upper hand. But humanities disciplines, and especially multimodal composition, are relevant to every profession, providing the much-needed critical and reflective skills everyone needs both in the workforce and beyond. So much of what multimodal composition is about is helping students and faculty use their writing in unique and creative ways to engage audiences beyond their workplaces. For more on what employers are looking for in a job candidate, especially pertaining to communication skills, see Anthony F. Arrigo's chapter 13 in this collection. As has been documented time and again, multimodal composition can tap into what makes each of us unique, demanding that we must be inclusive and sensitive to the diverse ways people make meaning.

REFERENCES

"About Digressions." 2020. *Digressions: Literary and Art Journal.* https://nsuworks.nova .edu/digressions/vol17/iss1/.

Arduini, Tina. 2018. "Cyborg Gamers: Exploring the Effects of Digital Gaming on Multimodal Composition." *Computers and Composition* 48: 89–102.

Artze-Vega, Isis, Melody Bowdon, Kimberly Emmons, Michele Eodice, Susan K. Hess, Claire Coleman Lamonica, and Gerald Nelms. 2013. "Privileging Pedagogy: Composition, Rhetoric, and Faculty Development." *College Composition and Communication* 65 (1): 162–84.

Blair, Kristine L. 2017. "ePortfolio Artifacts as Graduate Student Multimodal Identity Assemblages." In *Assembling Composition*, edited by Kathleen Blake Yancey and Stephen J. McElroy, 121–39. Urbana, IL: NCTE.

Butler, Janine. 2017. "Bodies in Composition: Teaching Writing through Kinesthetic Performance." *Composition Studies* 45 (2): 73–90.

Cedillo, Christina V. 2017. "Diversity, Technology, and Composition: Honoring Students' Multimodal Home Places." *Present Tense* 6 (2): 1–9.

DePalma, Michael-John, and Kara Poe Alexander. 2015. "A Bag Full of Snakes: Negotiating the Challenges of Multimodal Composition." *Computers and Composition* 37: 182–200.

Gray, Kellie, and Steve Holmes. 2020. "Tracing Ecologies of Code Literacy and Constraint in Emojis as Multimodal Public Pedagogy." *Computers and Composition* 55: 1–29.

Horner, Bruce. 2020. "Modality as Social Practice in Written Language." In *Writing Changes: Alphabetic Text and Multimodal Composition*, edited by Pegeen Reichert Powell, 21–40. New York: MLA.

Kalmbach, James. 2017. "Beyond the Object to the Making of the Object: Understanding the Process of Multimodal Composition as Assemblage." In *Assembling Composition*, edited by Kathleen Blake Yancey and Stephen J. McElroy, 60–77. Urbana, IL: NCTE.

Khadka, Santosh, and J. C. Lee. "Introduction: Extending the Conversation: Theories, Pedagogies, and Practices of Multimodality." In *Bridging the Multimodal Gap: From Theory to Practice*, edited by Santosh Khadka and J. C. Lee, 3–13. Logan: Utah State University Press.

Kitalong, Karla Saari, and Rebecca L. Miner. 2017. "Multimodal Composition Pedagogy Designed to Enhance Authors' Personal Agency: Lessons from Non-academic and Academic Composing Environments." *Computers and Composition* 46: 39–55.

Kohout-Tailor, Jessica, and Kelsey E. Sheaffer. 2020. "Using Open Educational Resources to Empower Student Creators." *Journal of Electronic Resources Librarianship* 32 (1): 11–18.

Lauer, Claire. 2009. "Contending with Terms: 'Multimodal' and 'Multimedia' in the Academic and Public Spheres." *Computers and Composition* 26: 225–39.

Lutkewitte, Claire. 2014. "An Introduction to Multimodal Composition Theory and Practice." In *Multimodal Composition: A Critical Sourcebook*, edited by Claire Lutkewitte, 1–8. Boston: Bedford/St. Martin's.

Lutkewitte, Claire, Juliette C. Kitchens, and Molly J. Scanlon. 2022. *Stories of Becoming: Demystifying the Professoriate for Graduate Students in Composition and Rhetoric*. Logan: Utah State University Press.

Nova Southeastern University. 2023. "M.A. in Composition, Rhetoric, and Digital Media." https://hcas.nova.edu/degrees/masters/composition-rhetoric-digital-media.html.

Opel, Dawn S., and Jacqueline Rhodes. 2018. "Beyond Student as User: Rhetoric, Multimodality, and User-Centered Design." *Computers and Composition* 49: 71–81.

Shepherd, Ryan P. 2018. "Digital Writing, Multimodality, and Learning Transfer: Crafting Connections between Composition and Online Composing." *Computers and Composition* 48: 103–14.

Teston, Christa, Brittany Previte, and Yanar Hashlamon. 2019. "The Grind of Multimodal Work in Professional Writing Pedagogies." *Computers and Composition* 52: 195–209.

Wysocki, Rick, Jon Udelson, Caitlin E. Ray, Jessica S. B. Newman, Laura Sceniak Matravers, Ashanka Kumari, Layne M. P. Gordon, Khirsten L. Scott, Michelle Day, Michael Baumann, Sara P. Alvarez, and Dànielle Nicole DeVoss. 2018. "On Multimodality: A Manifesto." In *Bridging the Multimodal Gap: From Theory to Practice*, edited by Santosh Khadka and J. C. Lee, 17–29. Logan: Utah State University Press.

Yancey, Kathleen Blake, and Stephen J. McElroy. 2017. "Assembling Composition: An Introduction." In *Assembling Composition*, edited by Kathleen Blake Yancey and Stephen J. McElroy, 3–25. Urbana, IL: NCTE.

11

"GO *MAKE* THINGS HAPPEN"
Professionalizing Graduate Students through Multimodal Composing

Shauna Chung, Stephen Quigley, and Tia Dumas

INTRODUCTION

Graduate schools around the world, tasked with facilitating the development of students across disciplines and, in many cases, on different campuses and locations, are increasingly asking one another how they can ensure their students' experiences prepare them for success in the early years of their professional careers. Yet, each graduate student's school experience is not anyone else's. Some schools may provide infrastructure and support for interdisciplinary collaborations and prepare students for the responsibilities of the classroom, developing the organizational, interpersonal, and technological skills for succeeding as an educator in diverse and distributed educational spaces. In other cases, graduate students might work in a research role, performing a single controlled activity over and over again towards a specific end, working as one among a small number of individuals inside an institution or lab, all similarly concerned with the same small set of problems. Some graduate students experience few cares outside their immediate program, or are simultaneously raising children, working another job, caring for a loved one in need, navigating the complexities of marriage, or getting divorced. Some may have completed their work on campus or online, synchronously or asynchronously, perhaps thousands of miles away in isolation. To ensure all students can fully access opportunities and collaborations across a university space, and to best leverage the unique skills of each individual student, graduate schools are increasingly seeking to provide training and experiences that extend beyond the narrow scope of students' specializations in an effort to address a multitude of academic, professional, and personal needs. While we echo the approaches recommended in this collection to develop institution-wide

https://doi.org/10.7330/9781646424184.c011

collaborations (see chapter 1) that incorporate the multivocality and lived experiences of diverse students in higher education (see chapters 2 and 3), implementing such programs at scale may prove difficult.

At Clemson University in 2016–17, Graduate School Associate Dean Dr. Tia Dumas developed GRAD 360°, a comprehensive model of professional development for graduate students and postdoctoral scholars that centers diversity, inclusion, and equity while focusing on four themes to support trainees and their development in an ever-changing global community: transferable skills and core curricula, learning and learner development, mentoring and building community, and tracking transformation. To flesh out the conceptual (i.e., the *what*) and practical (i.e., the *how*) components of these themes, Dr. Dumas identified nine focus areas—the Tiger 9—that encompass essential proficiencies at the core of graduate education and professional preparation for any employment sector. They include the following:

1. Career Development.
2. Personal Health, Wellness, and Financial Literacy
3. Research and Innovation
4. Professionalism and Ethics
5. Leadership and Management
6. Teamwork and Collaboration
7. Teaching and Learning
8. Oral, Written, and Intercultural Communication
9. Social and Global Responsibility (GRAD 360° 2020)

While the GRAD 360° program had incorporated these areas of focus into its ethos and engineered infrastructure for an expanded mentorship network, ad hoc trainings and workshops, and a student self-assessment tool, it had not yet built a comprehensive curriculum to address how students would develop these sets of skills.

In this chapter we relate a cross-curricular digital literacy program designed to address the above Tiger 9 skills for graduate students studying at Clemson University. While the practical aim of this digital writing and learning curriculum was to help students acquire new digital tools for writing webtexts and making instructional videos, podcasts, and other digital projects, its philosophical intent was to position multimodal composition as a conduit through which students develop relationships with key partners inside and outside the university; advance inclusive, equitable, and dynamic models for success; engage in professional development through training in transferable skills and core curricula; and excavate their identities as individuals, students, colleagues, and global citizens. More specifically, we discuss the personal, theoretical, and practical aspects of developing a digital-literacy curriculum that partners with the core values of graduate school education and works to provide students with opportunities to be active, civic-minded creators rather than passive consumers of information. We do this by sharing a transparent picture of our process, discussing the challenges encountered in our collaboration at the institutional, project, and interpersonal level in particular. We also unpack the theoretical framework that guided the development of our learning modules: Gregory Ulmer's theory of electracy and the mystory genre, which sees multimodal invention as a rearticulation of identity and positionality in relation to digital media and larger social contexts. Finally, we explicate and present samples of the five-module curriculum that emerged from our semester-long collaboration—comprised of a flexible assignment prompt, resources for students to execute the prompt, and a mentor text—to offer practical principles to promote digital literacy beyond our campus. We argue that any initiative in higher education that involves training in digital technologies would greatly benefit from an approach that nurtures not just proficiency in technical skills but, more important, operationalizes multimodal composition in service of personal, professional, and community-centered growth.

SITUATING CLEMSON'S DIGITAL-LITERACY INITIATIVE

To contextualize our digital-literacy curriculum at Clemson, we briefly address shifting definitions of workplace literacy as articulated by members of the New London Group and, along with scholars examining multimodal rhetorics, argue that prefixing *digital* and appending *curriculum* necessarily involves a movement away from skills-based training in electronic technologies as an end goal and toward the development of "a robust understanding of rhetoric and creative process" so learners can "apply and adapt to all the diverse forms of alphabetic, auditory, and visual composing they are likely to encounter in their lives" (Palmeri 2012, 153). Using our personal experiences developing a digital-literacy curriculum with graduate student professional-development and workplace proficiencies in mind—that is, the targeted site of "encounter"—we later illustrate that despite a few detours, our process of making ultimately cultivated such robust rhetorical and creative understandings.

In *Literacies*, Mary Kalantzis, Bill Cope, Eveline Chan, and Leanne Dalley-Trim (2016) note that literacies in professional settings have

216   CHUNG, QUIGLEY, AND DUMAS

shifted dramatically from industrial-era needs and logics. Veering away from rote, behavior-based competencies (e.g., the ability to receive and follow directions), employers in what the authors call the "knowledge-era" desire skills related to collaboration with and influence over others, finding solutions in innovative and creative ways, and both digesting and demonstrating "effective oral and written communication skills" (41). These qualities, explain Cope and Kalantzis (2009) in their ten-year retrospective on the New London Group's manifesto on multiliteracies, conceptualize literacy not as a passive, linear approach to comprehending and making meaning. Instead, developing "new" literacy, or practices and abilities that keep pace with social change, "is aimed at creating a kind of person, an active designer of meaning, with a sensibility open to differences, change and innovation" (175). In our media-saturated society, Kalantzis et al. (2016) contend, these *kinds of people* must be proficient as "multimodal communicators" who navigate difference and innovate solutions via "the oral, written, visual, gestural, tactile and spatial modes, shifting between modes as and when necessary" (46–47). Put another way, the twenty-first-century employee must not only be an agile worker with multimodal communication abilities but must also be savvy on when and how to use them.

This latter ability provides a natural entry point for scholarship in rhetoric and composition and, in turn, a clearer definition of "multimodal." Though scholars have persuasively argued multimodality brings registers of the oral, written, visual, gestural, tactile, and spatial through what Jody Shipka calls "purposeful engineering" of digital *and* analog technologies (Purdy 2014; Shipka 2005, 300; Shipka 2011), the field has generally associated multimodal composing and communication with digital technologies. Claire Lauer (2009) observes a conflation of terms like "multimodal" and "multimedia" in past scholarship, which further reinforces the connection between a variety of modes and electronic media. She also remarks that as definitions and disciplinary conventions have matured over time, multimodality—a term once limited to productions using "computers, video, audio, and interactivity"—now encompasses "the cognitive and socially situated work students do in the classroom" that involves thoughtful design and process-based learning (238). Multimodality, in other words, is not the mere use of digital technologies but, perhaps more important, attends to the cultural logics and social practices that arise from or motivate such use. Moreover, as Rick Wysocki, Jon Udelson, Caitlin E. Ray, Jessica S. B. Newman, Laura Sceniak Matravers, Ashanka Kumari, Layne M. P. Gordon, Khirsten L. Scott, Michelle Day, Michael Baumann, Sara P. Alvarez, and Dànielle

Nicole DeVoss (2019) argue in their manifesto on multimodality, "Writing and technology are not monolithic, determined, or static entities" but "dynamic and multilocal" (19). Thus, the cultural and social dimensions of multimodality remain fluid and rhetorically situated for each user, observer, and creator of multimodal compositions.

These aspects of multimodality are especially salient for professional-development efforts in higher education seeking to foster digital literacy, or what Renee Hobbs and Julie Coiro (2019) call "a set of competencies" acquired through critical examination of and intentional production in "information and communication technologies that are part of everyday life" (402). Through running the professional-development program at the University of Rhode Island's Summer Institute in Digital Literacy, Hobbs and Coiro observe a significant variance in the way participants conceptualize technology as it relates to *their* everyday lives. Participants begin the program with diverse and often unrelated needs and perceptions of digital technologies. In fact, Hobbs and Coiro report some recognize digital affordances as "limiting practices of reading and writing" while others view it as "extending and deepening these practices" (403). These experiences underscore the need to start any digital-literacy initiative by first recognizing the plurality of perspectives—the "dynamic and multilocal" characteristics of multimodal work—and "beliefs" that guide uses and perceptions of digital affordances (Tan and Matsuda 2020). Stuart Selber's (2004) *Multiliteracies for a Digital Age* speaks to a similar framing of digital-literacy efforts. He also notes the "myths" of technologies, primarily related to computers, casting electronic affordances as Terminator or Savior of society, the great divider or equalizer. Selber opts for a "post-critical stance toward technology" instead that does not negate critique of digital technologies and their social/cultural impact but couples this critical awareness with functional and rhetorical literacies (8). Functional literacy, he explains, teaches "effective ways to interact with computers and with those who are online" (23–24)—the baseline technical skills required to gain access to computing's networking abilities—while rhetorical literacy positions the individual as a creator, or an active, "reflective producer of technology" (135). He explains that these three literacies ideally exist alongside each other and that competency is not mastery of one but is becoming "skilled at moving among them in strategic ways" (24).

A TURN TOWARD TRANSFERABLE SKILLS

When seeking to cultivate multimodal compositional strategies and knowledge-era digital literacy, the impulse is often to begin with functional literacy and position the technicalities of technology as an end instead of a means. This was certainly our initial approach when developing a digital-literacy curriculum for graduate student professional development at Clemson University. At the beginning of this project, we—Stephen and Shauna—were PhD students in Clemson's rhetorics, communication, and information design (RCID) program, recruited neither for our curriculum design experience nor for our expertise in digital literacy, but for our digital-production acumen. Our initial task was small: address *one* facet of the Tiger 9, the "Oral Written, and Intercultural Communication" focus, to help students "develop *skills* for the effective *use* of digital devices" (GRAD 360° 2020; our emphasis). In early talks regarding our employment, Dr. Dumas and RCID professor Dr. Jan Holmevik, our liaison to the project, discussed potentially creating technical resources for using digital tools and techniques to lay the foundations for a digital making-knowledge hub—the "Purdue OWL" of digital literacy. We understood our (albeit ambiguous but nonprescriptive) task to be the production and organization of videos on specific topics made accessible to students working now or possibly in some distant time and place.

Because we had both taught and learned with various technologies in our respective roles as educators and students, we were uniquely positioned to tackle the task of creating digital-literacy resources, specifically for video and audio production and graphic design. Consequently, we adhered to Wysocki et al.'s (2019) call to "include student voices and, when possible, the ideas of other stakeholders in our curriculum-building processes" (22). Though the initial conception of our efforts did not involve an explicit curriculum and privileged the skills necessary for and uses of digital devices, we, as graduate students creating content for graduate students, understood the often-difficult process of developing technical know-how and using these proficiencies for multiple roles in a university context. Thus, we drew heavily from our personal production experiences and our coursework in information design and information technologies to determine how best to select, scaffold, and teach relevant skills to our peers. We were unknowingly developing what Jason Palmeri (2012) calls a "kind of pilot project to explore the development of interdisciplinary multimodal curricula," grown and realized through collaborations with entities across the university (155).

With this positionality and these unconscious intentions in mind, we began our work by shooting instructional videos that would walk students through available resources on campus and offer guidance on how to use different digital tools. Using greenscreens and picture-in-picture tutorials, we sought clean, scripted productions, thinking this approach would best convey our training. Critically reviewing our footage and learning outcomes, however, revealed the inauthenticity in our delivery. Our skills-based approach abstracted the user from a learning environment and instead put sole focus on using digital technologies. Similar to the graduate instructors' reflections in chapter 5 of this collection, we recognized "multimodal literacies is not simply delivering multimedia content but rather an active engagement with multimodality." Rather than operating via the nonlinear, participatory logics of Kalantzis et al.'s (2016) "new" literacy or Wysocki et al.'s (2019) dynamic conception of multimodality, we had reduced digital technologies to "someone else's software package" for which students would simply be "the invention of that package" (Yancey 2004, 320). Moreover, we recognized the problems Laurie Bedford (2019) and the authors of chapter 7 in this volume identify with professional development in higher education: that learning in professional learning communities (PLCs) is often a passive endeavor delivered via "long- and short-term workshops, courses, and seminars" and in the absence of "trusting learning environments that allow for engagement and interaction" (Bedford 2019, 121). Our tutorials would have facilitated a program consisting of checked boxes instead of active participants with functional, critical, and rhetorical digital literacy.

Considering these factors, we abandoned the idea of *just* creating technical tutorials and determined to develop a digital-literacy curriculum supporting our community of graduate students. To accomplish this task, we needed to better understand our graduate school community, their/our real-life concerns, goals, and "spheres of action," and recognize how multimodal composing using digital technologies could practically attend to and partner with their/our professional needs and trajectories (Wysocki et al. 2019, 19). Additionally, we needed to explore the unique rhetorical affordances of the digital technologies at our disposal—webtexts, audio, video, graphics, ePortfolios—in order to move away from template-based training and toward community-based learning that employed these affordances in more purposeful and contextually fluid ways. Finally, we identified a need to practice what we preached—to put ourselves into the program, to proceed with the same kinds of self-reflexivity we inserted into our own scholarly and pedagogical work—and to lean into the intuition that our content would better relate with students when inflected across first-person and story-driven dimensions. We were mindful of what Steph Ceraso (2014) argues: "In addition to semiotic approaches to multimodality, it is necessary to

Figure 11.1. Shauna's screenshot from the revised, personal approach

address the affective, embodied, *lived* experience of multimodality in more explicit ways" (104).

This shift towards narrative in our production methods established a different tone, less didactic and more personal and empathetic. We replaced our green-screen talking heads with b-roll featuring multiple parts of our campus and spliced in candid video from our personal lives, including coming-of-age shots, domestic and community scenes, and clips from our professional lives. We sought to situate our digital-literacy training and looked not only for candor in these scenes but also uncertainty—not the clean, professional shots that convey a measure of success but scenes that demonstrate the tension in our own becoming. In other words, we sought to connect with our audience by communicating our shared struggles as Clemson graduate students along with the complexity of, and diversity in, our respective journeys to, and through, this learning environment.

Our shift in focus from skills training to fostering connection and community—core tenets of the GRAD 360° model—marked a new and definitive direction for this emerging digital-literacy program. We sought to develop training resources that helped students discover in themselves the specific elements not solely corresponding to oral, written, and intercultural communication (i.e., just one facet of the Tiger 9) but across all the focus areas. When positioned in this way, digital literacy was not reduced to the simple use of technologies to communicate.

Figure 11.2. Stephen's screenshot from the revised, personal approach

Rather, it also encompassed research and innovation, professionalism and ethics, teamwork and collaboration, teaching and learning, and social and global responsibility, to name a few. To begin this process, we first assessed how a digital-literacy component could assist in efforts to promote holistic growth for graduate students at any point in their educational experience. We determined that a subcurriculum, rather than a repository of tool-based training assets, would better support GRAD 360°'s focus areas and that scaffolding this curriculum across modules would provide a clearer structure for technical, personal, and professional development. We also decided to base the learning outcomes and training on real-life situations students on our campus could encounter: adjusting to a new living and learning environment, collaborating with peers and faculty, engaging in teaching and research assistantships, presenting research to broader audiences, and preparing a professional profile online for the job market. These experiences turned into five modules that included a recommended implementation phase, a concept (i.e., deliverable), Tiger 9 focus areas, a production tool,[1] a level of difficulty, and learning outcomes.

To develop each module, we created scripted instructional videos that provided general training in technical skills, included specific prompts to guide students' making, and featured a sample (i.e., a "mentor text") that exemplified the module's deliverable. Every step of the way, we reminded students that we—"Stephen and Shauna, your digital-literacy

CHUNG, QUIGLEY, AND DUMAS

guides"—remained alongside and in solidarity with learners. This became an integral part of our instruction since it helped us understand the production process for ourselves and the personal impact the task would eventually have on other students, echoing what Cheryl Glenn and Melissa A. Goldthwaite (2014) say of pedagogy by way of Nancy Comley: "Never give an assignment you have not tried yourself" (177). Below, we detail the methodologies that guided these productions, informed how each module took shape, and worked over and with our identities.

A THEORETICAL FRAMEWORK FOR MAKING

> *Life is a series of moments: little ones, big ones, happy ones, sad ones. Some are filled with parents, siblings, spouses, children. Some involve friends, pets, special events. Music, performances, collaborations. First times, lifelong hobbies. Some are experienced alone—some with colleagues. Each comprise our identities. They work over and through us, orient and disorient us, transform us, position us to be better daughters, sons, parents, friends, makers, teachers, colleagues, STUDENTS . . . and now this moment: the beginning of a new academic journey. To know where you're going, perhaps it's important to know where you've been—to acknowledge these moments.*

> —Excerpt from draft 1 of the
> Module 1 instructional video

In his call to "develop flexible, multimodal strategies for inventing and revising alphabetic writing," Palmeri (2012) suggests the use of the *progymnasmata* in masters and doctoral programs, exercises students might undertake as training in inventing and performing (149, 152). In our exploration of this pedagogy, we discovered the *progymnasmata* technique of *ethopoeia*, which translates to a kind of "bringing *ethos* into being," or "performing the *ethos*" of another in an act of becoming. Alternatively, we wondered how we might design modules that asked students to recognize their emerging professional *ethos* not by aspiring to be "another" but through analyzing the self. To do this, we needed to conceptualize *ethos* as *éthea* as Charles E. Scott (1990) does in *The Question of Ethics: Nietzsche, Foucault, Heidegger*. He explains the *éthea* is a kind of "dwelling place" where animals return to graze, distinguishing it from *nomós*, or "a specific field for grazing" (143). The *éthea*, he clarifies, "are specific environments that are associated with patterns of actions peculiar to the animal" instead of prescribed locations designating where and who to be (143). When put in the context of our multimodal curriculum, we saw a return to the *éthea* as uncovering the discourse that languages the experience of who we are and what we think. In other words, transformation *is happening* not in spite of our own unique experiences but because of them.

Gregory Ulmer's (1989) theory of electracy provides a framework for beginning this process of self-examination and transformation through multimodal composition. Sarah Arroyo (2013) characterizes and extends Ulmer's electracy as "a worldview for civic engagement, community building, and participation" that arises through the emergence and ubiquitous use of electronic technologies. Electrate writing—what Arroyo calls "participatory composition"—emphasizes the "convergence of the visual, verbal, aural, and corporal" that champions "production and participation in every writing gesture, largely defined" (10). She and Ulmer stress that the purpose of such multimodal production and participation is not simply analysis but to call up personal insights that catalyze invention. In other words, composing through the combination of visual, verbal, aural, and corporal modes uniquely invites the individual not only to give attention to their experiences but also to create with them.

Ulmer's mystory genre, a compositional exercise originating in his 1989 *Teletheory: Grammatology in the Age of Video*, operationalizes the above premise by encouraging learners to reflect on their identities across four discourses: family, entertainment, community, and school. He encourages writers to use webtexts that incorporate visual and sonic media alongside alphabetic text to narrativize the four discourses and create a multidimensional "cognitive map of its maker's 'psychogeography'" that decodes and organizes the components that constitute being and knowledge (Ulmer 2003, 81). As the authors of chapter 13 in this collection aptly note, this exercise positions multimodal composition not as the simple use of multiple discursive modes but as "a social and cultural practice that allows communicators to draw on situated ways of knowing, meaning making, and identity to forge relationships across generational, cultural, economic, and geographic boundaries." Ulmer (2003) distills the connections and relationships made across discourses to a visual metaphor he calls a "wide image," which acts as a guide for creativity.

We began developing scripts and prompts for the modules with this theoretical framework in mind and built Module 1—"Telling Your Story" via a webtext—around Ulmer's mystory. Because we created a mentor text to accompany each module, we had to try out our curriculum, in this case examining our own identities in relation to the four discourses in search of a wide image. For Stephen, this symbol was the bicycle, which provided him with the means to leave home and to see the world, and his eventual interest in bicycle activism led him to graduate school. As he examined the four discourses, he also realized the important role his children were playing in his development as a scholar. Rather than living two lives, feeling like a student who had to take on a completely different role and set of responsibilities whenever he went home at night, he realized how much his experiences as a father and his connections with his children contributed to his work and even positioned him differently from others in his graduate school program. For Shauna, the symbol she located was strings, which physically appeared on her musical instruments but became a larger metaphor for connection to family history, teaching, and her work in digital rhetoric. Through the process of creating a mystory, Shauna similarly recognized that her seemingly disparate identities as a musician, an Asian American, a PhD student, and an educator converged when she began composing with multimodal affordances; in these media, especially as they informed her scholarly work, these identities were not mutually exclusive.

Storytelling in webtext form gave us profound insights on our emerging professional identities and also provided an opportunity to hone our skills embedding media and designing a webpage. Because this task cultivated both personal/professional development and proficiency using a digital tool, our first unit became a model for how we would produce training assets—that is, informative videos that introduced a task using a digital tool and more technical videos that demonstrated how to build skills—and mentor texts for every module going forward. As Drs. Dumas and Holmevik signed off on our work and direction, we proceeded with Ulmer's (2019) assumption in mind—that "the imagined future of education is not just 'media literacy,'" or the knowledge of how digital tools work, but involves acts of invention with these media in ways that do not deny the personal (xi). We saw acts of making as opportunities for students to explore the different roles they would be playing in their careers.

DEVELOPING THE MODULES

In every step of our production process, the goal was to establish an invention-forward ethos alongside goal markers for personal and professional development according to the Tiger 9 and our learning outcomes.

Figure 11.3. Shauna demonstrating how to edit audio in Adobe Audition for Module 2

Figure 11.4. A graduate student editing her own audio for Module 3

For our instructional videos, we conveyed these intentions primarily in the visuals we incorporated. These videos followed a narrative throughline, which continued (and could also stand alone) in all other videos for the modules. This throughline often involved recurring "characters," or students we recruited and filmed as they created mock versions of our modules. We also filmed ourselves as digital-literacy guides, both using and explaining various audio, video, and graphic editing software. We wanted to represent experiences with which students could both identify and connect. Additionally, we wanted to situate this on *our* campus—not just describing student transformation happening in our graduate school but demonstrating it.

Figure 11.5. The characters Shauna and Stephen as digital-literacy guides, sans green screen

Another key component of our modules was building community—recognizing that our university, despite departmental silos, could be a network of learners and that digital tools could be the medium to effectively foster this connection. Modules 1, 2, and 4 spoke directly to this purpose as we envisioned students creating content for their personal and professional development in addition to a wider scholarly community. In Module 1, for example, we intended for students to use webtexts as self-introductions, not just to colleagues in their discipline but across the graduate school. Dr. Dumas later referred to this as a "family reunion" concept wherein both new and returning students could post their stories during the summer and, by the beginning of the fall semester, already be acquainted with the names, faces, and experiences of their graduate student colleagues.

Module 2 worked toward similar ends as it sought to first build connections within disciplines in order to later share the fruits of these collaborations with audiences beyond that discipline. Students would do this by creating episodes for a hostless and genreless *Clemson Graduate School Podcast* that would enable each student to be their own host, select their preferred genre, and articulate knowledge from their field. These unique, department-specific episodes, housed on the same platform, could help individuals within and without those departments better understand and connect with both disciplinary content and each other. Module 4 fulfilled a related purpose, as students would create three-column posters in Adobe InDesign so they could participate in our campus's annual interdisciplinary graduate research symposium,

Figure 11.6. Footage of graduate students presenting at Clemson's annual Graduate Research and Discovery Symposium we captured on campus for Module 4

providing a forum to work within and across departments through their technical making.

In addition to work done and shared at the graduate level, we also saw classroom interactions as a ripe environment for building community through digital tools. With a significant portion of students on our campus occupying teaching assistantships or graduate instructor roles, and with the need to better support online learners, we recognized video editing as a helpful skill in making classroom content more accessible and engaging. Thus, the aim of Module 3 was to create a repository of video-mediated teaching resources geared toward an undergraduate population. Graduate students would learn principles of video editing in order to translate discipline-specific concepts to their own students, emphasizing once again this push to see the technology as a conduit for connection.

Module 5 synthesized these community-centric focus areas by incorporating a more deliberate, outward-facing component: creating a portfolio of work that showcased projects completed in previous modules. These portfolios would not only help students develop an online presence for the job market but would also make work visible to colleagues across campus—to highlight personal, professional, and technical development through participation in the digital-literacy curriculum. Similar to Module 3, the intent was to build repositories of student-created projects accessible to students across campus, as well as potential colleagues outside the university. Instead of a knowledge hub centered around technical skills, these portfolios would, instead, be demonstrations of technologies applied to relevant graduate student learning environments and situations.

By the end of our assistantship, we created five instructional videos, two supplementary video tutorials, a podcast episode, a three-column poster, and Behance/Portfolio profiles. At present, the Clemson graduate school is working through the logistics of moving from our design phase to institution-wide implementation. For access to our module materials, visit https://t.co/hVN8gM3PPx or use the QR code in figure 11.7.

Figure 11.7. QR code for digital-literacy modules.

MULTIMODAL COMPOSITION APPLICATIONS BEYOND CLEMSON UNIVERSITY

Aristotle (2019) reminds us our ends as designers are not necessarily the ends of our users. Oftentimes, when we undertake curriculum writing, we can focus too much on the front end, the skills *we* want to teach, the ideas *we* want to circulate, the outcomes *we* codify so as to measure student learning. Our students, meanwhile, are often happy enough to jump through the hoops of graduate school, proceeding through their coursework procedurally, to get that diploma. As designers of curricula, digital or otherwise, we have a profound opportunity to think creatively and critically about ways we can center learners and help them utilize their work and engagement to realize higher ends. Multimodal practices offer a multitude of opportunities to reach and professionalize these higher ends. While aspects of functional, critical, and rhetorical literacies prove useful in developing workplace preparedness and multimodal composing, these proficiencies must work to honor, not come at the expense of, students' identities and provide opportunities for personal and professional becoming.

By conveying the nitty-gritty process of developing a digital-literacy component for Clemson University's model of professional development, we argue that reaching these higher ends cannot stop at the acquisition of technical skills. A digital-literacy curriculum focused on tutorials geared towards learning specific software will be obsolete before it is ever implemented. Such tutorials have already been written—*that's what YouTube is for*. Thus, we join in critique of this skills-based approach in favor of efforts that place emphasis on student identities (Martin and Grudzieki 2006) and take into account the local needs of a student body to ensure success at the institutional level and beyond (Murray and Perez 2014).

Yet we also believe a professional curriculum should extend beyond rhetorical awareness or methods for critiquing technology. For us, the end of our curriculum was a beginning—that of student transformation and realization. The big question we needed to think through was, *How can we design a curriculum that harnesses the power of digital making to work as a catalyst for student becoming?* In our case, we couldn't have thought up these higher ends on our own. Addressing that question required collaboration with faculty who sought out and extended opportunities to graduate students to assist in campus-wide digital-literacy efforts; our administration and individuals like Dr. Dumas willing to remain open to uncertainty and taking risks without compromising core principles of graduate student education; and other students who graciously shared their stories and experiences and whom we took time to meet at campus events and workshops. Involvement and investment were crucial at all three levels to realize our curriculum.

Additionally, at the production level, achieving these higher ends required us as developers to proceed with radical self-reflexivity and to take note of the ways the curriculum and its components worked over *our own* identities as makers. As Ulmer (1989) suggests, we discover crucial ideas and interventions needed to navigate our increasingly media-saturated world when we recognize and legitimate "the personal and the popular as knowledge within the domain of historiography" in order to make "available experience as an alternative to the rule of method" (86). In our production process, such legitimation and self-reflexivity manifested through being mindful of the tension at play in our making and adopting a bricoleur's ethos to, as Jan Holmevik (2012) puts it in *Inter/vention*, "create through the act of re/making" (24). Rather than dismissing the feelings of inauthenticity in order to persist in a method we thought was right or expected, we leaned into the discomfort, inventing *with* it and, as a result, reconfiguring institutional, curricular, and personal expectations in ways that better suited the needs of our campus and our creator voice.

Such reconfiguration also required an extension of the personal to the communal. Like our critique of technical skills as digital literacy, we similarly understood student becoming through acts of making did not stop at a personal "aha!" moment; instead, it involved using that moment as a catalyst for engaging with colleagues, faculty, students, and broader scholarly and professional communities. Put another way, it brought the Tiger 9 focus areas—Dr. Dumas's core values for professional development in the graduate school—into clearer focus. For us, this partnership between the technical and the communal was a beautifully recursive process: through making comes community, and through community come more acts of making, all of which lead to potential pathways for personal and professional development. In that spirit, webtext design became an opportunity for graduate students across disciplines, especially those at the beginning of their graduate student journeys, to connect by sharing personal narratives; podcast production provided a platform for graduate colleagues to convey discipline-specific knowledge to a broader audience; video editing enabled graduate student educators to create resources for and connect with an undergraduate population; graphic design facilitated interdisciplinary, scholarly conversations between students at professional events; and online portfolios became repositories of digital work that could support future graduate student training in digital literacy. By sharing the process and justification for these pairings, we emphasize that a digital-literacy curriculum incorporating both technical skills and the personal does not promote or yield widespread navel gazing but rather encourages learners to position technical skills as an opportunity to visualize and language their becoming so they can transfer these skills to multiple professional environments and situations.

The sum of these insights can be encapsulated in a mantra Stephen repeated throughout our assistantship: "Go *make* things happen." Each of the processes, pivots, and realizations detailed above originated from acts of making that, in turn, supported our university's model of professional development. While this chapter describes how we *made things happen through multimodal composition* at Clemson University using our available technologies, the overall digital-literacy curriculum we present is largely platform agnostic and shifts focus from technical to soft, transferable skills. Had we built modules around digital tools and conventions as we had initially planned, our program could not have realized the community Dr. Dumas was trying to establish in the Clemson Graduate School. Instead, we considered how students could use multimodal composition as a method for looking inward, connecting with others, and scaffolding their own becoming—a framework we believe can extend well beyond our institution.

NOTE

1. Important to note is Clemson University's partnership with Adobe, which grants all students access to Creative Cloud tools. These include audio, video, and graphic-design software, as well as access to advanced features in cloud-based applications

like Adobe Spark. Because this was our university's affordance, we incorporated these tools into our curriculum, though we support (and often point our own students in the direction of) free and open-source resources like Audacity, OpenShot, Inkscape, and Wordpress.org.

REFERENCES

Aristotle. 2019. *Nicomachean Ethics.* Translated by Terence Irwin. Indianapolis: Hackett.

Arroyo, Sarah. 2013. *Participatory Composition: Video Culture, Writing, and Electracy.* Carbondale: Southern Illinois University Press.

Bedford, Laurie. 2019. "Using Social Media as a Platform for a Virtual Professional Learning Community." *Online Learning Journal* 23 (9): 120–36. https://files.eric.ed.gov/fulltext/EJ1228870.pdf.

Ceraso, Steph. 2014. "(Re)Educating the Senses: Multimodal Listening, Bodily Learning, and the Composition of Sonic Experiences." *College English* 77 (2): 102–23. https://www.jstor.org/stable/24238169.

Cope, Bill, and Mary Kalantzis. 2009. "'Multiliteracies': New Literacies, New Learning." *Pedagogies: An International Journal* 4 (3): 164–95. https://doi.org/10.1080/15544800903076044.

Glenn, Cheryl, and Melissa A. Goldthwaite. 2014. *The St. Martin's Guide to Teaching Writing.* New York: Bedford/St. Martin's.

GRAD 360°. 2020. "The Tiger 9." https://grad360.sites.clemson.edu/t9.php.

Hobbs, Renee, and Julie Coiro. 2019. "Design Features of a Professional Development Program in Digital Literacy." *Journal of Adolescent and Adult Literacy* 62 (4): 401–09. https://doi.org/10.1002/jaal.907.

Holmevik, Jan. 2012. *Inter/vention: Free Play in the Age of Electracy.* Cambridge: MIT Press.

Kalantzis, Mary, Bill Cope, Eveline Chan, and Leanne Dalley-Trim. 2016. *Literacies.* Port Melbourne: Cambridge University Press.

Lauer, Claire. 2009. "Contending with Terms: 'Multimodal' and 'Multimedia' in the Academic and Public Spheres." *Computers and Composition* 26 (4): 225–39. https://doi.org/10.1016/j.compcom.2009.09.001.

Martin, Allan, and Jan Grudziecki. 2006. "DigEuLit: Concepts and Tools for Digital Literacy Development." *Innovation in Teaching and Learning in Information and Computer Sciences* 5 (4): 249–67. https://doi.org/10.11120/ital.2006.05040249.

Murray, Meg Coffin, and Jorge Perez. 2014. "Unraveling the Digital Literacy Paradox: How Higher Education Fails at the Fourth Literacy." *Issues in Informing Science and Information Technology* 11: 85–100. http://iisit.org/Vol11/IISITv11p085-100Murray0507.pdf.

Palmeri, Jason. 2012. *Remixing Composition: A History of Multimodal Writing Pedagogy.* Carbondale: Southern Illinois University Press.

Purdy, James P. 2014. "What Can Design Thinking Offer Writing Studies?" *College Composition and Communication* 65 (4): 612–41. https://www.jstor.org/stable/43490875.

Scott, Charles E. 1990. *The Question of Ethics: Nietzsche, Foucault, Heidegger.* Bloomington: Indiana University Press.

Selber, Stuart. 2004. *Multiliteracies for a Digital Age.* Carbondale: Southern Illinois University Press.

Shipka, Jody. 2005. "A Multimodal Task-Based Framework for Composing." *College Composition and Communication* 57 (2): 277–306. https://www.jstor.org/stable/30037916.

Shipka, Jody. 2011. *Toward a Composition Made Whole.* Pittsburgh: University of Pittsburgh Press.

Tan, Xiao, and Paul Kei Matsuda. 2020. "Teacher Beliefs and Pedagogical Practices of Integrating Multimodality into First-Year Composition." *Computers and Composition* 58 (2): 102614. https://doi.org/10.1016/j.compcom.2020.102614.

Ulmer, Gregory L. 1989. *Teletheory*. New York: Routledge.

Ulmer, Gregory L. 2003. *Internet Invention*. New York: Longman.

Wysocki, Rick, Jon Udelson, Caitlin E. Ray, Jessica S. B. Newman, Laura Sceniak Matravers, Ashanka Kumari, Layne M. P. Gordon, Khirsten L. Scott, Michelle Day, Michael Baumann, Sara P. Alvarez, and Dànielle Nicole DeVoss. 2019. "On Multimodality: A Manifesto." In *Bridging the Multimodal Gap: From Theory to Practice*, edited by Santosh Khadka and J. C. Lee, 17–29. Logan: Utah State University Press.

Yancey, Kathleen Blake. 2004. "Made Not Only in Words: Composition in a New Key." *College Composition and Communication* 56 (2): 297–328. https://www.jstor.org/stable/4140651.

12

CENTERING TRANSLINGUALISM IN MULTIMODAL PRACTICE
A Reflective Case Study of a Linguistically Diverse Graduate Program

Megan E. Heise and Matthew A. Vetter

INTRODUCTION

Although writing, rhetoric, and applied linguistics fields have amassed a comprehensive body of research on multimodal communication and pedagogy (Devoss 2013; Lutkewitte 2014; Selfe 2007; Sorapure 2006), there remains a significant gap between our field's knowledge of theory related to multimodality and its professional and pedagogical practice. Santosh Khadka and J. C Lee (2019), for instance, have found that actual implementation of multimodal approaches remains "sporadic" at a programmatic level (4). While such a disconnect is undoubtedly related to a number of complex factors, this chapter looks at how academic-program culture informs multimodal practices in a doctoral-level course on digital rhetoric. Due to the demographic context of the doctoral program both authors are currently engaged in (one as a professor, one as student), this chapter focuses on the intersection of multimodal practice and translingualism. More specifically, we consider how transmodal pedagogies may be put into practice within a graduate program that attracts a majority of multilingual and transnational students.

To frame this consideration, we draw on Jody Shipka's (2016) conception of transmodality, which itself builds on and converses with Bruce Horner, Cynthia Self, and Tim Lockridge's (2015) definition. For Shipka (2016), the transmodal "bring[s] the translingual and multimodal . . . character of texts and communicative practices" forward, awakening a broader repertoire of communicative action (250). Drawing upon these full repertories of communication also works in opposition to standard language and modal norm (SL/MN) ideologies that have perpetuated more limited communication strategies (Horner, Selfe, and

https://doi.org/10.7330/9781646424184.c012

Lockridge 2015). Via the paradigm of transmodality, multimodality and translingualism augment and interact with one another in complex and beneficial ways and are fluid and dynamic systems rather than static, separate, and hierarchical entities (Horner, Selfe, and Lockridge 2015). Recognizing this fluidity and intersectionality allows us to build upon scholarship that has shown how multimodality can help linguistically diverse students develop advanced and expanded ways of communicating to multiple audiences with skill, nuance, and purpose (Bigelow et al. 2017; Emert 2014; Kim 2018). As Laura Gonzales (2018) writes, "If multilinguals cannot rely on words to convey an idea in a specific language, we are motivated to creatively come up with other solutions, using any available modality to make our thoughts heard and understood outside the boundaries of standardized language systems" (2). Transmodal pedagogical approaches also enact what Chizoba Imoka (2018) terms "equity pedagogy" in that they help "accommodate the learning styles and cultural diversity of students" (87).

This chapter contributes to conversations regarding the intersection of theoretical promises and embodied pedagogical practices of transmodality (Shipka 2016). By offering a highly contextualized case study within a uniquely situated graduate program, we forward a reflective account that invokes Laura Micciche's (2010) theorization of writing *as* feminist rhetorical theory, having the potential to interrupt: to "unstick normative conventions from fixed locations, making possible a questioning of what is in order to make claims for what might be" (177). Just as trends in composition theory in the twentieth century enabled and forwarded monolingual biases, much of the work in multimodality theory in the first two decades of the twenty-first century has neglected language diversity. "Despite their common points or origination," Horner, Selfe, and Lockridge (2015) note, "discussions of [multi/trans]modality have remained largely separate from discussions of translinguality, to the impoverishment of both." Our goal is to center translingualism by interrupting conversations regarding conventional theory and practice around multimodality.

To accomplish this, we reflect on the spring 2020 course at Indiana University of Pennsylvania (IUP), English 846: Digital Rhetoric, which we participated in as a doctoral student (Megan) or taught as the instructor on record (Matthew). The program in which this course is situated, the PhD in Composition and Applied Linguistics (CAL) at IUP, is one in which our graduate students are both learning to teach linguistically diverse students *and* comprise a linguistically diverse pool of students themselves. In the course explored in this chapter, for example, eight of twelve students (67%) identify as multilingual and international students. Given the program's emphasis on first and second language literacy within the context of composition and applied linguistics, students with diverse educational backgrounds in TESOL, rhetoric and composition, writing studies, and linguistics take courses such as Second Language Literacy, Research Methods in Composition and Applied Linguistics, Language and Social Context alongside the courses Theories of Composition, Research and Practice in the Teaching of College Composition, and Technology and Literacy.

Within this translingual landscape, however, as Cristina Sánchez-Martín, Lavinia Hirsu, Laura Gonzales, and Sara P. Alvarez (2019) maintain, there remain opportunities to more fully weave multimodality with translinguality through a distinctly transmodal approach. In this chapter, we make space for professor and graduate student reflection on implementing multimodal pedagogy within a linguistically diverse graduate course. As part of this reflection, we identify specific challenges and successes that help us better understand intersections between translingual and multimodal theories and practices, with the ultimate goal of informing future programmatic curricula. For instance, how *can* writing faculty, particularly those working with linguistically diverse students, better integrate multimodality in their curricula? While we value our positionality as professor and graduate student, we also acknowledge the limits of our own experience when it comes to issues of translanguaging, as we are both US citizens who identify as "native" English speakers (NES). In order to further highlight the embodied experiences of the diverse students making up the academic program, and in this case, the course, we also include qualitative data in the form of course reflections collected from three additional students, two of whom identify as either bi- or multilingual. By attending to these students' experiences (as well as our own), we exemplify how multimodal composition "tells a story about the people and materials that interact with one another . . . a story that must consider the histories of people and their cultures, the histories of materials, and the histories of time, places, and spaces" (Lutkewitte, in chapter 10 of this collection, pp.197–212). Furthermore, we also build on earlier chapters (1–3) in this collection that explore opportunities and challenges of representing diverse students' experiences.

Ultimately, our chapter answers Gonzales's (2018) call to "continue expanding our notions of writing beyond standard alphabetic modalities," with the more direct goal of attending to the professional practice of course design (114). In the following sections of this chapter, we offer reflective accounts regarding a doctoral course in digital rhetoric that provided opportunities for exploring the intersections of multimodality and translingualism and share recommendations and implications regarding the need for graduate programs' further professionalization in translingual and multimodal pedagogy.

PROFESSOR COAUTHOR REFLECTION: MATTHEW

My positionality as professor in both the course and academic program discussed in this chapter, combined with my embodied identity as cishet, white, male, and monolingual, informs my thinking and experience regarding language diversity in countless ways. Privilege and access to dominant forms of language, education, and other institutions have played a role in my professionalization, research, and career. My relative lack of experience with language diversity has limited my ability to completely engage students in terms of their translanguaging. Confronting the shift from a monolingual academic culture to one much more linguistically and culturally diverse has been a years-long process and has, in many ways, defined much of my teaching in the program. The course explored in this chapter represents one attempt to open up my pedagogical practice to linguistic variation. Yet I acknowledge it is still a beginning. I must continue listening to my students and the scholarship to understand how to best leverage my (in)experience towards approaches for transmodal pedagogies.

English 846: Digital Rhetoric emphasized three major design values: (1) open-access content, (2) student agency and decision-making, and (3) scholarship, especially by Black, Indigenous, and People of Color (BIPOC) scholars, that examines intersections among identity, languaging, and multimodal composition. In attempting to center the voices of BIPOC scholars, as well as women and queer scholars, I hoped to offset and challenge rhetoric's male-oriented tradition (Ratcliffe 2005; Schell and Rawson 2010) and to make room for diverse identity representations in a course (and program) whose demographic also reflected enormous diversity. While this scholarship is diverse in terms of the identities and positionalities of authors, their contributions also showcase how multimodal writing, as recognized by Kelly Moreland, Sarah Henderson Lee, and Kirsti Cole in chapter 2 of this collection, "decenters standard academic English while facilitating a focus on written expression in multiple, commonly used academic and nonacademic modes" (50).

The work produced by students in this course overall demonstrated scholarly insight, discovery, and rigor—especially in projects that enabled students to make explicit connections to identity, language, and digital literacy. The first major project in the course, the multimodal-essay assignment (MP1), encouraged students to experiment with various modalities and genres as an alternative to standard academic writing and toward the production of either a literacy narrative or academic memoir. This assignment afforded students the opportunity to reflexively engage their own histories and cultures towards a more nuanced understanding of their academic journey and identity. A Saudi woman whose culture and familial upbringing often discouraged advanced academic learning, for example, illustrated through multiple modalities and through translanguaging practices such as code mesh-ing (Canagarajah 2011) the ways she has challenged those social pres-sures in order to become more critical of gender roles and patriarchal expectations. For me, as the professor and designer of the course, this student's experience emphasized the importance of creative writing genres in a course on digital rhetoric (as well as in doctoral education in general). Although all students can benefit from challenging traditional academic forms and modalities, transnational and multilingual students especially need to be given explicit instruction to interrogate and break the boundaries of standard academic English (SAE)—especially since doing so can result in opportunities for rethinking culture, identity, and personal literacy history.

In addition to the multimodal essay, students were introduced to methods for rhetorical criticism and asked to write a brief rhetorical analysis of a digital artifact. The work produced led to a number of important realizations. One student examining the artwork of a multi-lingual, new-media artist, for example, was able to analyze this work from a sociomaterial semiotic approach and discover how translingualism and transmodality are enacted in mixed-media artistic expression (Ali 2020). This project seemed particularly well positioned to challenge SL/MN ideologies when examined in conjunction with the artist's biographical and aesthetic statement, which highlighted her own transnational expe-rience and multilingual identity. Furthermore, the student's analysis of translingualism and multimodality also enabled her appreciation and theoretical understanding of transmodality, especially the opportunities that emerge when we bring artistic compositions (especially those of transnational and multilingual artists) into the classroom as transmodal rhetorical artifacts. Reflecting on these and other opportunities and challenges, and combining Megan's insights with additional student perspectives, allows us to further explore the implications of the course for transmodal practice, offering recommendations and implications in the final section.

STUDENT COAUTHOR REFLECTION: MEGAN

I hold a complex positionality as both an insider—a PhD student who took ENGL 846: Digital Rhetoric in the spring 2020 semester—and an outsider—a nontranslingual, noninternational, NES. I frame these particular identities as lacks—what I am not—in an attempt to counter deficit discourses around translingual students and teachers, such as the use of the term *nonnative English speakers* (NNES). Of course, I also acknowledge the stickiness of such a choice; the world—and, poignantly, especially, the job market for English for speakers of other languages (ESOL) teachers—certainly hasn't moved away from the native and non-native speaker binary and false hierarchy, and perhaps by *not* using these words I run the risk of seemingly erasing these very real power dynamics. My intent is to align here with Suhanthie Motha, Rashi Jain, and Tsegga Tecle (2012), who advocate for such a reframing in order to recognize and honor "the considerable linguistic and pedagogical resources that translinguistic identity offers" (15). In other words, although I do not identify as translingual, I believe very much in the power of translingu-al*ity* (Robinson, Hall, and Navarro 2020) as a way of thinking about teaching language and writing.

From our first "reading" (Hidalgo 2018), I was struck by Shewanda Leger's (2018) and Naomi Sweo's (2018) video projects in doing the work of blurring the boundaries of what is and is not included in academic spaces such as the essay, and, as Leger (2018) puts it, "disrupt[ing] peda-gogical values." It was almost immediately clear to me how transmodal forms, such as the video memoirs in Hidalgo's (2018) collection, hold power to subvert academic and genre conventions. I resonated with these ideas deeply and drew upon them in eagerly crafting my own MP1—an academic "or not" memoir via a transmodal Wix site (Heise 2021). In this project I engaged in/with/across a variety of modalities, and I also shifted among informal, conversational, and slang forms of English and pushed back against SAE, all with the goal of disrupting what is considered typical or welcome in an academic space.

I realized through this course that there is something in particular about transmodality as both a form and a way of thinking that lends itself to work like this that subverts academic structures that so problem-atically reinforce hierarchies, inequalities, and injustices. For example, a recurring theme in our readings (Leger 2018; Reid and Hancock 2019) involved teachers pushing back against presumptions that their students in foundational writing classes lacked the skills and complex-ity of thought to engage in digital projects, particularly using language and communication gestures appropriate to such formats that veered away from SAE. As an instructor of introductory composition classes, I, too, bristled at such commonplace assumptions surrounding students' (in)abilities to code mesh informal and formal vernaculars in transmodal (including, but not limited to, digital) communicative spaces—as if they didn't do that work every day already.

The imperative to mesh multimodality and translingualism into a transmodal framework became more and more apparent as the course went on. In particular, Cruz Medina and Octavio Pimentel (2016) spurred important conversations in and outside the classroom about language, race, and multimodality. In considering creative expression as a meaningful tool of transmodality, I was struck by Medina's (2016) chapter, in which he writes, "Testimonios including digital ones, contribute to decolonial knowledge that breaks from—and often speaks against—dominant colonial narratives." He continues, "Testimonio functions in much the same way as counterstory, which Aja Martinez outlines for the fields of writing and rhetorical studies in Composition Studies, revealing the marginalized experience or cumulative experiences and testifying rhetorically in opposition to dominant, stock stories about minoritized and racialized experiences." Through our course projects, especially the digital-literacy narrative (Major Project 1, or MP1) and rhetorical analysis (Major Project 2, or MP2), we had these opportunities to work with and craft our own counterstories meaningfully and creatively across languages and modalities. For my MP2, for example, I conducted a rhetorical analysis of a transmodal project, "Redefining Refugee" (Youth Ritsona 2017), in which young residents of a refugee camp in Greece pushed back against common (mis)conceptions of the label *refugee* through disidentification (Muñoz 1999) strategies. This work—based on a project I helped facilitate while working alongside refugee youth in Greece in 2017—is one that has continued to inform my scholarship, community engagement, research, and teaching, especially as I enter into teaching first-year writing in the fall of 2021.

Through all our projects, readings, and discussions in Digital Rhetoric, I've come to understand on a much deeper level the connections among language, modality, and rhetoric and the need for further conversations around their intersections in transmodality. In other words, the lines of inquiry I followed in Digital Rhetoric around transmodality have woven their way into my professional identity through both research and teaching as a paradigm that bridges extant theories around multimodality and translingualism in ways that are deeply just, affirming, and equitable.

STUDENT REFLECTIONS: MARISOL, EMY, AND NINA

Because both coauthors identify as white, monolingual US nationals, and in order to garner further perspectives on the intersections between translingual and multimodal practices, we recruited students to reflect on the course via a learning-management system (LMS) discussion-board forum in preparation for writing this chapter. This activity was completely optional and was not weighted or assigned any type of value within the course. Furthermore, student permissions were obtained and methods for obtaining qualitative data approved by the author's IRB (Log #20-113). Three students posted to the discussion board in response to the following questions:

- What was your experience working multimodally on [Major Project 1, the "Multimodal Memoir"], particularly through a multi/translingual lens?
- More broadly, how have you experienced the interaction of multimodality and multi/translingualism in this class?

Students were also informed that the discussion board was "meant to be a very open space for subjective and freeform reflection" and instructed to "feel free to treat these prompts as ideas rather than instructions, and to modify or disregard them completely as feels best for you." Once the course was over, we initiated the IRB review process, gained consent from each student-participant, and also asked them to choose a pseudonym by which we could identify their responses. The main theme that emerged from these student narratives was how perceptions of and responses to transmodality varied based on the participant's relationship to and/or conceptualizations of translingualism.

In her contribution, Marisol, a CAL PhD student, expressed feeling marginalized as a Hispanic American monolingual student in an atmosphere dominated by transnational and multilingual students. Marisol writes about how she wasn't given space to focus on Hispanic identity and experience in her collaborative discussion leadership of Medina and Pimentel (2016), observing that the class conversation "shifted Hispanic culture from where it was supposed to be as the epicenter of the conversation to the back burner. When I did try to bring the conversation back around to the intended topic, I was met with general resistance from the class." These experiences of marginalization were further exacerbated by the transnational and translingual dynamics of our course, with Marisol writing,

> In some ways I also felt disrespected cause I felt like my opinion about my own people was being disregarded. No one was asking, "Well Marisol, as

a Hispanic American what do YOU think about the author's theories?" While my international classmates are considered experts on their own cultures and languages, no one was treating me like I was the expert on my own.

For Marisol, the focus on translingualism in our course and program led to further marginalization, with her reflecting, "Because everyone sees me as *just* an American, my culture feels very erased and thrown into a generalized category." This marginalization became quite embodied through a multimodal exercise using Google Docs to create a handout for her group-discussion leadership. Marisol writes, "My other group member literally deleted my entire section to make room for his. Having google docs are nice and all but it also made me feel more marginalized. Like . . . literally. I was squeezing my stuff in on the literal margins of the page." Without the (literal) space to share and celebrate her Hispanic American and monolingual identities, Marisol experienced these transmodal components of the course as frustrating and marginalizing.

Emy joined the class from a non-CAL graduate degree program and brought with her diverse disciplinary, modal, and linguistic knowledge and perspectives. For her, using multiple languages in our course, and especially in MP1, was a relatively matter-of-fact experience. She shares, "As a bilingual, I have to learn English by using Arabic alphabets. For example, 'I am tired,' would be written as 'دريت ما يا.' For me, I learned the English language through the use of Arabic alphabets." Even in her response, Emy meshes English and Arabic alphabets so casually, in fact, that Megan (who is learning Arabic) read through it a few times before realizing "دريت ما يا" is the phonetic Arabic spelling for "I am tired," not the actual translation of the phrase. This matter-of-fact demeanor does not suggest, however, that Emy's linguistic journey as a bilingual hasn't been fraught; Emy elaborates on her difficulty learning English through Arabic in both her MP1 and her reflection on it, writing,

> For me, in my MP1 I used 2D animation software to reflect my own experience in learning the English language and how my pronunciation affected me negatively on the personal, educational, and social levels. I wanted to tell my audience that my journey was not easy and still it is filled with difficulties and challenges. In my animation, I used a mix of Arabic and English to reflect part of this experience.

For Emy, a mix of languages made sense for a project that called on our class to engage with multiple modes. She reflects, "The blend between a 2D animation (Photos, Videos, Voiceover, Music) and my experience was a perfect interaction between both of them." Without using the disciplinary language of transmodality, Emy's work and reflection demonstrate

242   HEISE AND VETTER

the interweaving of modality and language in her work in this class as a self-identified bilingual student.

Nina, a CAL PhD student, also shared her insights as a self-described "multimodal speaker" and "translingual individual," clarifying that her conception of translingualism is "how we use language in communication/writing without any boundaries or obstacles." For Nina, using translingual strategies is tied to how to "convey my intention to the audience of this project" and is related to how she engages with different modalities for different effects. She explains, "I used various visual writing cues to showcase my identity of a transnational individual. I went back and forth using Ukrainian, Russian, English in my writing." In her MP1, which she identified as targeting a predominantly English-speaking audience, Nina made a video with voice-overs in Russian and Ukrainian, subtitles in English, personal and open-access images, and music. While Nina also doesn't use the term *transmodality*, she does explain that, to her, *all* writing is multimodal, elaborating,

> For example, we use not only pen, pencil, or paper, or computer to transform our ideas into writing, but also we use various forms of audio, video, visual cues, imagination, background to form this ideas and to deliver our thought in the ways we find persuasive or productive, according to the goal of writing.

She elaborates, "I use multimodality and translingualism simultaneously. They are both part of my identity." While drawing on her embodied identities, including as a translingual individual, Nina's recollections of her experiences in the class and with MP1 remain rather matter of fact, though deeply thoughtful, in highlighting the interplay between translingualism and multimodality.

DISCUSSION AND RECOMMENDATIONS

By offering a highly contextualized case study within a uniquely situated graduate program, we forward a reflective account, coauthored and drawn from student course reflections, of our own professional journeys at the intersection of multimodality and translingualism. Through these polyvocal reflections, we see this chapter as an opening, perhaps a beginning or "interruption" (Micciche 2010) of normative standards surrounding language and modality. In this final section, we circle back to the question that has most motivated us: How *can* writing faculty, particularly those working with linguistically diverse students, better integrate multimodality in their curricula?

Our experiences, combined with those of three students in the course, have highlighted the need to (1) center transmodality and translingualism within multimodal courses like digital rhetoric, (2) balance high demands and high support in transmodal pedagogies, (3) engage with transmodality in ways that interrupt SL/MN discourses, and (4) attend to complex intersections of privilege and power in highly contextualized ecologies.

Center Transmodality and Translingualism in Digital Rhetoric

The intersections of multimodality and translingualism in this course provided opportunities for transmodal thinking and practice. However, much of this intersection became apparent through course readings rather than course projects. In interactions with the class, it was the multilingual and transnational students, though certainly not all of them, who felt the most anxious about those projects. To support these students, and in order to actually *center* transmodality in future iterations of the course, titles of major assignments and the actual course syllabus should employ more specific language regarding translingualism and transmodality. Being explicit in the titling of these course documents could provide a much-needed grounding for students who are unfamiliar with rhetoric, an anchor into something that *is* familiar. Reframing the titles of each major project will also allow for a revision of the major projects that center transmodal work. In particular, we plan to make a number of changes to the course. (1) Retitle the course Transmodality in/and Digital Rhetoric. (2) Create a model for rhetorical criticism with options for translingual analysis of multimodal artifacts. Such an approach will help support international and multilingual students by explicitly showcasing how translanguaging works in tandem with multimodal composition to create meaning. Ali's (2020) website and artist statement, discussed in the previous section, will serve as an opening framework for this project. (3) Rearrange the curriculum so the multimodal academic memoir project (MP1) is placed at the end of the assignment sequence. Such placement will allow students to carry their experience and learning into the assignment while also emphasizing the significance of transmodal and translingual narratives as effective interrogations of conventional academic writing and publishing. (4) In terms of day-to-day instruction, emphasize language and language practices as significant modes of communication and knowledge creation, especially by connecting classroom activities and discussions to the goals of the larger projects.

244   HEISE AND VETTER

Balance High Demands and High Support in Transmodal Pedagogies

Within the dynamic context of our course, we also learned about the need for equal measures of challenge and support for students engaging in transmodal work. This balance in creating an environment both "inviting and demanding" (Emert 2014, 34) is difficult, but crucial. For example, Gonzales (2018) stresses the importance of scaffolding translation and translanguaging work in "a cultural-rhetorical environment that will facilitate these interactions" (119). In our coauthor conversations looking back on this class, we sometimes wondered whether that cultural-rhetorical scaffolding was fully there for all students.

Moving forward, we both plan to draw upon multimodality to support language learning *and* to take translingual orientations to multimodality in order to scaffold rhetorical learning and outcomes. As Pacheco and Smith (2015) found, through multimodal pedagogies, linguistically diverse students "leveraged and meshed multiple semiotic resources to not only connect multiple audiences to the distinct experiences of their subjects but also to connect their own identities to these experiences" (308). Transmodality, then, intersects with identity formation and expression *as well as* being a rhetorical attunement (Lorimer Leonard 2014) between speaker and audience. Strengthening these points of connectivity and metacognition to foster this rhetorical awareness is a priority for both of us moving forward in our teaching.

Interrupt Harmful SL/MN Discourses through Transmodality

In realizing the necessity of providing explicit instruction and productive environments (Gonzales 2018) for transnational and multilingual students—as well as national and/or monolingual students—we seek to foster a course context in which they may interrogate and work across the boundaries of SAE. Such scaffolding can further "unstick" (Micciche 2010, 177) the prevalent and enduring notions of SL/MN, and in ways accessible to both mono- and translingual students, particularly in a highly transnational context. Nina's and Emy's reflections on the ways languages and modalities intertwined in their course projects, for example, demonstrate the ways transmodality can facilitate such moments of unsticking.

Due in part to instances of border crossings related to experimental forms, genre remix, and code meshing, transmodality enables especially salient moments of unsticking and interrogation of SL/MN. These border crossings were especially apparent in a student's analysis of a multilingual artist's web portfolio. This student was able to analyze and demonstrate how transmodality is enacted in mixed-media artistic expression and how such work challenges SL/MN ideologies. Although this particular case may not be representative of all students' work on this assignment, it serves as a formative example of the potential for discovering and engaging transmodality in the work of artists. A brief elucidation can be found by examining the artist's statement included in their digital portfolio (Ali 2020). "My own multilingual lens," Ali (2020) explains, "has shown me how language can be a form of misinterpretation rather than a means of understanding. My immersive installations of light, pattern, and textiles seek to move past language to offer a more expansive, experiential understanding of self, culture, and nation." Ali's (2020) statement parallels what Bigelow et al. (2017) acknowledge: "Communication can be made more complex by exercising new, multimodal literacies, which draw on a multitude of semiotic resources made possible in digital environments" (185). At times, we must move beyond language, especially SL/MN language, to fully represent the complexity of experience. If we are to seriously grapple, in our pedagogical practice, with the notion of transmodality, composition ought to pay more attention to artistic practices and processes. Abstract visual and mixed-media art, in particular, can provide numerous theoretical and pedagogical entry points into transmodal composition. Accompanying artists' statements, furthermore, allow us access to the artists' self-described practices.

Attend to Power and Privilege Dynamics in Transnational Contexts

In the singular microcosm of our classroom, we experienced a unique inversion of the power and privilege dynamics around transnationality and translinguality. Given that our class was composed of a majority of both multilingual and transnational students, and that attention was focused on offering such students inroads for critiquing SAE, a Hispanic American monolingual student, Marisol, experienced marginalization. While transmodality can and often does subvert norms, in this case it may have reified it, as in Marisol's example of literally being pushed into the margins of a Google Doc by her translingual and transnational classmates. At the same time, Marisol's reflections, in response to our prompts, formed in themselves the sort of counterstory transmodality can foster, as she pushed back against the ways translingualism and transnationality were embodied as privileged positions in our classroom. Moving forward, our considerations of transmodality can and should attend to other intersections of marginalized identities beyond only language and modality.

Likewise, a more explicitly transmodal approach to digital rhetoric can be essential within a transnational context like our CAL PhD program at IUP. In Sujin Kim's (2018) study of one transnational youth, she found the participant "drew upon her entire semiotic repertoire in digital spaces to materialize relationships and identities across her local and transnational social fields" (39). By reflexively examining our own experience and the student reflections above, we have recognized how a transmodal approach to digital rhetoric can be self-empowering and relationship building for students in a transnational context. At the same time, we have also seen how important it is to expansively scaffold transmodality, and especially translingualism, as a paradigm. For example, through Marisol's reflection, it becomes clear that a broader definition of translingualism and translanguaging may have been helpful, that is, one in which self-identified monolingual students could feel empowered to translanguage through various dialects, registers, and vernaculars of their own Englishes. While we both perceive translanguaging as a broad and fluid communicative act that *can* include monolinguals' use of different dialects, this breadth may not have been clear in the course or shared across the program. Moving forward, we seek to create a space where monolingual students, and especially those with other marginalized identity positions, can feel self-empowered to bring their full repertoires of linguistic and literate resources in a multimodal, digital environment.

CONCLUSION

A recurring motif in this chapter, as well as the course, is that of dis- and/or interruption towards transmodal professionalization. For example, in our transnational classroom, transmodal texts that subverted the norms of academic writing (and identity), such as Jacqueline Rhodes and Jonathan Alexander (2015), created discomfort in the classroom, disrupting the typical chatter of the seminar and replacing it with silence and confused questions. Class became charged when discussing Medina and Pimentel (2016) as tensions arose between students' different experiences of race and racism across multiple national, ethnic, and racial contexts, as referenced in Marisol's reflection. Even discussions on language diversity itself, in particular while reading Gonzales (2018), brought up fraught and complicated reactions from monolingual students with other marginalized identity positions, like Marisol. These tensions are not necessarily to be avoided but are rather to be navigated in a compassionate and culturally and rhetorically responsive pedagogical context. Looking back, we can see these intersections are part of what makes the work of transmodality so rich and complex. It certainly might not have always felt comfortable, but we argue transmodality as a paradigm requests that we loosen our hold on the comfortable, engage in contact zones (Pratt 1991), and work within difference(s) rather than around it.

In our invocation of Micicche's (2010) writing as feminist rhetorical theory as a reflective methodology, furthermore, we sought to interrupt our own professional engagement in the PhD CAL program (as professor and student) by looking back to think more deeply about how multimodality and translingualism were actually enacted in the course and how they might be better emphasized. Such disruption and interruption parallel the unique capability of transmodality, as a developing and dynamic theoretical movement within composition, to interrupt and disrupt SL/MN ideologies toward the use of new models of composing that allow for the complexity and diversity of language and identity. Ultimately, making a commitment to these models in our teaching creates more space for communicative difference, opening up the profession to more diversity in terms of academic identity, scholarship, linguistic negotiation, and the sharing of knowledge.

REFERENCES

Ali, Alia. 2020. "X-Ray Artist Statement." Alia Ali. https:/www.alia-ali.com/filter/x-ray/Artist-Statement %7B%7BAU.

Bigelow, Martha, Jenifer Vanek, Kendall King, and Nimo Abdi. 2017. "Literacy as Social (Media) Practice: Refugee Youth and Native Language Literacy at School." *International Journal of Intercultural Relations* 60: 183–97. https://doi.org/10.1016/j.ijintrel.2017.04.002.

Canagarajah, Suresh. 2011. "Codemeshing in Academic Writing: Identifying Teachable Strategies of Translanguaging." *Modern Language Journal* 95 (3): 401–17. https://doi.org/10.1111/j.1540-4781.2011.01207.x.

DeVoss, Dànielle. 2013. *Understanding and Composing Multimodal Projects*. Boston: Bedford/St. Martin's.

Emert, Toby. 2014. " 'Hear a Story, Tell a Story, Teach a Story': Digital Narratives and Refugee Middle Schoolers." *Voices From the Middle* 21 (4): 33–39.

Gonzales, Laura. 2018. *Sites of Translation: What Multilinguals Can Teach Us About Digital Writing and Rhetoric*. Ann Arbor: University of Michigan Press. https://www.fulcrum.org/concern/monographs/0z708x360.

Heise, Megan. 2021. "Academic (Or Not): An Academic Memoir Troubling the Ivory Tower." *Inspiring Pedagogical Connections* 6: 15–16. https://mheise21.wixsite.com/academicornot.

Hidalgo, Alexandra, ed. 2018. *Pixelating the Self: Digital Feminist Memoirs*. Enculturation Intermezzo. http://intermezzo.enculturation.net/o8-hidalgo-et-al/contents/index.html.

Horner, Bruce, Cynthia Selfe, and Tim Lockridge. 2015. *Translinguality, Transmodality, and Difference: Exploring Dispositions and Change in Language and Learning*. Enculturation. http://intermezzo.enculturation.net/o1/ttd-horner-selfe-lockridge/index.htm.

248 HEISE AND VETTER

Imoka, Chizoba. 2018. "Training for 'Global Citizenship' but Local Irrelevance: The Case of an Upscale Nigerian Private Secondary School." In *Decolonial Pedagogy: Examining Sites of Resistance, Resurgence, and Renewal,* edited by Njoki Nathani Wane and Kimberly L. Todd, 73–91. London: Palgrave Macmillan.

Khadka, Santosh, and J. C. Lee, eds. 2019. *Bridging the Multimodal Gap: From Theory to Practice.* Logan: Utah State University Press.

Kim, Sujin. 2018. " 'It Was Kind of a Given That We Were All Multilingual': Transnational Youth Identity Work in Digital Translanguaging." *Linguistics and Education* 43: 39–52. https://doi.org/10.1016/j.linged.2017.10.008.

Leger, Shewonda. 2018. "Making Space for Myself While Making Space for My Students." In *Pixelating the Self: Digital Feminist Memoirs,* edited by Alexandra Hidalgo. Enculturation Intermezzo. http://intermezzo.enculturation.net/08-hidalgo-et-al/06-shewonda -leger-making-space/index.html.

Lorimer Leonard, Rebecca. 2014. "Multilingual Writing as Rhetorical Attunement." *College English* 76 (3): 227–47. http://www.jstor.org/stable/24238241.

Lutkewitte, Claire. 2014. *Multimodal Composition: A Critical Sourcebook.* Series in Rhetoric and Composition. Boston: Bedford/St. Martin's.

Medina, Cruz. 2016. "Digital Latinx Storytelling: Testimonio as Multimodal Resistance." In *Racial Shorthand: Coded Discrimination Contested in Social Media,* edited by Cruz Medina and Octavio Pimentel. Logan, UT: Computers and Composition Digital Press. https:// ccdigitalpress.org/book/shorthand/chapter_medina.html.

Medina, Cruz, and Octavio Pimentel, eds. 2016. *Racial Shorthand: Coded Discrimination Contested in Social Media.* Logan, UT: Computers and Composition Digital Press. https:// ccdigitalpress.org/book/shorthand/.

Micciche, Laura. 2010. "Writing as Feminist Rhetorical Theory." In *Rhetorica in Motion: Feminist Rhetorical Methods and Methodologies,* edited by Eileen E. Schell and K. J. Rawson, 173–88. Pittsburgh: University of Pittsburgh Press.

Motha, Suhanthie, Rashi Jain, and Tsegga Tecle. 2012. "Translinguistic Identity-as-Pedagogy: Implications for Language Teacher Education." *International Journal of Innovation in English Language Teaching* 1 (1): 13–28.

Muñoz, José Esteban. 1999. *Disidentification: Queers of Color and the Performance of Politics.* Minneapolis: University of Minnesota Press.

Pacheco, Mark B., and Blaine E. Smith. 2015. "Across Languages, Modes, and Identities: Bilingual Adolescents' Multimodal Codemeshing in the Literacy Classroom." *Bilingual Research Journal* 38 (3): 292–312. https://doi.org/10.1080/15235882.2015.1091051.

Pratt, Mary Louise. 1991. "Arts of the Contact Zone." *Profession* 91: 33–40.

Ratcliffe, Krista. 2005. *Rhetorical Listening: Identification, Gender, Whiteness.* Carbondale: Southern Illinois University Press.

Reid, Lynn, and Nicole Hancock. 2019. "Teaching Basic Writing in the 21st Century: A Multiliteracies Approach." In *The Archive as Classroom: Pedagogical Approaches to the Digital Archive of Literacy Narratives,* edited by Kathryn Comer, Michael Harker, and Ben McCorkle. Logan, UT: Computers and Composition Digital Press. https:// ccdigitalpress.org/book/archive-as-classroom/digital1.html.

Rhodes, Jacqueline, and Jonathan Alexander. 2015. *Techne: Queer Meditations on Writing the Self.* Logan, UT: Computers and Composition Digital Press. https://ccdigitalpress .org/book/techne/.

Robinson, Heather, Jonathan Hall, and Nela Navarro. 2020. *Translingual Identities and Transnational Realities in the U.S. College Classroom.* New York: Routledge.

Sánchez-Martín, Cristina, Lavinia Hirsu, Laura Gonzales, and Sara P. Alvarez. 2019. "Pedagogies of Digital Composing through a Translingual Approach." *Computers and Composition* 52: 142–57. https://doi.org/10.1016/j.compcom.2019.02.007.

Schell, Eileen E., and K. J. Rawson, eds. 2010. *Rhetorica in Motion: Feminist Rhetorical Methods and Methodologies.* Pittsburgh: University of Pittsburgh Press.

Selfe, Cynthia L. 2007. *Multimodal Composition: Resources for Teachers.* New York: Hampton.

Shipka, Jody. 2016. "Transmodality in/and Processes of Making: Changing Dispositions and Practice." *College English* 78 (3): 250–57. https://www.jstor.org/stable/44075115.

Sorapure, Madeleine. 2006. "Between Modes: Assessing Student New Media Compositions." *Kairos: A Journal of Rhetoric, Technology, and Pedagogy* 10 (2). http://kairos.technorhetoric.net/10.2/coverweb/sorapure/between_modes.pdf.

Sweo, Naomi. 2018. "Woman in Relation: On Sisterhood, Self, and Marriage." In *Pixelating the Self: Digital Feminist Memoirs,* edited by Alexandra Hidalgo. Enculturation Intermezzo. http://intermezzo.enculturation.net/08-hidalgo-et-al/08-naomi-sweo-woman-in-relation/index.html.

Youth Ritsona. 2017. "Redefining Refugee." *Ritsona Kingdom Journal* 2. https://www.lighthouserelief.org/ritsona-kingdom-journal.

13

MULTIMODALITY AS A KEY CONSIDERATION IN DEVELOPING A NEW COMMUNICATIONS DEGREE AT UMASS, DARTMOUTH

Anthony F. Arrigo

A MOVE TOWARD MULTIMODALITY

Over the past few decades, content creation has gone from the purview of a few people with specialized training in media and design to anyone with access to a desktop, laptop, tablet, or phone. In his book, *Literacy in the New Media Age*, Gunther Kress (2003) refers to the confluence of social, technological, economic, and communication changes as "so profound that it is justifiable to speak of a revolution in the landscape of communication" (9). Nearly twenty years later, that revolution continues unabated. Today, everyone from middle schoolers to grandmothers can quickly produce multimodal content to share across digital and print platforms. Image manipulation is commonplace. Video editing can be done in seconds on a mobile device and instantly shared on social media with potentially millions of people. Memes that combine images with text to make humorous or satirical messages are ubiquitous on social media and private messaging platforms. Gifs, emojis, hashtags, and inventive uses of traditional text are commonplace ways to express emotional reactions to information or situations. For example, ASCII art uses the 128 characters of the ACII text standard for connotative and denotative meanings that range from feelings and emotions to depictions of animals, electronics, weapons, and more (https://www.asciiart.eu/).

Even web and document design are becoming accessible to anyone with basic digital-literacy skills. Webhosting companies provide WYSIWYG drag-and-drop graphical user interfaces and thousands of free templates for easy web design with no coding required. Graphic-design companies provide downloadable predesigned templates for everything from business cards to resumes to corporate quarterly reports. Podcasts,

https://doi.org/10.7330/9781646424184.c013

videos, music mashups, animations, and more can all be produced and consumed from the comfort of one's home. With online video tutorials, anyone can become proficient with nearly any skill or technology without formal education. I'm a testament to this. I became proficient in Adobe InDesign, Photoshop, and Illustrator, DIY home remodeling, and playing Beatles songs on the guitar simply by watching hours upon hours of free tutorial videos on YouTube!

Because of the dramatic change in the digital-media landscape and the ease with which we can acquire various literacies, there has been a corresponding increase in multimodal composition and analysis in the classroom. Writing and composition, rhetoric, and communications curricula now regularly include studying and producing materials for digital and online spaces, print publications, video games, podcasts, and more. Students in composition classrooms, for example, are regularly asked to produce texts that, along with writing, include aspects of art, photography, film, video, and graphic design. If we take Kress and Theo van Leeuwen's (1996) definition that multimodal texts are "any text whose meanings are realized through more than one semiotic mode," it is clear multimodal composition in and out of the classroom is now commonplace.

As many other departments have no doubt noticed, students are looking to gain the academic skills that come with writing and communications courses, coupled with professional skills directly applicable to workplace needs. Moreover, companies now want to hire graduates with more than just superb grammar and the ability to turn a phrase; they want employees who can deploy a range of communication skills that include visual, oral, digital, and multimedia.

One example that elucidates this point comes from the Association of American Colleges and Universities, which periodically surveys business leaders to assess what they desire in new students coming out of college. Contrary to the prevailing narrative and push for more STEM-related expertise, these surveys show that indeed communication, critical thinking, and integrative and applied knowledge are most desirable. According to its most recent surveys (https://www.aacu.org/leap/pub lic-opinion-research/2015-survey-results), more than 90 percent of respondents said "a demonstrated capacity to think critically, communicate clearly, and solve complex problems is *more important* than [a job candidate's] undergraduate major." More than 75 percent said students should get *more* training in critical thinking, written and oral communication, and applied knowledge. Among the most important requirements for new hires across all those surveyed are oral and written communication skills, technological skills, information literacy, and integrative and applied knowledge in real-world settings.

Consequently, for new PhDs moving into the current academic landscape, it is no longer enough to come away from a graduate program with a strong theoretical grounding; they also need a ready toolbox of multimodal communication techniques and technologies for teaching and research. Writing and communications educators must move nimbly between traditional writing instruction and, for example, usability studies (UX), media studies, content-management systems, visual communication and graphic design, writing for social media, web design, and audio and video production.

In the sections that follow, I outline how we have conceived of multimodality in our new communications BA curriculum, some of the trends toward multimodality, and challenges and opportunities for multimodal scholarship and pedagogy going forward.

MULTIMODALITY IN OUR COMMUNICATIONS CURRICULUM

The University of Massachusetts, Dartmouth, is a small public research university on the south coast of Massachusetts. Nestled between the economically struggling cities of Fall River and New Bedford, whose days of prosperity peaked in the nineteenth century during the heyday of whaling and textiles, UMass Dartmouth enrolls approximately 9,000 total students, with 7,295 undergraduates and 1,621 graduate and law-school students. Nearly 40 percent of our undergraduates have significant enough financial need to qualify for Pell Grants, and 85 percent of our students receive some form of financial aid. Nearly half are the first in their family to attend college, and nearly 30 percent of our students identify as people of color.

For decades the English department at UMass Dartmouth was like many across the country: bifurcated into a two-track system we generally referred to as "literature" and "writing," with a roughly two to one ratio of writing to literature majors. Although many departments have long ago waded through the painful process of breaking off disciplines from English departments into communications, rhetoric, writing studies, media studies, and various other concentrations, we had managed to hold out. Nevertheless, the reality of national trends, student demand, business needs, competition in the academic marketplace, and scholarly movement in the field forced our hand.

This process provided a unique opportunity to reimagine our curriculum. Rather than nibbling around the edges, we were able to develop new pathways through the major and new courses based on our values and the realities of employment opportunities for our students. In our case, since we actively sought to connect contemporary trends in digital communication and writing with education and professionalization opportunities for our students, we are now offering courses that cover both the theoretical and practical training students need to enter an increasingly digitally and visually mediated world.

Three broad assumptions frame multimodality in our curriculum. First, it is a fundamentally interdisciplinary subject that requires multiple literacies: verbal, digital, cultural, visual, gestural, aural, and so forth. To encourage students to cross over the borders of conventional academic disciplines and break out of the box of traditional composition, educators need tools and training in not only writing but also areas such as graphic design, computer science, and social and mass media, among others. Multimodal composition is not an academic discipline in the traditional sense but instead is an approach, an area of study, an interpretive framework that draws on many disciplines. Second, multimodality is a social and cultural practice that allows communicators to draw on situated ways of knowing, meaning making, and identity to forge relationships across generational, cultural, economic, and geographic boundaries. Third, multimodal composition is rhetorical. Many of our faculty were trained in rhetoric, writing studies, rhet-comp, or technical communication programs with strong rhetorical traditions. We believe rhetorical theory provides explanatory power and pedagogical frameworks that enhance multimodal composition opportunities for students. Below I offer some rationale for each of these assumptions.

Multimodal Composition Requires Multiple Literacies

Kress and van Leeuwen (1996) write that if language, until now the most valued and policed code in our society, is changing over to visual communication, educators should "perhaps begin to rethink what 'literacy' ought to include, and what should be taught under the heading of 'writing' in schools" (32).

Digital texts require us to interpret a complex landscape of iconography, hyperlinks, tabs, colors, images, sound, and so forth. We also interact with digital texts using embodied gestures such as hand and finger movements with a keyboard, mouse, and/or trackpad, which allows us to navigate, interact with, and manipulate the screen.

Multimodal composition requires various literacies and different patterns of thought. Instead of the *linear* thinking associated with traditional text composition, students need *lateral* thinking to move freely among modes and make *connections* between disparate types of information. Instead of merely collecting the *content* of ideas, they need to understand the *relationships* between concepts. Thinking across and between associations, translating between different cultural ways of knowing, accessing social knowledge, and communicating it across platforms to diverse audiences unmoored from regional or generational or political boundaries— these are the literacy skills needed to negotiate today's global and multimodal public sphere.

We also must accept that disinformation—distorted and intentionally misleading misinformation and propaganda, what Rubin (2019) describes as "a socio-cultural technology-enabled epidemic in digital news, propagated via social media" (1014)—is part of our new-media landscape. Consequently, students need to be taught not just literacies but critical literacies that allow them to process persuasive messages and understand their interpellation and historical and cultural context (Newfield 2011).

Multimodal Composition Is a Social and Cultural Practice

Building on the idea of multiliteracies is the idea that those literacies are also embedded in a range of social and cultural practices. In *Negotiating Spaces for Literacy Learning: Multimodality and Governmentality,* Mary Hamilton, Rachel Heydon, Kathryn Hibbert, and Roz Stooke (2015) argue that multimodality is largely reliant on various conceptions of literacy, which are themselves social practices. To them, literacy is a kind of technology and thus subject to all the nonneutral and culturally specific characteristics and power structures of other types of technologies. They situate multimodal literacy within the broader term *multiliteracies* and point to three key strands that include multilingual movement between and among diverse communities, digital literacies in which meaning making is both produced and consumed in digital environments, and cultural literacies focused on ethnographic work studying situated literacy practices.

Others argue multimodality and social and cultural practices are inextricably intertwined. Bill Cope and Mary Kalantzis (2000) suggest that the best multimodal pedagogy calls for several things: draw on past and present experiences, consider learners' sociocultural identities, and create safe spaces that promote trust and risk (329). Linda Scott (1994) argues that "pictures are not merely analogues to visual perception but symbolic artifacts constructed from the conventions of a particular culture" (252).

Kress (2003, 2010) describes the semiotic resources we use to create multimodal messages as socially constructed because communicators use their existing frames of reference and knowledge to both interpret their meanings and redeploy them in new ways to make new meanings. They can do this across the same mode (what he calls "transformation") or various combinations of modes and communicative contexts ("transduction").

An advantage of starting with the baseline understanding of multimodal communication as being social and cultural provides an opportunity to overcome one of the significant problems with traditional approaches to composition instruction, namely that it treats composition as though it's occurring in a social and cultural vacuum. Many composition textbooks are formulaic and stocked with what is professed to be professionalizing moves writers should make. They often consider students an empty vessel, ahistorical, homogenous, culturally neutral, and free of ideology, which is clearly not the case.

Multimodal Composition Is Rhetorical

The composing process is one of invention. That is, it makes new connections from existing knowledge by blending modes and resources to create new meanings. Rhetorical invention provides communicators with heuristics that let them create arguments appropriate for a given situation by taking ideas they already have, examining the positions of others, and arranging arguments in novel and imaginative ways to find the best available means of persuasion.

Visual rhetoric looks at how image producers draw on shared vocabularies, desires, values, cultural knowledge of the audience, and the audience's ability to infer the producer's intentions within their particular sociohistorical context. In visual rhetoric, as in multimodal communication, images cannot be examined in isolation but instead must be considered alongside their circulation, distribution, and reception by the audience within their historical context (Arrigo 2014; Finnegan 2005).

A rhetorical approach also has many advantages over traditional process composition pedagogy. According to Cynthia Selfe (2009), "The history of writing in U.S. composition instruction, as well as its contemporary legacy, functions to limit our professional understanding of composing as a multimodal rhetorical activity and deprive students of valuable semiotic resources for making meaning" (617). Dislodged from their typical modes of communication once in the composition classroom, students are often not given the opportunity to think and act laterally or ask probing questions. They often feel as though they do not have anything new to say or that what they do have to say lacks importance. However, rhetorical training such as learning about commonplaces, stasis theory, *dossoi logoi*, and invention can provide students disciplinary means to develop arguments, try out opinions, and test those opinions against intellectual scrutiny.

Rather than teaching the standard five-paragraph essay, which students will likely never use outside a college classroom, it would be better to equip students with the fundamentals of invention, arrangement, style, memory, and delivery—concepts they can apply to any subject and modality. Some scholars like Collin Brooke (2009) have reconsidered the rhetorical canon, adapting and changing it to better conform with how people interact with new media. Students should become adept at recognizing enthymemes and using them in their compositions. Enthymematic arguments are just as potent in visuals, videos, and mixed-mode communications as they are in formal argumentation (Finnegan 2001). Rather than focusing on text-based rules like thesis statements and topic sentences (which are somewhat foreign to classical rhetoric), students would be better off learning to compose in socially and culturally accepted genres of communication appropriate for specific times, events, and occasions.

This, of course, is not to say students should never learn how to write a thesis sentence or an introduction but that rules and expectations for one mode of communication do not necessarily apply to all others. This view also recognizes the reality that with students and faculty now tethered to smartphones, tablets, and computers for much of their waking lives, knowledge-making practices in our lived experiences are firmly ensconced in the digital and multimodal realms, which should be reflected in our pedagogy, too.

Communication Curriculum

At the department level, when thinking about moving to more emphasis on multimodal composition in the classroom, faculty will need to consider curricular design issues such as whether to use a foundational approach, in which students are offered a series of specific courses to gain skills that can then be later used in other courses, or a permeated approach, in which the tenets of multimodal composition are taught in all (or nearly all) courses offered in the major. Regardless of the approach, students will need to be taught how to use the tools and deploy their compositions.

Because we were afforded the opportunity to develop a holistic approach with the new major, we decided that since multimodal communication permeates so many of our courses, we did not need as strong a focus on required stand-alone technical instruction. Instead, students will gain exposure to these skills and ideas throughout the curriculum and in a range of topics and environments. Although we do still offer mode-specific classes with the intention that those skills will follow students throughout their coursework, the expectation in upper-level courses is that since students have been repeatedly exposed to multimodal composition in the lower-level courses, they will come into the upper-level class already familiar with a range of modalities and technologies.

Learning Outcomes: With these assumptions in hand, we set about restructuring our program. Our learning outcomes include modes of visual, textual, oral, and digital communication. Not every class is digital or multimodal, but to qualify as a communication course, it must meet at least four learning outcomes. Consequently, each class includes at least two modes of communication from this list:

- Create written texts using appropriate supporting materials and theories in communication and rhetoric.
- Communicate ideas orally within multiple contexts.
- Use information design principles to produce texts appropriate for an audience, purpose, and context.
- Summarize and apply key concepts in communication and rhetorical theory.
- Evaluate the historical and/or cultural contexts of communication practices and describe their ethical, social, or environmental implications.
- Evaluate messages from a variety of media and technologies using methodologies in communication and rhetoric.

Foundations Courses: We have four foundations courses covering rhetoric, ethics, digital and media literacy, and speech communication. Each of these courses is fundamental to the rest of the curriculum, and all are required and prerequisites for other courses in the major. Digital and media literacy is focused on developing basic multimodal communication skills that can be applied throughout a student's matriculation. Our decision to require such a course early in our curriculum was a conscious effort to encourage students to continue to hone their skills in subsequent courses. Most upper-level courses assume students come into the class able to create basic digital films and infographics, use online collaborative platforms, use digital mapmaking tools, and so

258   ARRIGO

Table 13.1. Required courses

Foundations	1. Introduction to Rhetoric and Communication (prerequisite for all subsequent courses in the major) 2. Ethics in Communication (prerequisite for capstone) 3. Digital and Media Literacy (prerequisite for all upper-level classes in the major) 4. Speech Communication (prerequisite for Capstone)
Intermediate writing	5. Any department Intermediate Writing course (prerequisite for all 300-level classes in the major) Communicating in the Sciences Business Communication Technical Communication Introduction to Strategic Communication Introduction to Journalism
Cultural context and theory	6–7. Any two upper-level literature courses 8. Any one of the following Advanced Rhetoric Language and Culture Special Topics in Rhetorical Studies Visual Communication
Electives	9–12. Elective Pathways (any four upper-level courses)
Capstone	13. Capstone in Communication

forth. This provides instructors across the department wide latitude to encourage multimodal assignments without spending onerous amounts of time teaching technical skills.

Intermediate Writing: Our university employs a university studies core curricular requirement that applies across the campus. Part of this requirement is Intermediate Writing. In our department, classes that fulfill this requirement include journalism, as well as business, science, technical, and strategic communications. These courses also provide springboards to the various pathways (some might call them *concentrations*) in the major.

Cultural Context and Theory: Because we are a multimajor department with literature, professional writing, and communications, students get a broad spectrum of courses that include literature and writing. We understand this is not common for communication departments. Nonetheless, our students have a requirement of two upper-level literature courses and one additional choice of advanced writing or rhetoric, or visual communications.

Elective Pathways: We wanted to provide as much flexibility as possible for students. Consequently, they are able to take any combination of electives they choose. However, we also understand students appreciate some guidance, so we grouped courses into logical bundles depending

Table 13.2. Elective pathways through the communication major

Journalism	Strategic communication
Foundations	Foundations
Intermediate Writing Introduction to Journalism	Intermediate Writing Introduction to Strategic Communication OR Business Communication
Cultural Context and Theory Two literature courses Advanced Rhetoric OR Language and Culture OR Special Topics in Rhetorical Studies	Cultural Context and Theory Two literature courses Advanced Rhetoric OR Language and Culture OR Special Topics in Rhetorical Studies
Electives (any 4) Sports Writing Writing Reviews Special Topics in Journalism Feature Story and Article Writing Writing about Popular Culture Magazine Writing	Electives (any 4) Public Relations Writing Special Topics in Writing and Comm Women Writing and Media Copywriting Tutoring Writing Environmental Communication
Capstone	Capstone
Multimodal and visual communication	*Technical communication*
Foundations	Foundations
Intermediate Writing Technical Communication OR Communicating in the Sciences	Intermediate Writing Communicating in the Sciences OR Business Communication OR Technical Communication
Cultural Context and Theory Two literature courses Visual Communication OR Advanced Rhetoric OR Special Topics in Rhetorical Studies	Cultural Context and Theory Two literature courses Advanced Rhetoric OR Visual Communication OR Special Topics in Rhetorical Studies
Electives (any 4) Multimodal Communication Internet Communication and Culture Document Design Digital Filmmaking Screenwriting Writing for Social Media	Electives (any 4) Report and Proposal Writing Usability Studies Special Topics in Writing and Comm Document Design Environmental Communication Special Topics in Communication
Capstone	Capstone

on what career path a student might wish to take. Because of our new learning outcomes that embed multimodality in all communications courses, we were able to move away from legislating specific multimodal or digital requirement categories and instead provide courses we feel students will want to take, with the expectation that each course will build various types of communication skills.

CHALLENGES TO TEACHING MULTIMODAL COMPOSITION

One of the main challenges for those in academic departments is whether digital and multimodal work is considered a legitimate currency in tenure and promotion decisions. Faculty structure their long-term research plans based on what is acceptable and preferable within their home institutions. Moreover, even if acceptance of such work is stated somewhere in one's tenure and promotion guidelines, there is a question of whether those in decision-making positions (such as deans and provosts) will genuinely consider the work to be on par with text-dominant publications. Thus, there can be a sense of risk in pursuing this kind of scholarship.

James Purdy and Joyce Walker (2010) wrote nearly a decade ago in "Valuing Digital Scholarship: Exploring the Changing Realities" that academic departments were attempting to consider how work in modalities outside traditional text-only formats could be considered scholarship, but that academic institutions were merely trying to find ways to accept digital work as equivalent to text instead of considering how it is transforming knowledge-making practices themselves. They argue that statements supporting digital publication by governing bodies like CCCC and MLA are well intentioned but they "perhaps unintentionally, place digital and print scholarship into narrowly constructed, oppositional genres that often privilege print and reinscribe the creative-scholarly split that has long been a problem for English studies" (178).

Concerns about digital and multimodal scholarship do not stop there. In many cases, the digital work requires official sanctioning through follow-up publications in traditional text modalities. This also has the knock-on effect of digital publications needing to be legitimated as equivalent to text by passing through preexisting processes and criteria set up to evaluate scholarship in the print-only modality. Moreover, multimodal scholarship is often seen as "creative" work, which in some institutions is accepted as legitimate scholarship but not at others.

Mills Kelly (2013) suggests that for digital scholarship to "count," it must meet three criteria: "It is the result of original research; it has an argument of some sort and that argument is situated in a preexisting conversation among scholars; it is public, peer-reviewed, and it has an audience response" (51). He outlines several obstacles that can prevent digital projects from meeting this bar of scholarship.

First is that some digital projects do not make an argument; only their follow-up journal articles accomplish that. Kelly gives examples of some well-known digital endeavors such as Tufts University's Perseus Project or the University of Virginia's Valley of the Shadow, which to him do not meet the scholarship criteria because they are not arguments but instead are merely large repositories of information.

The second is that there is little infrastructure in the humanities for peer review that adjudicates multimodal and digital projects' worthiness or unworthiness. Some ideas to change this have been proposed by humanities departments, and some professional organizations have put forth guidance, such as the MLA's *Guidelines for Evaluating Work in Digital Humanities and Digital Media*, which was last updated in 2012. Some peer-reviewed journals such as *Kairos* and *Vectors* have embraced multimodal scholarship, too.

Kelly also suggests that the traditional chronology of scholarship (submit the work, wait for feedback, adjust the work, resubmit, publish) simply does not work for digital projects. He suggests peer review of digital scholarship happens after the project is released to the public and offers analogues in various disciplines for that rationale.

An essential point in the "Does it count?" debate is made by Steve Anderson and Tara McPherson (2011) when they write, "It is increasingly important that we scholars . . . continue to translate existing guidelines like those of the MLA into terms and practices that are meaningful for our home departments and universities" (147). Our new communication major, along with increased scholarship by faculty in this area, provided the impetus to also examine our tenure and promotions standards. To our shock, we found our standards had not been updated in decades and had no language regarding major grant awards or digital scholarship. It cannot be stressed strongly enough that language supporting multimodal and digital scholarship must be included in department tenure and promotion standards.

The educational system itself also includes numerous structural barriers to multimodal literacy and proficiency. Though today's students expertly use digital devices to navigate modal boundaries and creatively mix and match semiotic resources to meet needs in their everyday lives, it is in the classroom where disciplinary partitions are introduced and enforced through the curriculum. Serafani (2015) points out that the multimodal texts students most frequently encounter outside school, such as graphic novels, video games, and comic books, are largely ignored as having any scholarly value in an educational setting and are thus pushed to the periphery of the curriculum—if not ignored outright—in favor of language-dominant texts (420). Consequently, students use fewer multimodal texts in school than outside school (Fleckenstein 2002).

262   ARRIGO

Another challenge is the frequency with which technologies, platforms, user interfaces, websites, and hardware requirements change. This places a burden on instructors to continually update their skills and to monitor their tools for changes.

The design process itself is a critical feature of composing, and instructors (or departments) must to spend as much time on this aspect as they do the actual crafting of the messages. Instructors must to guide students through choosing appropriate fonts or single or multicolumn layouts. Students need to learn about white space, where to place images, and how colors have emotional meanings for readers. Consequently, instructors must engage in what Eva Brumberger (2007) calls "demystifying design" and making the strange familiar.

OPPORTUNITIES IN TEACHING MULTIMODAL COMPOSITION

While there are challenges to embracing multimodal composition, for individual teachers or researchers or as a broader aspect of a department's curriculum, there are many opportunities in this area. Although concerns about multimodality as a scholarly activity continue, there is strong interest in the topic among academics. For example, multimodality was a popular topic at the 2019 Conference on College Composition and Communication (CCCC), which featured over sixty panels that included the term *multimodal, transmodal,* or *multimedia.* The 2018 Rhetoric Society of America (RSA) conference included over fifty panels and papers using the words *digital* or *multimodal* in the title, while the 2018 National Communication Association (NCA) conference had over seventy-five panels and papers with those terms.

Academic job listings show numerous positions open in departments of English, communications, media studies, rhetoric, writing studies, and writing centers, among others. They are looking for graduates with expertise in digital humanities, digital cultural studies, technology and digital media, digital rhetorics, emerging media, new media, social media, visual rhetorics, visual communication, visual design, information technologies, new communication media, digital texts, and more. A recent National Communication Association survey found that academic employment opportunities for communication faculty with digital competencies continue to increase, with the number more than doubling from 2009 to 2015.

Scholarly venues continue to become more accepting of digital and multimodal work. *Kairos, enculturation, Computers and Composition, Vectors,*

Multimodality as a Consideration in Developing a Communications Degree   263

and *Across the Disciplines* are just a few of the venues where scholars can publish multimodal work. Often this work is not just a critique or comment on multimodality but is itself multimodal. One of the first to cut through in this way was Anne Frances Wysocki's (2002) "A Bookling Monument," which was explicitly designed to disrupt our print-based reading practices.

A byproduct of all the recent scholarly interest in multimodality is that there are abundant resources available through books, journal articles, and websites that outline best practices and provide a wellspring of ideas for educators and scholars. These range from examining multimodality for language learners (Satar 2016; Yang 2012) to composition and communication scholars who have explored sound as their primary modality (Ahern 2013; Heydon and O'Neill 2016). There are resources on visuals and multimodal composition in children's literature and primary classrooms (Cloonan 2011; Hassett and Curwood 2009; Sipe 2007; Stafford 2011), photography and imagery (Fleckenstein, Calendrillo, and Worley 2002; Wiseman, Mäkinen, and Kupiainen 2016), design (Ball, Sheppard, and Arola 2018), pedagogy, (Palmeri 2012; Walsh 2010), and even the design of the multimodal composition spaces themselves (Black et al. 2012; Carpenter 2014). These make ups just a small fraction of the available examples, as the literature on multimodality is far too expansive to recount here and continues to grow.

Some challenges are also opportunities for growth and continued research. One example is in the area of theory. We do not yet have a recognizable and constitutively multimodal theory. Instead, we have an assortment of theories from rhetoric, composition, media studies, semiotics, comparative studies, and so forth that all started as linguistically based and then were adopted (or co-opted) for other modes.

There are also many opportunities in new and evolving media. For example, there are nearly unlimited opportunities for researchers to develop explanations and predictions for how immersive and digitally enhanced modalities communicate information and make meaning both inside and outside the classroom (Fowler 2015). For example, Julia Daisy Fraustino, Ji Young Lee, Sang Yeal Lee, and Hongmin Ahn (2018) found that 360-degree video used in the aftermath of a natural disaster "yields enhanced attitudes toward the helpful impact of the content" (331) Their paper is a response to a lack of academic research into how "modalities or delivery features play in publics' responses to public relations content" (332). They go on to say, "To the best of the researchers' knowledge, no found academic research in public relations examines outcomes of 360° video viewing."

There has also been significant research into areas of what might be considered fully immersive multimodality for teaching and learning, such as augmented and virtual reality and virtually enhanced education and training. These areas have been shown to improve both cognitive and noncognitive skills. Several studies conclude a clear outcome advantage for pairing traditional learning with immersive learning environments over traditional delivery (Merchant et al. 2014; Passig 2015; Yoon et al. 2012).

This kind of research seems particularly primed for humanities extension in and out of the classroom and opens up nearly unlimited possibilities for multimodal composition and communication. For example, there are opportunities for cross-disciplinary collaboration examining how socioeconomics, race, and gender influence students' perceptions of themselves and whether positive reinforcement in VR can help counterbalance negative aspects of social identity (Peck et al. 2018). This research can lead to more areas of opportunity with traditionally underrepresented groups, English-language learners, and low socioeconomic status groups who have typically been shut out of cutting-edge technologies in their classrooms. More research is also needed to validate previous studies' outcomes, particularly across more diverse groups of learners and locations (Smith et al. 2016).

CONCLUSION

Rachel Heydon and Sujsan O'Neill (2016) describe the holistic and positive impacts of multimodal literacy: "Our study findings also lead us to understand wellbeing through a qualitative lens of *flourishing* and *possibility*" (134). Multimodal literacy matters. It influences our identity, the way we understand the world around us, the way we interact with others, and the ways we make meaning. It is cross-disciplinary and cross-pollinating. It is both generative and receptive. Multimodal literacy has power, and with that power comes agency. At its best, it can build community and encourage our noblest ideals. However, at its worst, it creates division and hatred, otherness, and fear. That is why it is vitally important that we arm ourselves and our students with the tools to fight against our worst tendencies. If we are illiterate, we have no defense, no agency, no power.

I hope we can take a cue from the New London Group's 1996 manifesto *A Pedagogy of Multiliteracies: Designing Social Futures*, in which they state, "Access to wealth, power, and symbols must be possible no matter what one's identity markers." They argue states, schools, and literacy pedagogy must be "strong as neutral arbiters of difference. . . . This is the basis for a

Multimodality as a Consideration in Developing a Communications Degree   265

cohesive sociality, a new civility in which differences are used as a productive resource and in which differences are the norm" (Cazden et al. 1996, 69). The kinds of opportunities discussed here can allow students with different ways of knowing to express themselves by drawing on all the visual, cultural, oral, and textual resources available to them and participating in civil debate and the democratic process. Multimodal composition can give students agency by allowing them to assess the rhetorical situation and participate in asserting their power, celebrating their history, and changing the makeup of our civic spaces for the better. By teaching multimodal composition, we allow our students to make meaning across racial, ethnic, and political boundaries, promoting political and social engagement, upholding democratic principles, and encouraging social interconnection. Multimodal composition itself cannot save us from society's ills, but a more literate, empathetic, and understanding populace can.

APPENDIX X.A

University of Massachusetts Dartmouth Communication Major
  (13 courses, 39 credits)

Mission

Communication at UMass Dartmouth is committed to teaching twenty-first-century written, oral, and visual communication knowledge and skills grounded in rhetorical theory and critically engaged with diverse social, environmental, and technological perspectives.

Learning Outcomes

Upon completing the degree, students will be able to

- create written texts using appropriate supporting materials and theories in communication and rhetoric;
- communicate ideas orally within multiple contexts;
- use information design principles to produce texts appropriate for an audience, purpose, and context;
- summarize and apply key concepts in communication and rhetorical theory;
- evaluate the historical and/or cultural contexts of communication practices and describe their ethical, social, or environmental implications;
- evaluate messages from a variety of media and technologies using methodologies in communication and rhetoric.

*All UMD Communication courses must meet at least four of the learning outcomes.

266   ARRIGO

Required Courses

Foundations	1. Introduction to Rhetoric and Communication (prerequisite for all subsequent courses in the major) 2. Ethics in Communication (prerequisite for capstone) 3. Digital and Media Literacy (prerequisite for all upper-level classes in the major) 4. Speech Communication (prerequisite for capstone)
Intermediate Writing	5. Any department Intermediate Writing course (prerequisite for all 300-level classes in the major) Communicating in the Sciences Business Communication Technical Communication Introduction to Strategic Communication Introduction to Journalism
Cultural Context and Theory	6–7. Any two upper-level literature courses 8. Any one of the following Advanced Rhetoric Language and Culture Special Topics in Rhetorical Studies Visual Communication
Electives	9–12. Elective Pathways (any four upper-level courses)
Capstone	13. Capstone in Communication

Elective Pathways to Major Completion

Pathways are *potential tracks*. Students can take *any* combination of Intermediate Writing, Cultural Contexts and Theory, and four elective courses.

Journalism	Strategic Communication
Foundations	Foundations
Intermediate Writing Introduction to Journalism	Intermediate Writing Introduction to Strategic Communication OR Business Communication
Cultural Context and Theory Two literature courses Advanced Rhetoric OR Language and Culture OR Special Topics in Rhetorical Studies	Cultural Context and Theory Two literature courses Advanced Rhetoric OR Language and Culture OR Special Topics in Rhetorical Studies
Electives (any 4) Sports Writing Writing Reviews Special Topics in Journalism Feature Story and Article Writing Writing about Popular Culture Magazine Writing	Electives (any 4) Public Relations Writing Special Topics in Writing and Comm Women Writing and Media Copywriting Tutoring Writing Environmental Communication
Capstone	Capstone

Multimodal and visual communication	Technical communication
Foundations	Foundations
Intermediate Writing Technical Communication OR Communicating in the Sciences	Intermediate Writing Communicating in the Sciences OR Business Communication OR Technical Communication
Cultural Context and Theory Two literature courses Visual Communication OR Advanced Rhetoric OR Special Topics in Rhetorical Studies	Cultural Context and Theory Two literature courses Advanced Rhetoric OR Visual Communication OR Special Topics in Rhetorical Studies
Electives (any 4) Multimodal Communication Internet Communication and Culture Document Design Digital Filmmaking Screenwriting Writing for Social Media	Electives (any 4) Report and Proposal Writing Usability Studies Special Topics in Writing and Comm Document Design Environmental Communication Special Topics in Communication
Capstone	Capstone

REFERENCES

Ahern, Katherine Fargo. 2013. "Tuning the Sonic Playing Field: Teaching Ways of Knowing Sound in First Year Writing." *Computers and Composition* 30 (2): 75–86.

Anderson, Steve, and Tara McPherson. 2011. "Engaging Digital Scholarship: Thoughts on Evaluating Multimedia Scholarship." *Profession*, 136–51. http://www.jstor.org/stable /41714115.

Arrigo, Anthony F. 2014. *Imaging Hoover Dam: The Making of a Cultural Icon.* Reno: University of Nevada Press.

Ball, Cheryl E., Jennifer Sheppard, and Kristin L. Arola. 2018. *Writer/Designer.* 2nd ed. Boston: Bedford/St. Martin's.

Black, John B., Ayelet Segal, Jonathan Vitale, and Cameron Fadjo. 2012. "Embodied Cognition and Learning Environment Design." In *Theoretical Foundations of Learning Environments,* edited by Susan Land and David Jonassen, 2nd ed., 198–223. New York: Routledge.

Brooke, Collin Gifford. 2009. *Lingua Fracta: Toward a Rhetoric of New Media.* Cresskill, NJ: Hampton.

Brumberger, Eva R. 2007. "Making the Strange Familiar: A Pedagogical Exploration of Visual Thinking." *Journal of Business and Technical Communication* 21 (4): 376–401.

Campbell, Terry A. 2018. "Why Multimodal Literacy Matters: (Re)Conceptualizing Literacy and Wellbeing through Singing-Infused Multimodal, Intergenerational Curricula: By Rachel Heydon and Susan O'Neill. Sense Publishers, Rotterdam, 2016." *International Review of Education* 64 (2): 283–85.

Carpenter, Russell. 2014. "Negotiating the Spaces of Design in Multimodal Composition." *Computers and Composition* 33 (September): 68–78.

Cazden, Courtney, Bill Cope, Norman Fairclough, and Jim Gee. 1996. "A Pedagogy of Multiliteracies: Designing Social Futures." *Harvard Educational Review* 66 (1): 60–92.

Cloonan, Anne. 2011. "Creating Multimodal Metalanguage with Teachers." *English Teaching: Practice and Critique* 10 (4): 23–40.

Cope, Bill, and Mary Kalantzis, eds. 2000. *Multiliteracies: Literacy Learning and the Design of Social Futures.* 1st ed. New York: Routledge.

Finnegan, Cara A. 2001. "The Naturalistic Enthymeme and Visual Argument: Photographic Representation in the 'Skull Controversy.'" *Argumentation and Advocacy* 37 (3): 133–49.

Finnegan, Cara A. 2005. "Recognizing Lincoln: Image Vernaculars in Nineteenth-Century Visual Culture." *Rhetoric and Public Affairs* 8 (1): 31–58.

Fleckenstein, Kristie. 2002. "Inviting Imagery into Our Classrooms." In Kristie Fleckenstein, Lina Calendrillo & Demetrice Worley (eds.), *Language and Images in the Reading-Writing Classroom*, 3–26. Mahwah, NJ: Erlbaum.

Fleckenstein, Kristie S., Linda T. Calendrillo, and Demetrice A. Worley, eds. 2002. *Language and Image in the Reading-Writing Classroom: Teaching Vision*. 1st ed. Mahwah, NJ: Lawrence Erlbaum.

Fowler, Chris. 2015. "Virtual Reality and Learning: Where Is the Pedagogy?" *British Journal of Educational Technology* 46 (2): 412–22.

Fraustino, Julia Daisy, Ji Young Lee, Sang Yeal Lee, and Hongmin Ahn. 2018. "Effects of 360° Video on Attitudes toward Disaster Communication: Mediating and Moderating Roles of Spatial Presence and Prior Disaster Media Involvement." *Public Relations Review* 44 (3): 331–41.

Hamilton, Mary, Rachel Heydon, Kathryn Hibbert, and Roz Stooke, eds. 2015. *Negotiating Spaces for Literacy Learning: Multimodality and Governmentality*. New York: Bloomsbury Academic.

Hassett, Dawnene D., and Jen Scott Curwood. 2009. "Theories and Practices of Multimodal Education: The Instructional Dynamics of Picture Books and Primary Classrooms." *Reading Teacher* 63 (4): 270–82.

Heydon, Rachel, and Susan O'Neill. 2016. *Why Multimodal Literacy Matters: (Re)Conceptualizing Literacy and Wellbeing through Singing-Infused Multimodal, Intergenerational Curricula*. Rotterdam, The Netherlands: Sense.

Kelly, Mills. 2013. "Making Digital Scholarship Count." In *Hacking the Academy*, edited by Daniel J. Cohen and Tom Scheinfeldt, 50–54. New Approaches to Scholarship and Teaching from Digital Humanities. Ann Arbor: University of Michigan Press.

Kress, Gunther R. 2003. *Literacy in the New Media Age*. New York: Routledge.

Kress, Gunther R. 2010. *Multimodality: A Social Semiotic Approach to Contemporary Communication*. Milton Park, Oxfordshire: Taylor & Francis.

Kress, Gunther, and Theo van Leeuwen. 1996. *Reading Images: The Grammar of Visual Design*. New York: Routledge.

Merchant, Zahira, Ernest T. Goetz, Lauren Cifuentes, Wendy Keeney-Kennicutt, and Trina J. Davis. 2014. "Effectiveness of Virtual Reality-Based Instruction on Students' Learning Outcomes in K–12 and Higher Education: A Meta-Analysis." *Computers and Education* 70 (January): 29–40.

National Communication Association (2016). A profile of the communication doctorate IV. https://www.natcom.org/sites/default/files/publications/Reports_on_the_Discipline _2015_NCA_Report_SED.pdf.

Newfield, Denise. 2011. "From Visual Literacy to Critical Visual Literacy: An Analysis of Educational Materials." *English Teaching: Practice and Critique* 10 (1): 81–94.

Palmeri, Jason. 2012. *Remixing Composition: A History of Multimodal Writing Pedagogy*. Carbondale: Southern Illinois University Press.

Passig, David. 2015. "Revisiting the Flynn Effect through 3D Immersive Virtual Reality (IVR)." *Computers and Education* 88 (October): 327–42.

Peck, Tabitha C., My Doan, Kimberly A. Bourne, and Jessica J. Good. 2018. "The Effect of Gender Body-Swap Illusions on Working Memory and Stereotype Threat." *IEEE Transactions on Visualization and Computer Graphics* 24 (4): 1604–12.

Purdy, James P., and Joyce R. Walker. 2010. "Valuing Digital Scholarship: Exploring the Changing Realities of Intellectual Work." *Profession* 2010 (1): 177–95.

Rubin, Victoria L. 2019. "Disinformation and Misinformation Triangle: A Conceptual Model for 'Fake News' Epidemic, Causal Factors and Interventions." *Journal of Documentation* 75 (5): 1013–34.

Satar, H. Müge. 2016. "Meaning-Making in Online Language Learner Interactions via Desktop Videoconferencing." *ReCALL* 28 (3): 305–25.

Scott, Linda M. 1994. "Images in Advertising: The Need for a Theory of Visual Rhetoric." *Journal of Consumer Research* 21 (2): 252–73.

Selfe, Cynthia. 2009. "The Movement of Air, the Breath of Meaning: Aurality in Multimodal Composition." *College Composition and Communication* 60 (4): 616–63.

Serafini, Frank. 2015. "Multimodal Literacy: From Theories to Practices." *Language Arts* 92 (6): 412–22.

Sipe, Lawrence R. 2007. *Storytime: Young Children's Literary Understanding in the Classroom.* Illustrated ed. New York: Teachers College Press.

Smith, Sherrill J., Sharon Farra, Deborah L. Ulrich, Eric Hodgson, Stephanie Nicely, and William Matcham. 2016. "Learning and Retention Using Virtual Reality in a Decontamination Simulation." *Nursing Education Perspectives* 37 (4): 210–14.

Stafford, Tim. 2011. *Teaching Visual Literacy in the Primary Classroom: Comic Books, Film, Television and Picture Narratives.* 1st ed. New York: Routledge.

Sullivan, Patricia Suzanne. 2012. *Experimental Writing in Composition: Aesthetics and Pedagogies.* Pittsburgh Series in Composition, Literacy, and Culture. Pittsburgh: University of Pittsburgh Press.

Walsh, Maureen. 2010. "Multimodal Literacy: What Does It Mean for Classroom Practice?" *Australian Journal of Language and Literacy* 33 (3). 10.1007/BF03651836.

Wiseman, Angela M., Marita Mäkinen, and Reijo Kupiainen. 2016. "Literacy Through Photography: Multimodal and Visual Literacy in a Third Grade Classroom." *Early Childhood Education Journal* 44 (5): 537–44.

Wysocki, Anne Frances. 2002. "A Bookling Monument." *Kairos* 7 (3).

Yang, Yu-Feng (Diana). 2012. "Multimodal Composing in Digital Storytelling." *Computers and Composition* 29 (3): 221–38.

Yoon, Susan A., Karen Elinich, Joyce Wang, Christopher Steinmeier, and Sean Tucker. 2012. "Using Augmented Reality and Knowledge-Building Scaffolds to Improve Learning in a Science Museum." *International Journal of Computer-Supported Collaborative Learning* 7 (4): 519–41.

EPILOGUE
Multimodal Professionalization during and after the COVID-19 Pandemic

Santosh Khadka and Shyam B. Pandey

We drafted this section during the week Shyam was attending a hybrid conference of the Association of Computing Machinery's Special Interest Group: Design of Communication (ACM SIGDOC) 2021, which had eight meet-up locations across the globe (Brazil, China, Ireland, and Portugal, and Michigan, Arizona, North Carolina, and Washington in the United States), and its sessions were run both synchronously and asynchronously. Some of its plenary sessions and workshops were in a synchronous mode, while the concurrent sessions and student posters were held in an asynchronous mode. The ACM SIGDOC moved its conference to virtual and hybrid mode immediately after the world was hit hard by the COVID-19 pandemic. The same week, Santosh packed his luggage, stored all his teaching materials on a large hard drive, and traveled internationally to celebrate one of his biggest festivals, Dashain, in Nepal. Santosh, his teaching assistant, and students were located transnationally, but he could still run his Digital Writing class while his students collaborated to produce documentary projects utilizing inter-active digital tools and platforms accessible to them remotely.

These two instances provide small snippets of how deeply embedded multimodality is in our professional lives and how important writing teachers' multimodal professionalization and engagements are to suc-cess in post-COVID-19 work environments. This pandemic has not only changed how we professionalize or engage multimodal composition in the present contexts but is also going to have a decisive impact on the mode or form of multimodal professionalization going forward. As we highlight in our introduction, despite neoliberal tendencies govern-ing many institutions of higher education, multimodal composition has been an unstoppable force in both writing curricula and various professionalization initiatives. While the precarity of writing faculty still

https://doi.org/10.7330/9781646424184.c014

remains a burning issue throughout the country, we are left with no option but to adopt a multimodal approach in our teaching and professionalization if we are to succeed in the post-COVID-19 world. Whether multimodal instruction or professionalization happens at the programmatic, institutional, national, or individual level, it must be informed by evolving technologies and their communicative affordances.

Therefore, the big takeaway for writing teachers and scholars is that we stand at a crossroads in the present moment from where we must make some clear choices. Either we professionalize and adopt multimodality in our research and teaching or we run the risk of becoming irrelevant to our students' expectations and the communication needs of the globalized world. The good news is that we have made significant progress in terms of multimodal composition research, but multimodal instruction is still lagging behind, particularly at the programmatic and institutional levels. This book is an intervention to inspire many fellow scholars and teachers to design and launch multimodal initiatives at the curricular, programmatic, departmental, and even institutional levels, wherever possible.

In this book, contributors from fifteen different universities detail various professionalizing initiatives around multimodal composing scholars, faculty, and academic leaders can emulate in their own institutional contexts. Drawing ideas from this book, they can also increase familiarity with multimodal composing, create programs that center multimodality, design courses incorporating multimodal components, or run multimodal professional-development programs in their own institutional contexts.

More important, contributors in this book, collectively, highlight what resources individuals need to professionalize multimodally. Infrastructures, no doubt, are at the center of multimodal professionalization, but human resources and faculty incentives through pay packages, release time, and research and teaching opportunities are not any less critical for change to happen. And, academic leaders can play a critical role in the process of multimodal professionalization. From pulling funds from other sources to allocating dollars from within the department, academic leaders can work to set up infrastructures, get teams together to offer multimodal professional-development events, give committees a charge to develop multimodal curricula or programs, and fight on behalf of the faculty for additional resources to offer as incentives to be involved in multimodal professionalization. Finally, this book draws our attention to the curricular principles for which we should strive. Our curriculum must keep up with the changing technology landscape and respond to the composing and communication needs of our students, which is to say our curriculum must coevolve with the changing dynamics in composition, communication technologies, and media and the ever-shifting needs of our students in the globalized world.

Looking forward, it's clear the demand for multimodal research and pedagogy is going to skyrocket across all kinds of institutions. The rapid development of technologies, such as 3D animations and AR and VR simulations, has only added urgency for unconditional adoption of multimodality and digitality in our writing instruction and research. Here is hoping academic leaders, faculty, and students all realize the value of multimodal composing sooner than later and work to make it a part of their curricula, programs, departments, and institutions. Whether at the institutional, programmatic, or course level, as discussed in this collection, there should be more initiatives for multimodal professionalization in order to bridge the glaring theory-praxis gap in multimodal composition.

INDEX

Academia.edu, 117
academic leadership, 9, 15, 16, 18
academic technologies (AT), 143–54
Adobe Spark, 35
Advanced Writing with Technologies, 206
African American and African Studies, 30
African American studies, 125
alphabetic literacy, 6
American studies, 30, 125
AmeriCorps, 159
annual interdisciplinary graduate research
  symposium, 226
antiracist and anti-ableist pedagogy, 61–75
antitechnology, 7
AR and VR, 5, 273
Arizona, 271
artificial intelligence, 5
Asian American studies, 125
assessment protocols, 44
assessment (re)design, 54
Association of American Colleges and Universities, 160, 251
Association of Computing Machinery's
  Special Interest Group: Design of Communication (ACM SIGDOC), 271
audacity, 35
audio-recording hardware/software, 101

Ball, Cheryl, 3, 80, 161, 176
Black, Indigenous, and People of Color
  (BIPOC), 165, 236
boot camps, 9
Brazil, 271
business communication, 258–67
business management, 125

California State University, 65
campus employment, 182
Canva, 35
Capstone Showcase, 188–89
career services, 35, 172
Carroll County, 168
certifications, 11, 12, 129
Chamber of Commerce, 167–72
China, 111, 271
code of ethics, 11
collaborative curricular work, 48

College English, 11
College of Arts and Letters, 30
communication technologies, 5, 217, 273
community-engaged projects, 115, 136
community engagement, 116, 120, 131, 168,
  178, 239
community writing center, 57
composing praxis, 5
Composition and Applied Linguistics
  (CAL), 19, 233–35
composition curriculum, 3–4, 46, 50, 177
Composition Forum, 29
composition pedagogy, 52, 57, 62, 79, 255
composition, rhetoric, and digital media
  (CRDM), 19, 197–211; faculty, 199–211
*Computers and Composition: An International
  Journal*, 116
Computers and Composition Online, 91, 116,
  140, 262
computers in writing intensive classrooms
  (CIWIC), 116–18, 140
Conference on College Composition and
  Communication (CCCC), 3, 7, 29,
  139–42, 162–66, 260–62
content/genre-informed decision-making,
  71–72
contingent faculty, 8, 11, 12, 28, 142
conventional rhetorical principles, 82
Council of Writing Program Administrators (CWPA), 7, 29
coursework, 82–90, 106, 198, 218, 228, 257
Courtney, Jennifer, 146
COVID-19, 25, 119, 136, 166, 271
creative writing, 52, 81, 125, 159, 183, 237
critical friendship, 52–54
critical literacy, 84
critical race studies, 124–25
cross-campus collaborations, 154
Cultural Context and Theory, 258–67
cultural-literacy model, 104
cultural studies, 125
curricula, 3–18, 23, 30–69, 108–13, 136–78,
  191–242, 273
Cushman, Jeremy, 96
CWPA. *See* Council of Writing Program
  Administrators

276   INDEX

D2L Brightspace, 50
Dashain, 271
data visualization, 182
Department of English, 30, 115, 144–47
digital collaborative writing (DCW), 4
digital composition, 3, 4, 5, 7, 10
Digital Environments, 13, 139, 245, 254
Digital Filmmaking, 259–67
digital flagship, 146–52
digital humanities, 125, 261–62
digital literacy, 3–19, 84, 115, 147, 195, 214–37, 250
digitally savvy, 162
Digital Media and Composition Institute, 13, 18, 113, 115–36, 140, 150
digital rhetoric, 4, 19, 26, 161, 195, 224–46, 262
digital writing, 4–29, 141–63, 214, 271
Dilger, Bradley, 144
disability studies, 124–25
disciplinary/professional, 35, 178, 181
Disciplinary Writing Consultant, 181
discourse negotiation, 49
DMAC. *See* Digital Media and Composition Institute
documentary, 5, 117, 147, 271
document design, 34, 250, 259, 267
dossoi logoi, 256
Dutta, Debarati, 151

Elon University, 18, 178–84
embedded expertise, 206
embodied approach, 61
emerging expertise, 78
emerging media, 3, 5, 6, 10, 262
emojis, 250
Enculturation, 262
ENG 101 course, 45, 46
English departments, 123, 142–45, 160, 173, 253
English studies, 4, 12, 30, 108, 109, 115, 140, 260
environmental communication, 259–67
ePortfolios, 81–90, 186–205, 219
executive committee, 176
exit dinners, 186–87

Facebook, 28
faculty preparedness, 9, 15, 16, 23
faculty-development initiative, 10, 15, 23
faculty-student collaboration, 53
Fall River, 252
Feenberg, Andrew, 29
feminist researchers, 98
film, media, and popular culture, 125
filmmaking, 5, 259, 267

first-year composition, 4–16, 23, 61, 64–67, 164–68, 177, 179
first-year writing (FYW), 17, 31–37, 95–110, 139–55; curriculum, 35; symposium, 35
Fishman, Jenn, 145
Florida, 160
four-year colleges, 8, 121, 122, 134
Fourzan, Judith, 147
Freire, Paolo, 66
functional literacy, 23, 84, 88, 217–18

gender and sexuality, 125, 127
general education, 178, 182
genre project, 67–71
George, Diana, 161
George Washington University, 164
gifs, 250
Global Arts and Humanities Discovery Theme, 136
Global Libraries Initiative Impact Planning and Assessment Road Map, 119
GNU Image Manipulation Program, 35
Google Docs, 98, 241–45
Google Forms, 69
Google Image, 26
Google Sheets, 26
graduate instructors, 23, 95–109, 219
graduate students, 14–97, 106–62, 202–30, 234
Graduate Teaching Assistant (GTA): and development workshop, 47; training, 50, 53, 81, 90; workshop, 44, 55

Haas, Angela, 31, 39, 65
hashtags, 250
HBCU (Historically Black Colleges and Universities), 115, 122
health sciences, 182
high-bridge, 86–87
high-school, 72, 136
higher education, 4–16, 121–34, 158, 183, 195, 209–19, 271
Hispanic, 65
Hispanic-serving institution, 142, 198

iMovie, 32
imposter syndrome, 56
infographic, 5, 30, 162, 180, 188, 257
infrastructures, 11, 113, 142, 154, 272
institutional levels, 272
institutional support, 6, 9, 118, 127, 175, 177
integrated internship model, 173
intermedia writing, 146, 258–67
Internet Communication and Culture, 259–67
internship-based courses, 18, 113, 158–73

intersectionality, 234
Introductory Composition at Purdue (ICaP), 144
iPad, 110, 146, 148
Ireland, 271

Jasken, Julia, 166
journalism, 125, 180, 258–66

Kairos, 91, 261–62
Kelly, Shannon, 96
Koger, Tara, 150
Kress, Gunther, 3–19, 250–55

L2 (second language) writing, 43, 44, 49, 51, 55
labor-based grading, 57, 68, 87
language and culture, 258–66
lateral thinking, 254
learning-management system (LMS), 147, 240
Let's Remix, 35
liberal arts, 30, 65, 115, 158, 175–85
linear thinking, 253
LinkedIn profiles, 117
literacy studies, 125
literature, 125, 131, 159–83, 208–67
low-bridge software, 85–87

marketable skills, 79
Marquette University, 113, 141–49
Maryland, 160, 167
MA students, 32, 97–100
McDaniel College, 158–73
media labs, 88–89
memes, 5, 250
memoir project, 243
Mendeley, 117
mentorship programs, 100
Miami University, 4
Michigan, 271
Michigan State University, 30, 38, 39, 177
Michigan Technological University, 116
Microsoft PowerPoint, 26
Microsoft Word, 85
Mina, Lilian, 29
Minnesota, 179
mixed-methods, 29
Modern Language Association Job List, 80
MSU Libraries, 33
MSU Museum, 35
Mullin, Joan, 147
multigenre project, 67
multilingual, 16, 23, 47–57, 107, 234–45, 254

multiliteracies, 5, 46, 61, 79, 84, 104, 216–64
multimedia, 28–104, 179–90, 208, 219–51, 262
multimodal communication, 5, 47, 216, 233, 252–57
multimodal element, 80
multimodality, 3–19, 28–40, 45–55, 61–212, 216–47, 250–73
multimodal literacies, 14, 95–109, 162, 176, 219, 245
multimodal pedagogy, 23, 63–109, 176–91, 235–54
multimodal program, 4, 191
multimodal projects, 5, 39–56, 74–135, 175–203
multimodal scholars, 6, 81, 116, 132, 134, 135
multimodal training, 81
multimodal writing center (MWC), 33–35
multiple modes, 43–64, 105, 159–82, 200–6, 241
multivocal and multimodal: framework/ approach, 49–58; writing, 23
musing-sharing site, 26

narrative theory, 125
National Council of Teachers of English (NCTE), 3, 7, 29, 139, 155, 162, 176
neoliberalization, 8
Nepal, 271
networked world, 38
New Bedford, 252
New London Group, 3, 61, 176, 216, 264
new media, 13, 28, 173, 237–62
new-media composing, 28, 107–8
new-media design, 80
nondominant language, 49
non-Eurocentric academic genres, 107
non-tenure-track faculty/position, 30, 122, 134, 145, 147
normative linguistic practices, 107
North Carolina, 190, 271
Northern Arizona University, 79
Nova Southeastern University, 18, 197–209
novice teachers, 44–51, 107

observations, 98, 129
Ohio State University (OSU), 113, 115, 141
online writing instruction (OWI), 45, 47
open-source web platforms, 85

PD model. *See* professional development
pedagogical inquiry, 97–99
pedagogy of the oppressed, 66
Pell Grants, 252
PhD programs, 43, 199, 209, 210

278 INDEX

Pickavance, Jason, 150
Pinterest, 32
podcast, 5, 26, 68–109, 226, 228
policy studies, 125
polymodal writing practice, 56
Portugal, 271
Position Statement on Multimodal Literacies, 162, 176
post-COVID-19, 23, 271, 272
practicum course, 17, 52, 89–99, 148–50
principal investigator (PI), 26
professional and technical communication, 124–25, 163
professional development (PD), 6–19, 23–40, 48, 90, 108–89, 214–72; institutes, 118; model, 14; programs, 7–14, 217, 272
professionalization initiatives, 271
professional organization, 7–11, 51, 139, 261
professional websites, 117
Professional Writing and Rhetoric (PWR), 18, 175–90
programmatic, 3–15, 27, 40, 95, 133, 143–60, 171, 183–85, 233–35, 272
protechnology, 7
PSA (public service announcement), 5, 68, 91
public relations writing, 259–66
Purdue University, 142–54

Quality Enhancement Plan (QEP), 177

reciprocal, recursive mentoring model, 14
reflective inquiry, 45, 49, 50
religious studies, 126
remixes, 5, 35, 36
Remix Project, 31–36, 145–46
report and proposal writing, 259–67
research methods course, 200
research symposium, 146
ResearchGate, 117
rhetorical approach, 105, 185, 255
rhetorical expertise, 32
rhetorical literacy, 84, 217
rhetorical principles, 82
rhetorical theory, 126
Rhetoric and Communication Initiative, 177
rhetoric and composition, 4–43, 65–92, 116, 161–77, 216, 235
ROLE, 91

Salt Lake Community College (SLCC), 113, 141–46
scaffolding exercises, 82–89
scholarship of teaching and learning (SOTL), 55

Schools of Arts/Sciences, 182
screenwriting, 259–67
second language writing. *See* L2 writing
Selfe, Cynthia, 3–7, 28–61, 82–83, 113–16, 176, 233, 255
semester-long workshop, 49
semiotic activity, 161
semiotic approach, 219–37
semiotic modes, 5, 80, 188, 251
semiotic resources, 245–61
Shipka, Jody, 65
single-authored study, 98
Singleton, Edgar, 146
small-stakes assignments, 88
Snapchat, 28
social media, 165
social media literacies, 5
Sonoma State University, 65–69
Southern Association of Colleges and Schools (SACS), 178–90
standard language and modal norm (SL/MN) ideologies, 233
Standard Written English, 48
Stanford, 179
STEM, 211, 251
Student Athlete Support Services, 33
student composers, 61
students' statements of goals and choices (SOGCs), 87
subject-matter expertise, 123–24
Summer Writing Institute, 181–82

teacher training, 4, 28–39, 85, 177
teaching assistants, 8–17, 23–27, 78, 227, 271
teaching documents, 98
Teaching Information Design, 182
teaching multimodal composition, 11–25, 50, 79, 80–95, 132
technical communication, 108–24, 258–67
technological and instrumental composing, 33–34
technological expertise, 34, 142
technological professional development (TPD), 7, 139–55
Technology Professional Development in Rhetoric and Composition, 116

tenure-line faculty/position, 8, 115, 122, 140, 145
Texas Tech, 95–96, 105–9
text-based analysis, 103
theory-praxis, 9, 273
TikTok, 28
TPACK framework, 13
TPD. *See* technological professional development

translingualism, 19, 63, 233–47
transmodality, 233–47
transnational, 48, 233–46, 271
tutoring writing, 259–66
twenty-first century, 17, 23, 66–82, 160–79, 209–16, 234, 265
Twitter, 28
TYCA, 139

Undergraduate Publishing and Information Design (CUPID), 184–91
University of California, Berkeley, 165
University of Massachusetts (UMass) Dartmouth, 19, 252, 265
University of New Mexico (UNM), 78, 81, 90
University of North Carolina–Charlotte (UNCC), 113, 141–47
University of Texas El Paso (UTEP), 142–54
upper-division writing, 13, 16, 195
usability studies, 252–67

vectors, 262–62
veteran faculty, 12, 14
video-conferencing platforms, 136
visual and spatial, 5
visual communication, 252–67

WAC Clearinghouse, 155
Washington State University, 177
Washington, 271
WCONLINE, 34

Western Washington University, 96
white spaces, 5
World English, 107
WPAs. See writing program administration
writing about writing (WAA), 45
writing across the curriculum, 57, 126, 180, 181
Writing Across the University, 179–81
writing center practice and theory, 126
writing center, 16, 26, 180–99, 262
Writing Excellence Initiative (WEI), 178–91
writing faculty, 7–16, 61, 182–95, 235–71
Writing for Main Street, 159–70
Writing for Nonprofits, 159–69
Writing for Social Media, 259–67
writing instructors, 10–17, 23, 48, 49, 163
writing-intensive, 15, 16, 33, 140, 145, 195
writing program administration (WPA), 8–18, 23, 28, 48, 58, 78–99, 109–50, 135
writing program certificate of excellence (WPCE), 142
writing transfer, 45
Written Communication VALUE Rubric, 179
written reflections, 98

Yancey, Kathleen Blake, 3, 87, 162, 176, 201
Young, Vershawn Ashanti, 66
YouTube, 26, 28, 228, 251

Zoom, 26, 44, 50, 159

ABOUT THE AUTHORS

Josh Ambrose, Johns Hopkins University

Kristin Arola, Michigan State University

Anthony F. Arrigo, University of Massachusetts, Dartmouth

Tiffany Bourelle, University of New Mexico

Christina Boyles, Michigan State University

Lauren Brawley, Texas Tech University

Shauna Chung, New York City College of Technology, CUNY

Kirsti Cole, Minnesota State University, Mankato

Morgan Connor, Texas Tech University

Meghalee Das, Texas Tech University

Aliethia Dean, Texas Tech University

Dànielle Nicole DeVoss, Michigan State University

Scott Lloyd DeWitt, The Ohio State University

Claudia Diaz, Texas Tech University

Tia Dumas, Clemson University

Michael J. Faris, Texas Tech University

Michelle Flahive, Texas Tech University

Wilfredo Flores, Michigan State University

Kerri Hauman, Transylvania University

Megan E. Heise, Indiana University of Pennsylvania

Sarah Henderson Lee, Minnesota State University, Mankato

John Jones, The Ohio State University

282 ABOUT THE AUTHORS

Stacy Kastner, University of Pennsylvania

Santosh Khadka, California State University

Maeve Kirk, Texas Tech University

Max Kirschenbaum, Texas Tech University

Joshua Kulseth, Texas Tech University

Alfonsina Lago, Texas Tech University

Jennifer Lanatti Shen, Sonoma State University

Kristina Lewis, Texas Tech University

Li Li, Elon University

Lance Lomax, Texas Tech University

Claire Lutkewitte, Nova Southeastern University

Brook McClurg, Texas Tech University

Megan McIntyre, Sonoma State University

Kelly Moreland, Minnesota State University, Mankato

Zachary Ostraff, Texas Tech University

Shyam B. Pandey, Sam Houston State University

Stephen Quigley, University of Pittsburgh

Anthony Ranieri, Texas Tech University

Paula Rosinski, Elon University

Daniel Schafer, McDaniel College

Sierra Sinor, Texas Tech University

Rebekah Smith, Southern Utah University

Michael Strickland, Elon University

Matthew A. Vetter, Indiana University of Pennsylvania

Teresa Williams, Michigan State University

Alison Witte, University of Dayton

Yifan Zhang, Baylor University